PLANNING FOR A CONTINENT OF CITIES

I0093690

First published in 2025 by
UWA Publishing
Crawley, Western Australia 6009
www.uwap.uwa.edu.au

UWAP is an imprint of UWA Publishing,
a division of The University of Western Australia.

THE UNIVERSITY OF
WESTERN
AUSTRALIA

This book is copyright. Apart from any fair dealing
for the purpose of private study, research, criticism
or review, as permitted under the Copyright Act 1968,
no part may be reproduced by any process without
written permission. Enquiries should be made
to the publisher.

Copyright Julian Bolleter and Robert Freestone © 2025
The moral right of the author has been asserted.

ISBN: 978-1-76080-306-3

Design by Upside Creative
Printed by Lightning Source

UWAP

CELEBRATING
90 YEARS

Julian Bolleter
Robert Freestone

PLANNING FOR A CONTINENT OF CITIES

Long-range scenarios for Australian urbanisation

UWA PUBLISHING

THE AUTHORS

Julian Bolleter

Julian Bolleter is the Director of the Australian Urban Design Research Centre (AUDRC) at the University of Western Australia and is the program director of AUDRC's Master of Urban Design course.

Robert Freestone

Robert Freestone is a professor of planning in the School of Built Environment at the University of New South Wales and a City Futures Research Centre Fellow.

FOREWORD

Planning for a Continent of Cities: Long-range scenarios for Australian urbanisation is a timely and valuable contribution to better managing future urban growth. This book sets the stage with population estimates for Australia expected to reach 53 million by 2100. As the authors somewhat provocatively suggest, by 2100, this could mean 59 more Canberra's, five more Melbourne's or 13 more Perth's and everything in between. Julian Bolleter and Robert Freestone identify several key challenges for planning urban and regional futures in a more sustainable and equitable way. These include the density wars, nimbyism, environmental issues, social segregation and climate change.

Helpfully, the authors explore the potential spatial patterns of urban settlement through a range of scenarios, including secondary capital cities, satellite cities, rail cities, sea change cities, megacities, and more. These spatial scenarios push us to think more deeply about how and where we could place urban development in the context of climate change, housing demand, labour mobility, technological change, infrastructure, biodiversity and more.

In many ways, this book proposes a national framework that brings all these elements into consideration to support states, territories and local governments across the nation. This is timely given the Australian government's recommitment to a national urban policy to support more sustainable urban and regional futures.

I commend the authors for their courage, foresight and scholarly contribution in providing an excellent platform for lively discussion and debate on what could be the most sustainable and equitable pattern of urban settlement in Australia over the 21st century. I encourage readers to engage in these critical discussions concerning urban communities nationwide.

Emeritus Professor Barbara Norman
University of Canberra and Honorary Professor, Australian National University.

CONTENTS

IMAGE BY AUTHORS

1

INTRODUCTION

The problems of our moment are as unprecedented as they are vast. The solutions will have to be unprecedented and vast.[1]

BACKGROUND

R ecent United Nations estimates show that the global population will surge from 7.9 billion to 10.4 billion by the late twenty-first century.[2] To put such grand projections in perspective, the constantly whirring world population clock shows that if you take 15 minutes to read this introduction, the global population will have increased by over 2200 people.[3]

The effect of such alarming projections can be paralysing for those who anticipate some imminent Malthusian collapse, and not without some cause, it should be said. Alternatively, this growth can be cast as an unparalleled creative opportunity. Indeed, the early twenty-first century will experience more urbanisation than all of human history, suggesting a considerable possibility to profoundly shape future cities on a grand scale.[4] Moreover, this window of opportunity is time limited, as the population is projected to stabilise post 2100. Because the bulk of the projected population increase will reside in cities, the solutions to some of humanity's most bedevilling issues (poverty, climate change and ecological collapse, to mention just a few) must also be found in cities.[5] This is no small challenge.

So, what do all these grand projections mean for the Australian narrative? Australia is essentially a microcosm of global pressures arising from population growth in cities. While the increase in population seems almost trivial on a planetary scale, and it did slow down through the COVID-19 pandemic when international migration was virtually zero, population growth from 2020 has resumed and continues apace.

Given that the future is riddled with uncertainty, what are the most credible projections for future populations? The Australian Bureau of Statistics (ABS) provides a mid-range forecast for 2101 (Series B) for the national population to double, reaching 53,600,000. his would represent an effective doubling of the current national population of 27,000,000. The more extreme Series A projection is that Australia's population could triple to

1   Fuller, 212
2   United Nations, 'World Population Prospects'
3   The World Counts
4   Seto et al.
5   United Nations, 'Sustainable Cities: Why They Matter'

70,100,000 in this period.[6] While on a global scale such figures are paltry, in relative terms, the projected proportional increase in Australia's urban population is enormous. Australia's population growth rate eclipses the world average and, surprisingly, the rate for major developing nations, including China and India.[7]

In all these scenarios, the population increase primarily stems from net overseas migration, not bountiful birth rates.[8] This pattern conforms to a long-term trend; indeed, the late, well-respected demographer Graeme Hugo estimated that in 2014, Australia's population of 23 million would have been only a lonely (and primarily White) 13 million without post-war migration.[9]

Furthermore, ABS's Series B projections for the capital cities estimate that their population will almost double in size by 2066 (Figure 1.1).[10] As of 2020, more than 76% of Australians lived in major cities with a population of more than 100,000 (Table 1.1), and the number of people in rural and remote urban areas across all Australian states and territories is generally flatlining or free-falling.[11]

6   Australian Bureau of Statistics, 'Population Projections, Australia, 2012 (base) to 2101'
7   Hill et al.; Raupach et al.
8   Australian Bureau of Statistics, 'Population Projections, Australia, 2017 (Base) - 2066'
9   Hugo, 'Population Distribution, Migration and Climate Change in Australia'
10 Australian Bureau of Statistics, 'Population Projections, Australia, 2017 (Base) - 2066'
11 Hill et al.

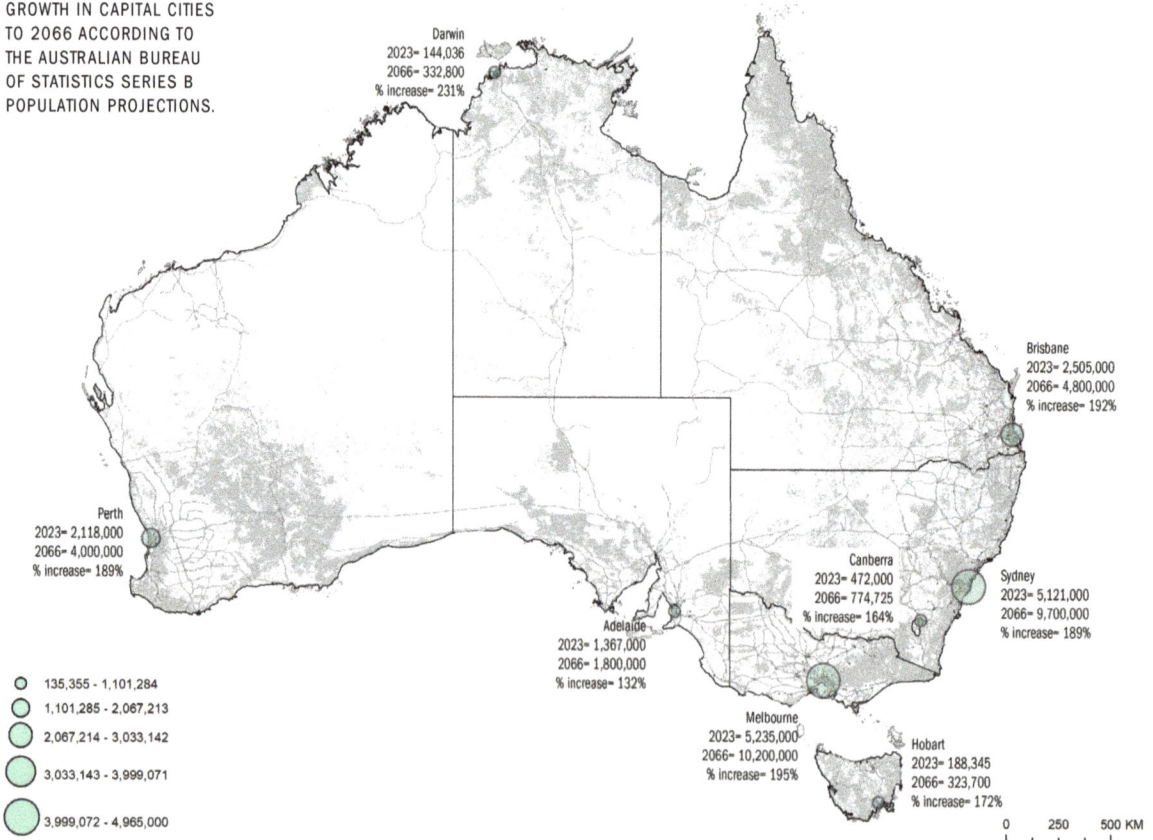

FIGURE 1.1: POPULATION GROWTH IN CAPITAL CITIES TO 2066 ACCORDING TO THE AUSTRALIAN BUREAU OF STATISTICS SERIES B POPULATION PROJECTIONS.

Darwin
2023= 144,036
2066= 332,800
% increase= 231%

Brisbane
2023= 2,505,000
2066= 4,800,000
% increase= 192%

Perth
2023= 2,118,000
2066= 4,000,000
% increase= 189%

Canberra
2023= 472,000
2066= 774,725
% increase= 164%

Sydney
2023= 5,121,000
2066= 9,700,000
% increase= 189%

Adelaide
2023= 1,367,000
2066= 1,800,000
% increase= 132%

Melbourne
2023= 5,235,000
2066= 10,200,000
% increase= 195%

Hobart
2023= 188,345
2066= 323,700
% increase= 172%

135,355 - 1,101,284
1,101,285 - 2,067,213
2,067,214 - 3,033,142
3,033,143 - 3,999,071
3,999,072 - 4,965,000

0   250   500 KM

Rank	City	State	Population
1	Melbourne	Vic	5,235,000
2	Sydney	NSW	5,121,000
3	Brisbane	Qld	2,505,000
4	Perth	WA	2,118,000
5	Adelaide	SA	1,367,000
6	Gold Coast-Tweed Heads	Qld/NSW	716,186
7	Newcastle-Maitland	NSW	517,811
8	Canberra-Queanbeyan	ACT/NSW	493,435
9	Sunshine Coast	Qld	397,205
10	Central Coast	NSW	345,481
11	Wollongong	NSW	309,345
12	Geelong	Vic	295,077
13	Hobart	Tas	252,693
14	Townsville	Qld	184,313
15	Cairns	Qld	158,178
16	Toowoomba	Qld	146,955
17	Darwin	NT	135,982
18	Ballarat	Vic	114,103
19	Bendigo	Vic	103,733

TABLE 1.1: AUSTRALIAN CITIES WITH A POPULATION OVER 100,000 IN 2021. DATA COURTESY OF THE AUSTRALIAN BUREAU OF STATISTICS.

Of course, demographic fallout from dramatic exogenous forces, such as out-of-control climate change and geopolitical upheaval, could blow these numbers out considerably, but these are not factored into official projections. That said, it's conceivable that 2101 populations could be below projections. History shows such forecasts are almost always incorrect to some degree. Indeed, demographic predictions are a notoriously tricky area, with enough variables to 'make fools of many'.[12] One unpredictable variable will be a possible surge in climate change refugees.[13] Estimates of the swell in environmental migrants in aggregate by 2050 variously include projections of 100 million by the World People's Conference,[14] 150 million[15] and then 200 million[16] by Norman Myers and the International Organization for Migration,[17] 309 million by The University of Sussex,[18] 750 million by Peter Singer[19] and 1 billion by Christian Aid.[20] Moreover, there is massive uncertainty about where these streams of environmental refugees will flow.[21]

All of this abstract population data prompts the question: What population could Australia actually support? The answers have been all over the place for over a century – veering between the boosterism of 'Big Australia' thinking and more guarded assessments given environmental constraints at a continental scale.

In the inter-war years, Griffith Taylor depicted most of the continent as 'almost useless', with a population carrying a modest 20 million capacity (Figure 1.2). While probably accurate for European agricultural practices, such a characterisation was predicated on the erasure of thousands of years of Indigenous knowledge that would have produced a very different assessment. Nonetheless, the historical geographer J.M. Powell captured Taylor's central position in these terms:

> The contemporary margins of settlement in Australia already closely approximated the limits which had been set by the very nature of the physical environment: whether people, plants or animals were considered, the appropriate environmental 'controls' could be ignored only at a cost.[22]

Such estimations were considered treasonous in an age when the dominant mood was expansionist, fuelled by a 'populate or perish' mentality, often with racist overtones.[23] However, a chorus of later commentators reaffirmed Taylor's assessment. Population biologist Professor Paul Ehrlich very conservatively claimed:

12 Murray, 34
13 Bolleter et al., 'Preparing Australia'
14 In Bettini
15 Myers, 'Environmental Refugees in a Globally Warmed World'
16 Myers
17 International Organization for Migration
18 Black et al.
19 In McAdam and Blocher
20 Christian Aid
21 Wennersten and Robbins
22 Powell, 87
23 Strange and Bashford

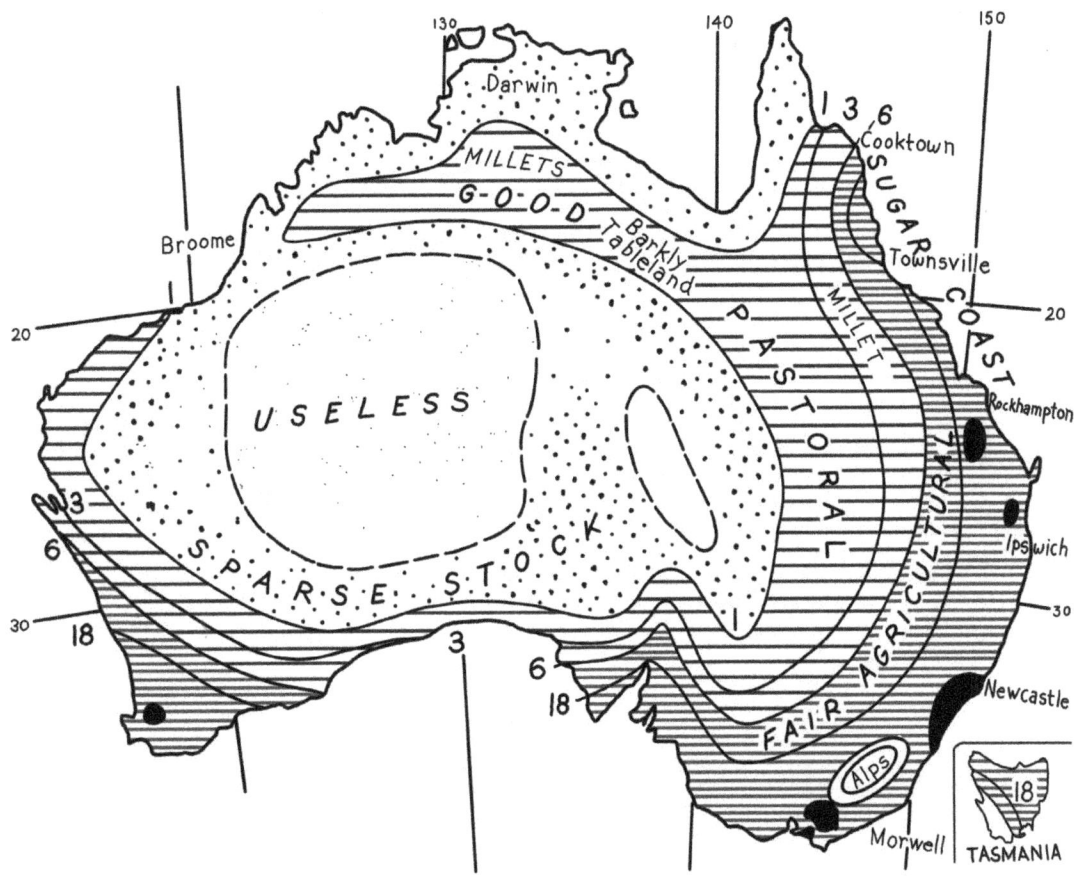

FIGURE 1.2: BASED ON AN ASSESSMENT OF HABITABILITY, GRIFFITH TAYLOR'S MAP OF AUSTRALIA REVEALED MUCH OF THE CONTINENT TO BE USELESS OR SUITABLE ONLY FOR SPARSE STOCK. IMAGE BY GRIFFITH TAYLOR (1937). TRACED BY SHUBHAM GAUTAM.

Australia's already in deep trouble, way beyond its carrying capacity and I'm afraid that not only are we not going to see 40 million or 100 million Australians, we are likely to see many fewer than 20 million, and many may have to evacuate.[24]

In 1975, a Commonwealth Scientific and Industrial Research Organisation team took up the 'carrying capacity' challenge. It concluded that Australia could feed around 60 million people, but assuming that food exports would continue, they saw a much lower domestic population of 30 million as supportable.[25] Even more conservative estimates are on record. The Australian Conservation Foundation recommended an optimal population of 17 million for Australia.[26] Well-known scientist Tim Flannery proposed that Australia's population would serve its ecology best at 6 to 12 million people.[27]

Australians themselves are also typically pessimistic (or perhaps realistic). In 2009, *The Age* published results of a poll on attitudes to an Australia of 35 million, and a substantial 40% thought the number too high.[28] As this attests, the debate about the optimum population of Australia has been rattling back and forth for at least a century and has yielded no consensus.[29] Clearly, such estimations are riddled with uncertainty – in part because the carrying capacity of Australia depends on the lifestyle of future Australians, where they live, how they travel, how much they consume and even what they eat. While variously surging and waning, population increase continues regardless

Uncertainties around ultimate carrying capacity aside, at least the ABS numbers provide an authoritative basis for long-range thinking – and planning. For example, the Series B projection implies that Australia must build an urban area equivalent to almost 59 Canberras (a particularly provocative metric) or (somewhat less politically charged) 5.3 Melbournes (Figure 1.3) or 13.2 Perths (Figure 1.4) in the next eight decades to accommodate population growth. In area terms, this equates to 6905 square kilometres of new suburban fabric (Figure 1.5) or 866 square kilometres of urbanism at the considerable density of Melbourne's urban core (Figure 1.6). It is tempting to be flippant about such benchmarks in city building, but this is a monumental undertaking (considering all the required parks, roads, houses, offices, shops, infrastructure, etc.). Furthermore, such development must occur within a restless public policy environment, including an unfolding climate emergency, a movement against increasing urban densification, resource shortages and calamitous destruction of biodiversity, the so-called sixth mass extinction.[30]

24 In Bolleter and Weller, 17
25 Harding
26 Harding
27 In Fincher
28 Betts
29 Hellicar; Stone
30 MacFarlane

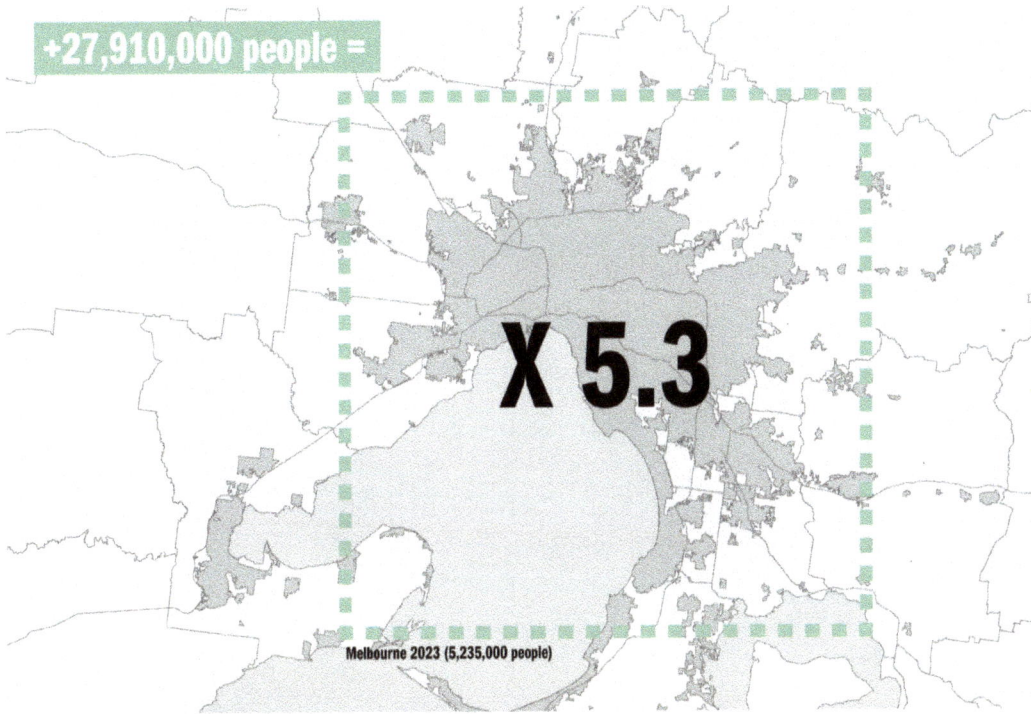

+27,910,000 people =

X 5.3

Melbourne 2023 (5,235,000 people)

FIGURE 1.3: THE EQUIVALENT OF 5.3 CURRENT-DAY MELBOURNES WOULD BE NEEDED TO ACCOMMODATE PROJECTED POPULATION GROWTH BY 2101.

+27,910,000 people =

X 13.2

Perth 2023 (2,118,000 people)

FIGURE 1.4: THE EQUIVALENT OF 13.2 PERTHS IS NEEDED TO ACCOMMODATE PROJECTED POPULATION GROWTH BY 2101.

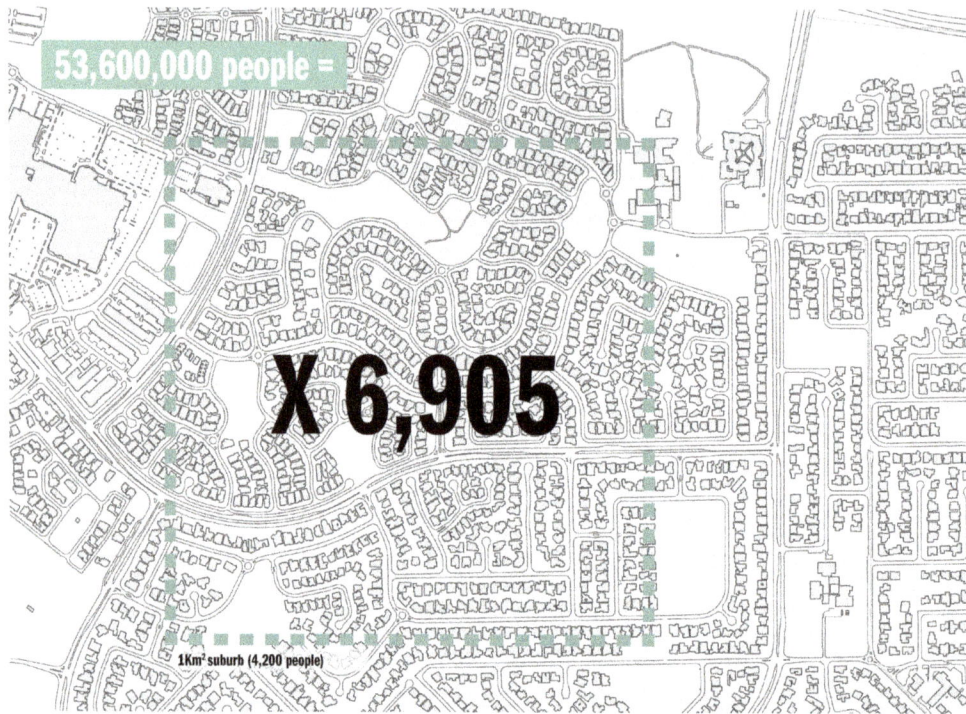

53,600,000 people =

X 6,905

1Km² suburb (4,200 people)

FIGURE 1.5: THE EQUIVALENT OF 6905KM² OF NEW SUBURBS IS NEEDED TO ACCOMMODATE PROJECTED POPULATION GROWTH BY 2101. THE PERTH SUBURB OF MIRRABOOKA IS PICTURED.

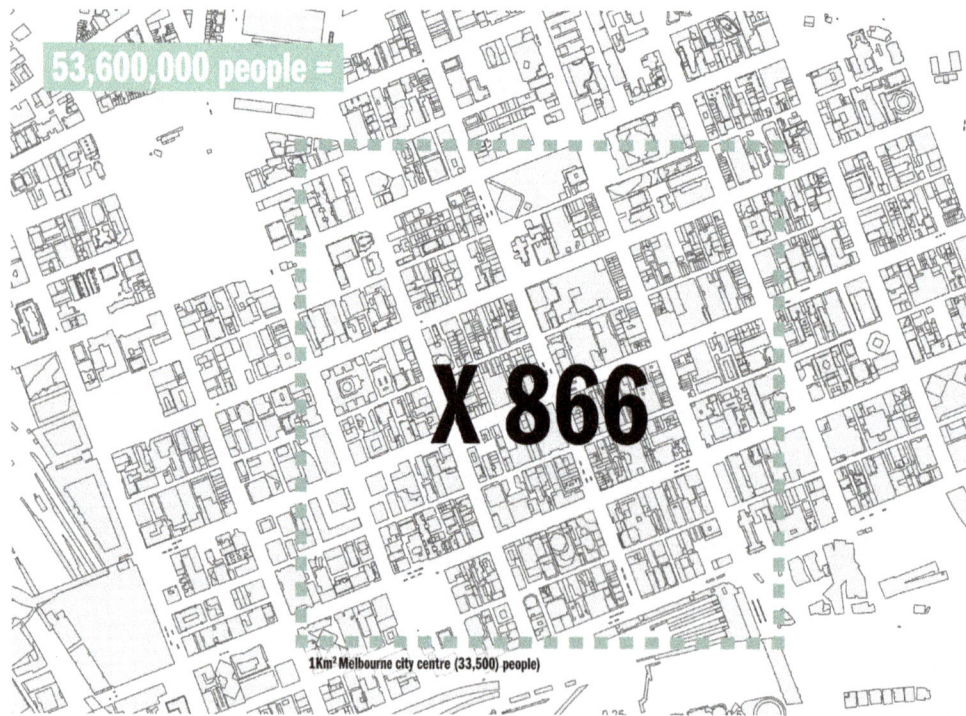

53,600,000 people =

X 866

1Km² Melbourne city centre (33,500) people)

FIGURE 1.6: THE EQUIVALENT OF 866KM² OF MELBOURNE'S CITY CENTRE IS NEEDED TO ACCOMMODATE PROJECTED POPULATION GROWTH BY 2101.

Incremental urbanisation is occurring in the absence of any continental settlement strategy which could inform where and how such a massive building program should happen in the national interest. While a new national urban policy framework was released by the Labor Government in November 2024, its major focus is on generic 'urban places' rather than the national urban system. While the Malcolm Turnbull–led Coalition government did establish a Centre for Population within the Treasury portfolio, its mission has been in macro-demographics without any explicit nexus to spatial policy. Given Australia's growth pressures this century, the longer-term benefits from a national systemic plan for urbanisation are readily apparent, especially where citizen opinion informs and supports such an initiative.

We intend this book to positively contribute to the contentious population debate in Australia by proposing a representative range of continental-scale settlement scenarios for consideration that could inform a prospective national settlement strategy (Figure 1.7). These scenarios do not emerge out of a vacuum, but rather mirror and extend the various kinds of future possibilities tabled in academic and policy literature.[31]

The national population forecast for 2101 employed to underpin the scenarios explored in this book is the authoritative ABS mid-range (Series B) projection of 53 million.[32] This projection represents about a 27 million person increase in the current national population. To understand the implications of this scale of growth in terms of settlement patterns, we presumed that half of this increase would naturally disperse across existing towns and cities.[33] This reflects the political reality that Australia's democratically elected governments do not have the levers outside regional dispersion immigration programs to direct people to places (in other words, they have limited carrots and even fewer sticks).[34] Essentially, this leaves around 14 million people to allocate in each settlement scenario. This approach results in scenarios for 2101 comprised of cities and towns with massively boosted populations. The scenarios were not mutually exclusive, so some cities could have multiple designations. You might find these proposals for massive population growth simplistic or even unduly alarmist. However, without a radically curtailed policy of zero population growth (which we don't propose), growth, either fast or slow, is inevitable. Sceptical readers should also note that Sydneysiders, say, 80 years ago, would have also been incredulous that their then-fair city of 1.5 million would ever surge to over 5 million. Such is the dominance of our lived experience of our cities, it is difficult to imagine them dramatically transformed, but they inevitably will be.

Given the scenarios' need for distinctly different spatial outcomes to clarify assessment and their geographic breadth, the settlement scenarios were presented as singular choices.

31 See for example: Australian Government Our North, Our Future; Australian Government 'Our Plan for Population, Migration and Better Cities'; SGS Economics and Planning; Bolleter and Weller

32 Australian Bureau of Statistics, 'Population Projections, Australia, 2012 (base) to 2101'

33 Bolleter et al, 'Evaluating Scenarios'

34 Australian Government, Planning for Australia's Future Population

+0.5 million people

+1 million people

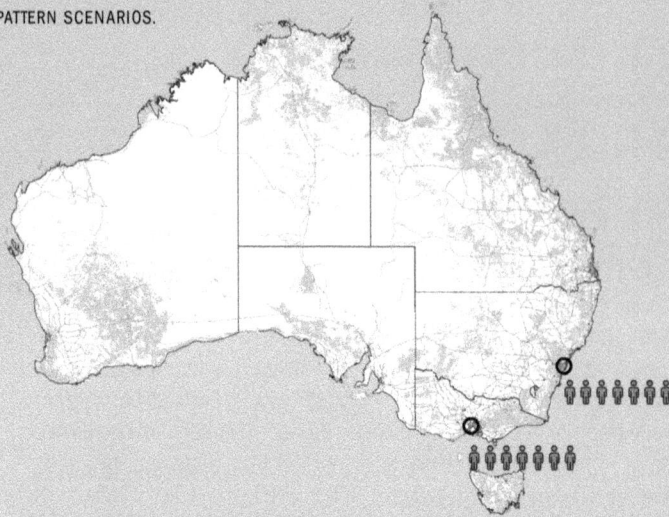
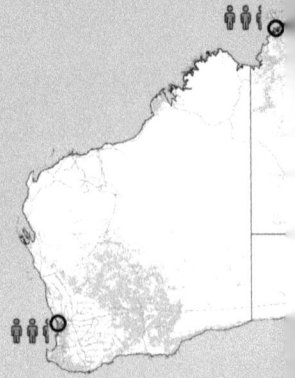

Mega Cities

Secondary Capital Cities

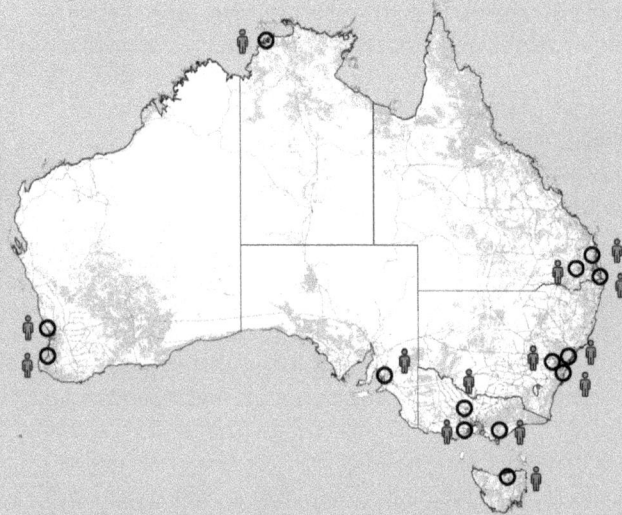
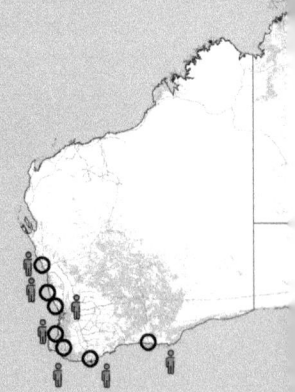

Satellite Cities

Rail Cities

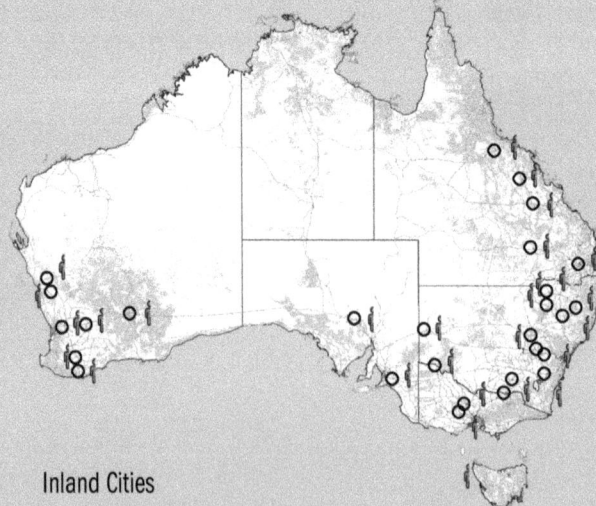
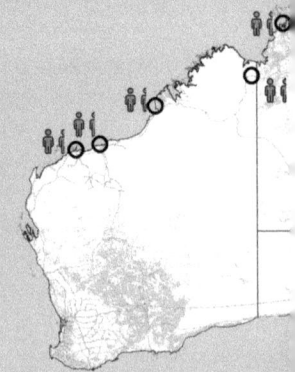

Inland Cities

Northern Cities

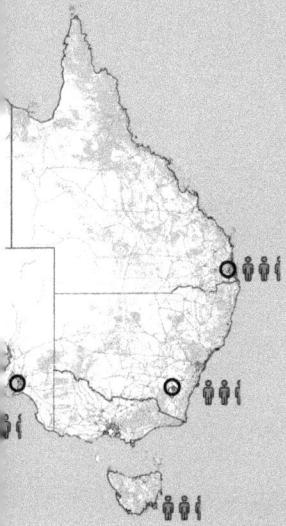

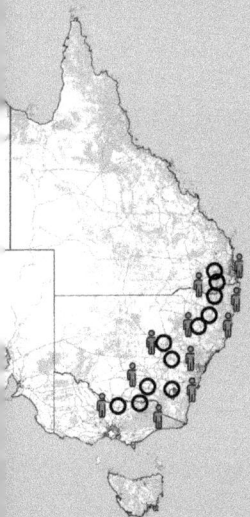

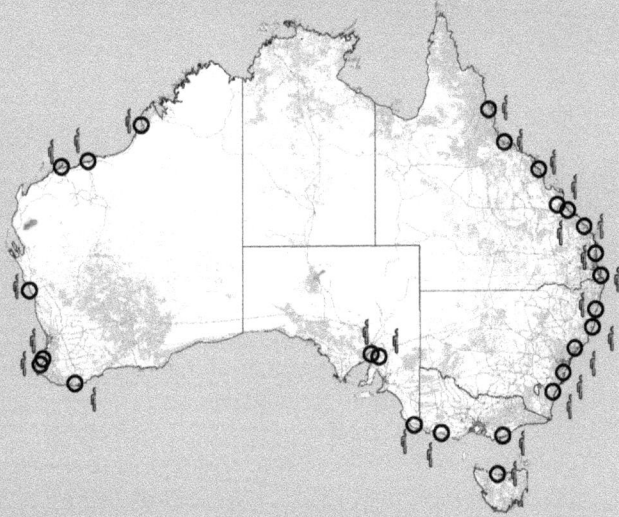

Sea Change Cities

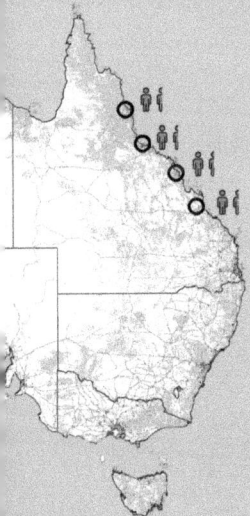

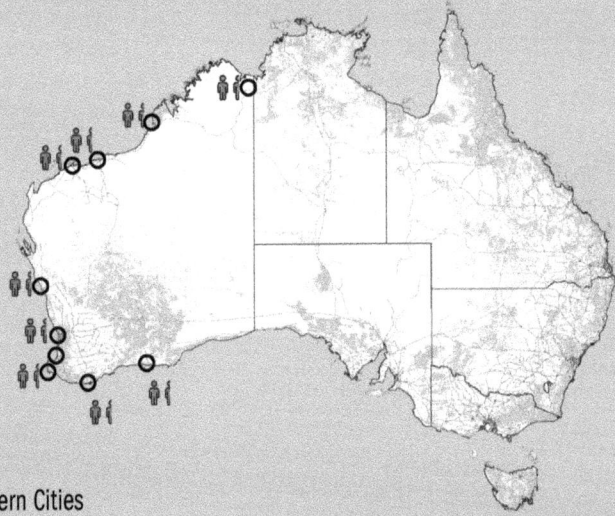

Western Cities

It was intended that such simplified propositional scenarios would allow clarity of vision and evaluation.[35] The eight scenarios are Megacities, Secondary Capital Cities, Satellite Cities, Rail Cities, Sea Change Cities, Inland Cities, Northern Cities and Western Cities.[36] We will not discuss them here, as later chapters explore them in detail.

Rather than leaving the scenarios as enigmatic possible futures, we submit them for systematic evaluation in this book. This critical analysis is essential because future populations will live with our planning decisions as twenty-first-century population, societal, economic, biodiversity and climate challenges unfold, and they will make or break Australia as a successful nation.[37] We conduct the evaluation in two ways: first, community and expert surveys, then a multi-factor suitability analysis.

THE PLAN *MY* AUSTRALIA SURVEYS

While a notable feature of local planning is its reliance on extensive public consultation processes[38] (town hall–style meetings, design charrettes and endless surveys), public consultation is rarely extended meaningfully to the metropolitan,[39] let alone the state or national, scale. However, given the general lack of state power to 'direct' populations to particular cities or regions that can be found in more authoritative systems, such as China, planning for population growth will be unlikely to yield outcomes 'on the ground' without broad alignment to – or at the very least a nuanced appreciation of – community preferences and sentiment.[40]

To address the lack of knowledge, in 2020, we tested the scenarios against expert and community sentiment through two surveys. Firstly, we shared them in consultation with 284 planning experts (the Plan *My* Australia expert survey).[41] The settlement scenarios embodied the national population forecast for 2101 of 53 million people.[42] To be clear, and as noted on page 11, presuming that half of this 28-million-person increase could disperse across existing Australian cities and towns, the survey asked respondents where they would support another 14 million Australians residing (Figure 1.8).

Secondly, we tested the scenarios in a national-scale survey of over 1000 Australians (the Plan *My* Australia community survey).[43] We developed this latter survey to unpack community preferences for long-term national-scale settlement scenarios. Our surveys – rating competing scenarios and inviting comment along the way – are the first to

35 Costanza et al.
36 Bolleter et al., 'Long-Term Settlement Scenarios'
37 Gleeson, The Urban Condition
38 Murphy, 'The Metropolis'
39 Murphy, 'The Metropolis'; Hopkins
40 Bolleter et al., 'Long-Term Settlement Scenarios'
41 Bolleter et al., 'Long-Term Settlement Scenarios'
42 Australian Bureau of Statistics, 'Population Projections, Australia, 2012 to 2101'
43 Bolleter et al., 'Long-Term Settlement Scenarios'

systematically integrate public and expert opinions to assess future spatial scenarios at this scale and understand how expert and public views align or differ.

The results of the surveys are discussed in subsequent chapters, with a particular focus on the community survey. Nonetheless, we have included a snapshot of the results in Table 1.2. The findings indicate a penchant for 'visionary' schemes for population decentralisation from state capital cities to regional areas, and resonate with urban-to-regional migration kindled by the pandemic.[44] Conversely, compounding population growth in the most significant capital cities, Sydney and Melbourne, was reviled. Laypeople also loathed the idea of substantial further population growth in the secondary capital cities (e.g., Perth or Adelaide).

SUITABILITY ANALYSIS

We also tested the settlement scenarios with reference to a continental-scale 'suitability analysis', which maps different factors to assess the suitability of potential regions for urbanisation. There is a long history of attempts to determine the habitability of the continent for more intensive occupation. As we've seen, these include the hand-drawn continental-scale maps of geographer Griffith Taylor in the 1920s as well as several metropolitan and district-scale suitability analyses using more sophisticated multivariate techniques conducted by a later generation of researchers.[45] In the early 1970s, Melbourne research planner Richard Arnot investigated the prospects for urban dispersal for a future national population of 30 million in relation to macro-climatic zones and major drainage basins. The intent was to underline the importance of securing a 'national spatial ordering plan ... without a wholly revolutionary change in technology with regard to energy and water resources'.[46] However, the first rigorous, but limited, national-scale analysis was carried out by a CSIRO research team in the early 1980s.[47] Human ecologist Doug Cocks reported on this work nearly a decade later to identify promising areas for major settlement initiatives, which included the Mackay (Queensland) and Geraldton (Western Australia) regions.[48]

Building on such pioneering work, our national-scale analysis is based on four different 'sub-models', namely climatic; natural and cultural heritage; infrastructure; and economics.[49] Alone and together, these help to identify potential regions where policymakers might direct future urban development. We briefly introduce each in turn below.

44 Bolleter et al., 'Implications of the Covid-19 Pandemic'
45 Pettit et al.; Chen; Weller; Strange and Bashford
46 Arnot
47 Arman et al.
48 Cocks
49 Bolleter et al., 'Informing Future Australian Settlement Planning'

If half disperse, where should we put the remaining 14 million people...?

Help us decide...

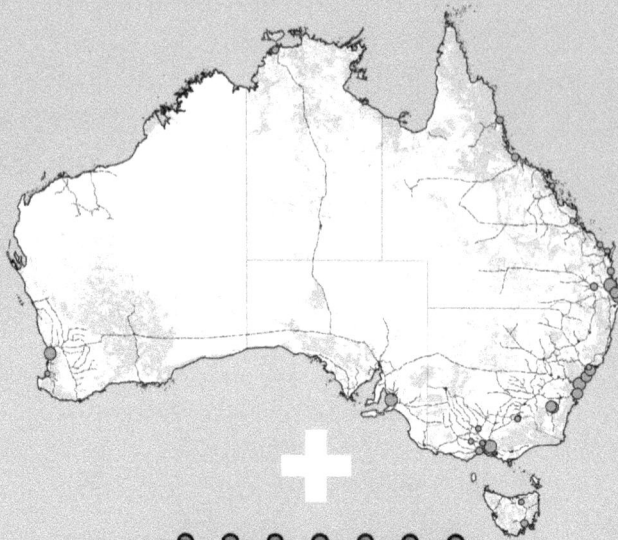

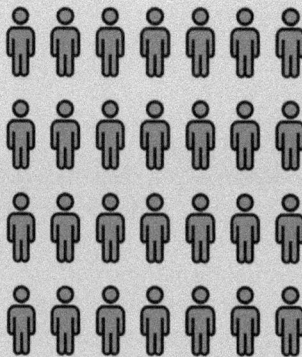

+27,910,000 by 2101.

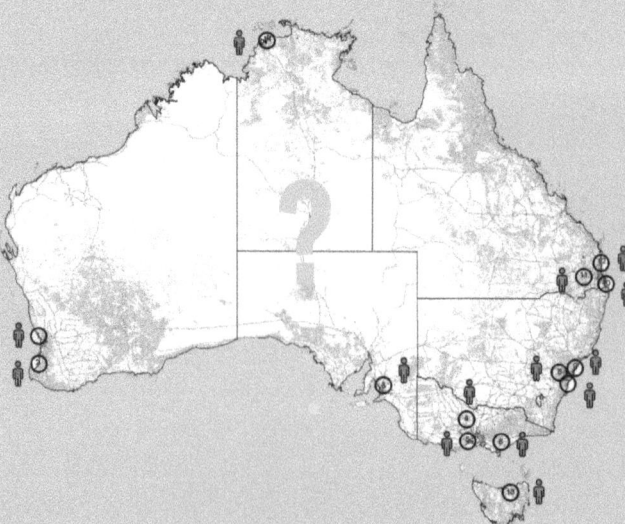

FIGURE 1.8: THE PLAN
MY AUSTRALIA SURVEY
INTRODUCTORY GRAPHIC.

Scenario	Community survey ranking	Expert survey ranking
Satellite Cities	1	1
Rail Cities	2	3
Inland Cities	3	N/A
Western Cities	4	7
Northern Cities	5	5
Sea Change Cities	6	4
Secondary Capital Cities	7	2
Megacities	8	6

TABLE 1.2: RESULTS OF THE PLAN MY AUSTRALIA COMMUNITY AND EXPERT'S SURVEY. THE EXPERT SURVEY DID NOT INCLUDE AN INLAND CITIES SCENARIO.

CLIMATE

As the climate crisis unfolds, climate will become an increasing driver of population distribution. Under the climate sub-model, we identify three factors constraining Australia's future urban development (Figure 1.9).[50] The first is *heat stress*, which derives from heat and humidity.[51] The second is the *annual rainfall*.[52] The third is areas that currently experience *cyclone risk*.[53]

NATURAL AND CULTURAL HERITAGE

Nineteenth- and twentieth-century city building occurred at great expense to ecosystems and Indigenous culture, a situation that can no longer be condoned or perpetuated. Accordingly, for our natural and cultural heritage sub-model, we select several factors that constrain urban development: significant native vegetation, conservation reserves, native title determinations, hydrological features and slope (Figure 1.10).[54] In addition to 'determinations', there are currently 128 outstanding native title claims. Many, if not most, will lead to determinations, so our analysis somewhat underestimates Indigenous claims to native title.

50 Bolleter et al., 'Informing future Australian settlement planning'
51 Davidson
52 Bureau of Meteorology
53 Bureau of Meteorology
54 Geoscience Australia; National Native Title Tribunal

Heat stress

Very hot very humid
Very hot not ness humid
Hot very humid
Hot not ness humid
Warm very humid
Warm not ness humid
Mild very humid
Mild humid
Mild not humid

0   290   580 KM

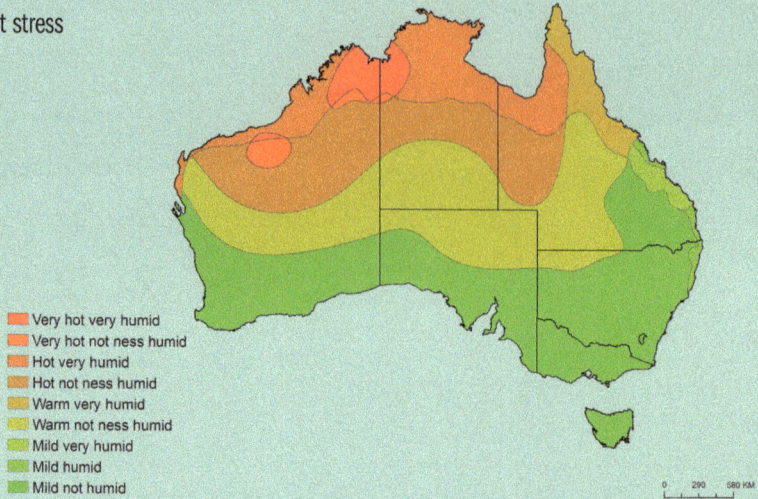

Average annual rainfall

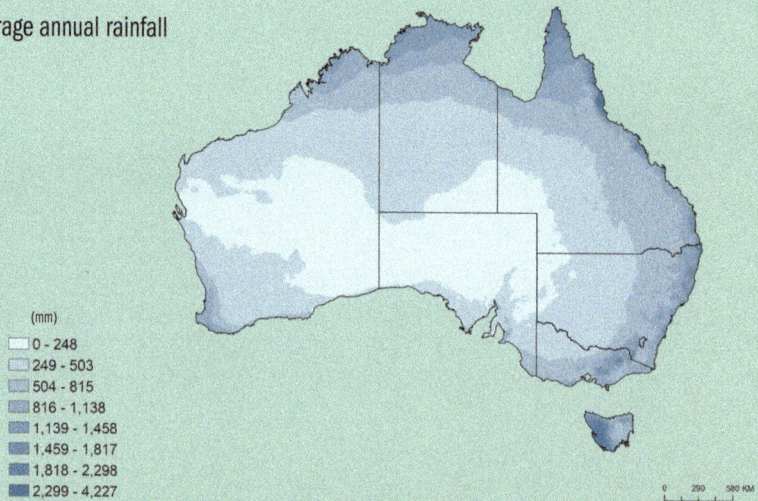

(mm)
0 - 248
249 - 503
504 - 815
816 - 1,138
1,139 - 1,458
1,459 - 1,817
1,818 - 2,298
2,299 - 4,227

0   290   580 KM

Cyclone Incidence

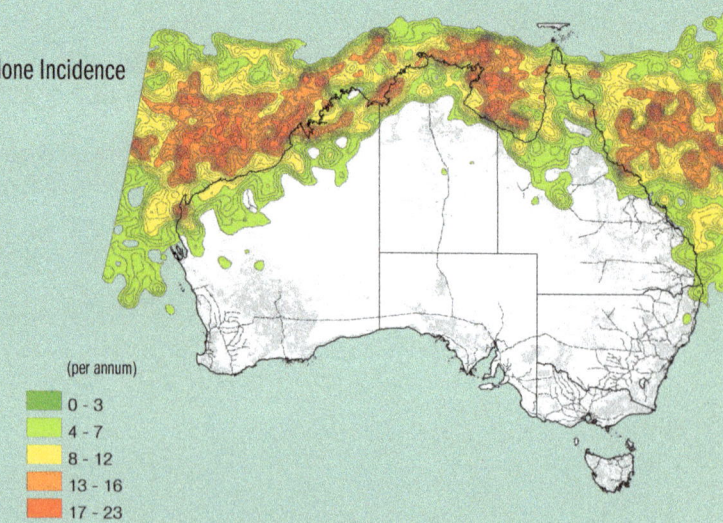

(per annum)
0 - 3
4 - 7
8 - 12
13 - 16
17 - 23

FIGURE 1.9: MAPPING
UNDERPINNING THE CLIMATIC
SUB-MODEL. RAINFALL AND
CYCLONE INCIDENCE MAPS
COURTESY OF THE BUREAU OF
METEOROLOGY.

INFRASTRUCTURE

Urbanisation will – as much as possible – need to be grafted onto existing infrastructure to boost both development feasibility and sustainability. Under the infrastructure sub-model, we identify several vital infrastructures that present opportunities for urban development at a continental scale. These are proximity to major ports, airports, regional railway lines, principal roads, water pipelines, major power lines and telecommunications (captured by the National Broadband Network [NBN]; Figure 1.11).[55] Urban development can, and will to some degree, occur without existing infrastructure capacity. However, it will be an exorbitantly expensive exercise, and constrained government budgets will weigh heavily on development feasibility.[56]

ECONOMICS

Finally, big and bold settlement plans will only gather dust in government libraries unless planned urbanisation is interwoven with economic opportunities in the form of jobs.[57] While remote working and fly-in fly-out (FIFO) commuting have stretched the umbilical cords between home and work, for most workers, physical proximity to work remains desirable, if not essential. As such, under the economics sub-model, we map two representative indicators: average weekly household incomes as a proxy for well-renumerated employment opportunities, and proximity to the capital cities – Australia's significant population and employment nodes (Figure 1.12).[58] Indeed, 80% of Australia's economic activity occurs in large cities, serving as 'the backbone of our economy'.[59]

    The various factors underlying each sub-model can be combined into four thematic suitability maps based on different weightings reflecting the importance of particular factors (Figure 1.13). In turn, these can be incorporated into a single synthesis suitability map against which we can assess the settlement scenarios (Figure 1.14).[60] As a snapshot, this map reveals that five principal regions are most suitable for twenty-first-century Australian urban development, to a large degree mirroring where settlement has occurred. Starting from the west is a region surrounding Perth and extending southwards to the coastal town of Busselton, northwards to the coastal town of Cervantes and southeast to Wagin. The second region encompasses Adelaide and extends to the Yorke Peninsula to the west. A third region to the east forms an almost contiguous area extending from Melbourne through Canberra, Wollongong, and Sydney to Newcastle. A fourth region encompasses Tasmania. A fifth region surrounds Brisbane and extends to Bundaberg in the north and Coffs Harbour in the south.[61]

55 Bolleter et al., 'Informing future Australian settlement planning'; Geoscience Australia
56 Arman et al.
57 Bolleter et al., 'Informing Future Australian Settlement Planning'
58 Australian Bureau of Statistics, 'Census'; Bolleter et al., 'Informing Future Australian Settlement Planning'
59 Kelly and Donegan, 23
60 Bolleter et al., 'Informing Future Australian Settlement Planning'
61 Bolleter et al., 'Informing future Australian settlement planning'

Native vegetation

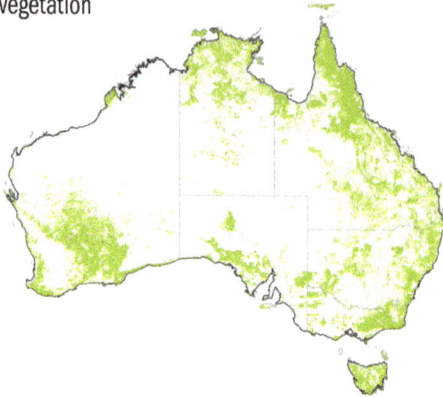

Hydrology

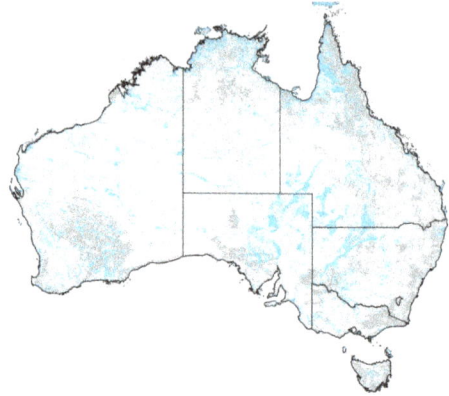

Conservation Reserves

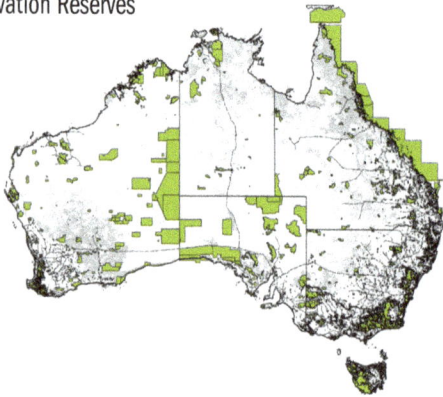

Slope (%)

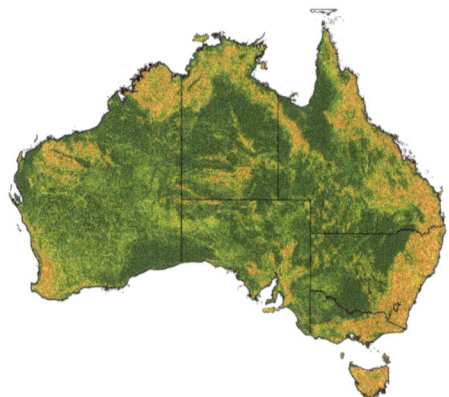

■ 0 - 2
■ 3 - 5
■ 6 - 9
■ 10 - 10
■ 20 - 30

Native Title Determinations

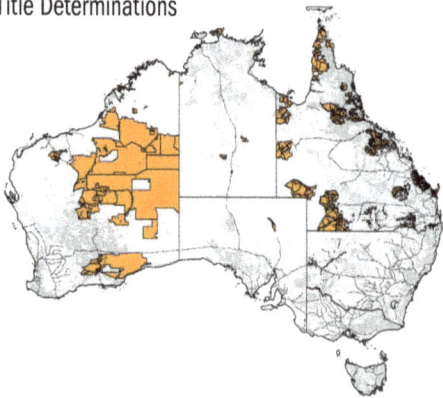

FIGURE 1.10: MAPPING UNDERPINNING THE NATURAL AND CULTURAL HERITAGE SUB-MODEL. MAPPING COURTESY OF GEOSCIENCE AUSTRALIA.

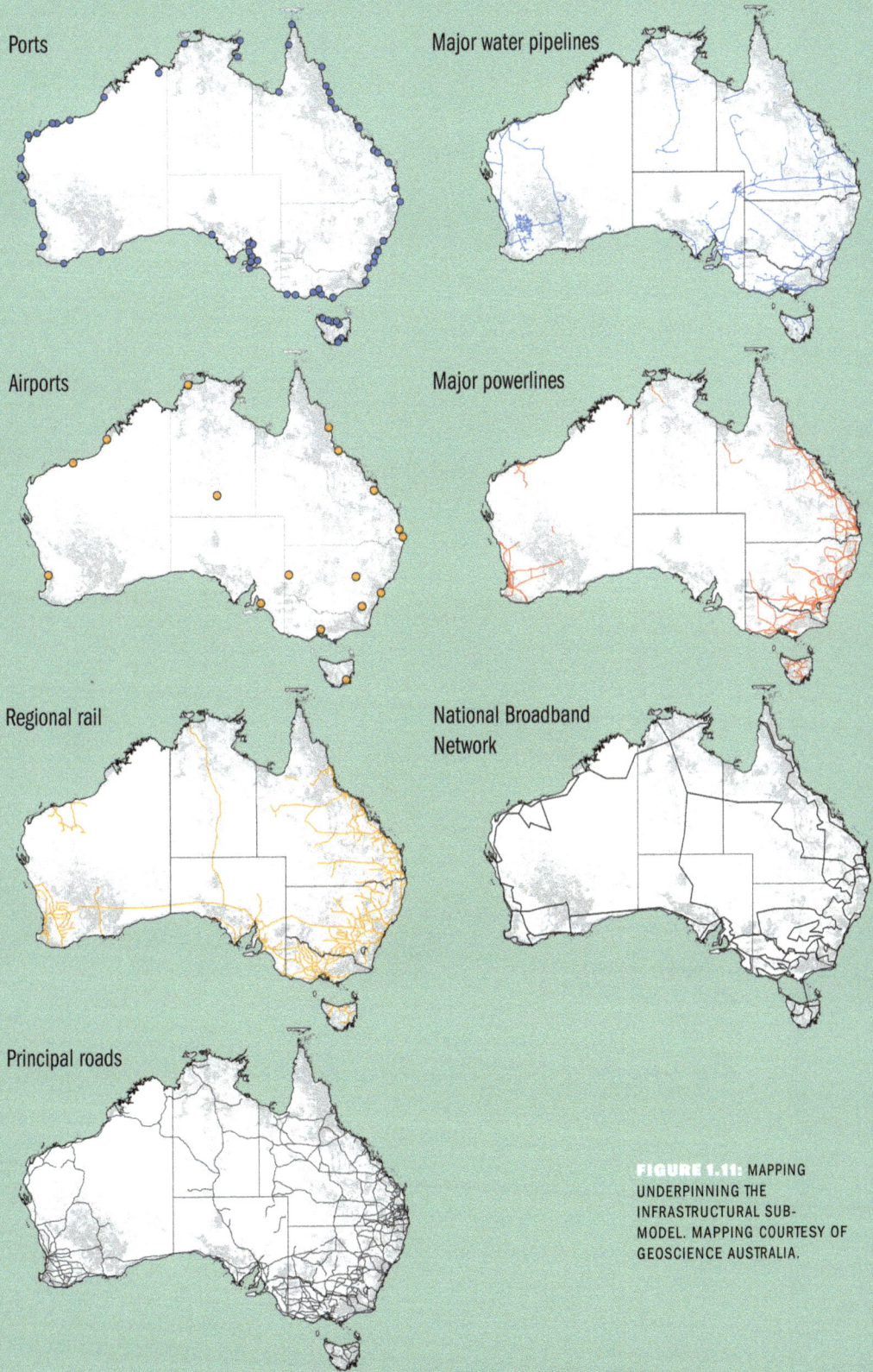

Ports

Major water pipelines

Airports

Major powerlines

Regional rail

National Broadband Network

Principal roads

FIGURE 1.11: MAPPING UNDERPINNING THE INFRASTRUCTURAL SUB-MODEL. MAPPING COURTESY OF GEOSCIENCE AUSTRALIA.

Capital cities

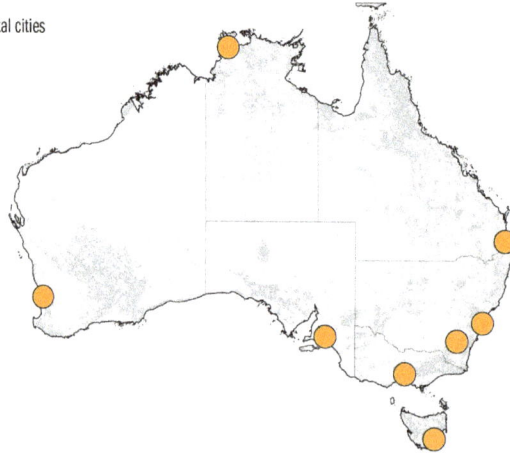

Average weekly income

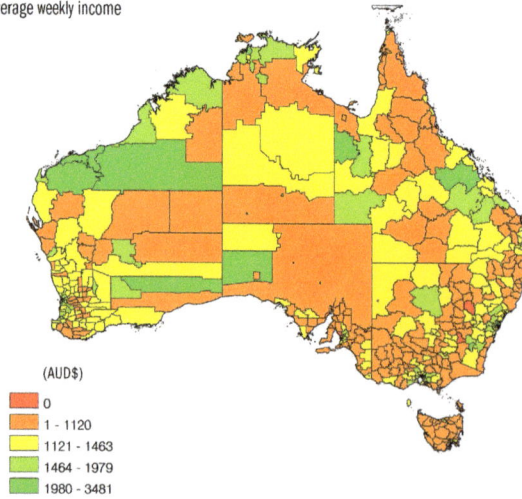

(AUD$)

- 0
- 1 - 1120
- 1121 - 1463
- 1464 - 1979
- 1980 - 3481

FIGURE 1.12: MAPPING UNDERPINNING THE ECONOMIC SUB-MODEL. MAPPING COURTESY OF GEOSCIENCE AUSTRALIA AND THE AUSTRALIAN BUREAU OF STATISTICS.

Climatic

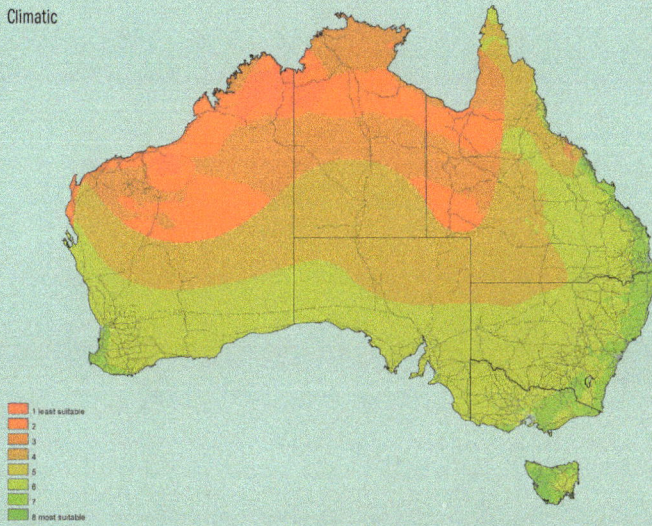

Natural and cultural heritage

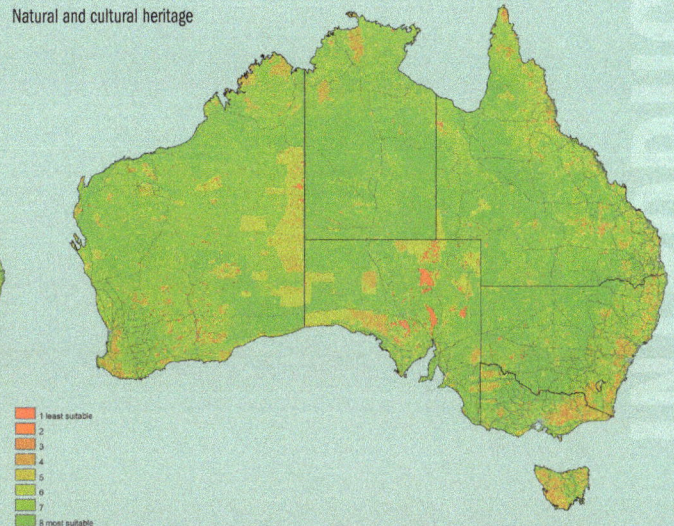

Infrastructural and economic

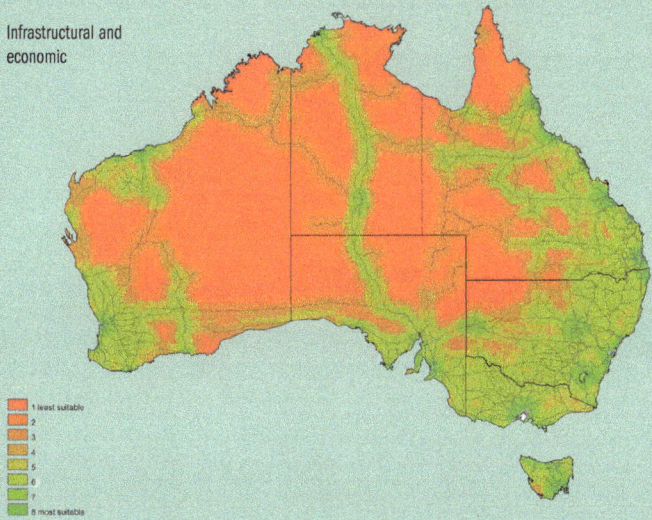

Urbanisation

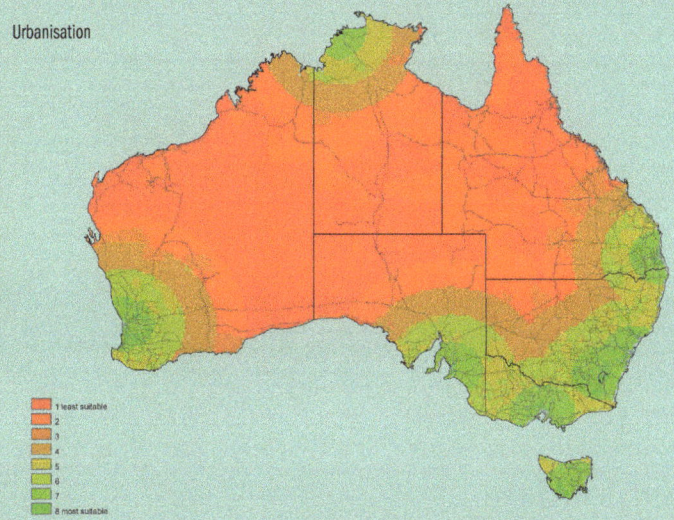

FIGURE 1.13: NATIONAL-SCALE ANALYSIS SUB-MODELS. GREEN AREAS ARE MORE FERTILE FOR URBANISATION, RED REGIONS LESS.

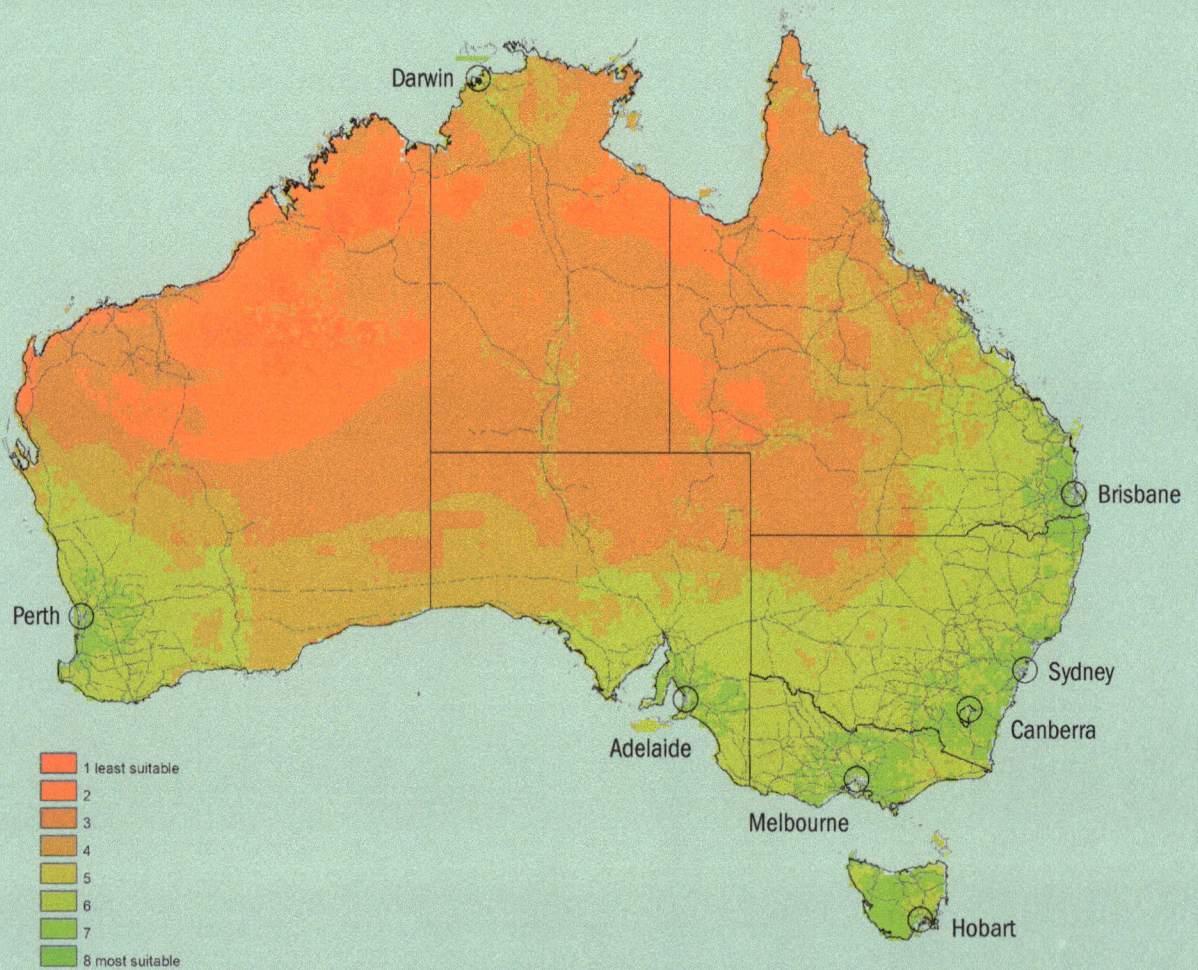

Darwin

Brisbane

Perth

Sydney

Canberra

Adelaide

Melbourne

Hobart

1 least suitable
2
3
4
5
6
7
8 most suitable

FIGURE 1.14: OUR
NATIONAL-SCALE SUITABILITY
ANALYSIS IS BASED ON
SYNTHESISING THE CLIMATIC,
NATURAL AND CULTURAL
HERITAGE, INFRASTRUCTURAL
AND ECONOMIC SUB-MODELS.

These broad regions typically offer some proximity to the capital cities – the powerhouses of the Australian economy – and reflect proximity to employment, but also existing infrastructure, such as major ports and international airports. Centres on rail networks and other major infrastructures connecting Melbourne and Sydney are also well placed for future urban development. Finally, a temperate climate and reasonable rainfall characterise the regions suited to urban growth. Conversely, the north and the interior appear likely to repel urbanisation, perhaps unsurprisingly. In later chapters, we will dive into the details of how the settlement scenarios rate against this overall suitability map.

BOOK STRUCTURE

Here, we sketch the book's structure to enable you to dip in and out as per your interests. Chapter 2 presents the plethora of problems that bedevil Australia's major cities. Despite its enduring allure, the Australian Dream is increasingly unattainable for many. Indeed, home ownership among young people is declining, while renters face worrying insecurity. As the population spreads further from city centres, traffic clogs arteries and commuting becomes a waking nightmare. Social isolation worsens while polarisation between rich and poor, young and old, and the inner city and outer suburbs deepens.[62] On top of these woes, Australia's multicultural melting pot model also shows signs of strain. Population growth, while ebbing and flowing, remains relentless globally. Australia must negotiate its future against this backdrop. In response, in Chapters 3 to 5 of this book, we introduce and interrogate the eight scenarios for how Australia, at the continental scale, could accommodate an extra 14 million 'new' Australians. The settlement pattern scenarios are organised thematically. Chapter 3 includes scenarios that advocate for continuing growth in Australia's dominant state and territory capital cities. Chapter 4 presents scenarios for decentralising the population from the chief capital cities to regional centres. In Chapter 5, we propose scenarios to deliver urbanisation in frontier regions, such as northern Australia and inland Australia. With the various scenarios described, interpreted and critiqued, in Chapter 6 we take a different tack by exploring what this new urban settlement might look like. Here, we draw from winning entries in an international student competition, organised by the authors and their colleagues, to design a future Australian city. In Chapter 7, we synthesise the scenarios into options for a continental settlement pattern that could inform a prospective national settlement strategy.

62 Kelly and Donegan

IMAGE BY YMGERMAN COURTESY OF SHUTTERSTOCK (STOCK PHOTO ID 1979945306)

2

CHALLENGES AHEAD

Second only to the problem of keeping world peace is that of coping with urban expansion.[1]

BACKGROUND

History reminds us to be cautious about how 'visionaries' use constructed 'crises' to legitimise extreme planning solutions.[2] One key example is the mid-twentieth-century modernist messiah Le Corbusier and his ideal of razing congested and tumorous historic city centres in favour of serried ranks of high-rise office towers and apartment blocks. Of course, such totalising ideals never really work, although they have influenced the course of urban development. In a similar mode, smart city proponents argue that we have created cities that are too large, polluted, unsafe and fundamentally out of control, and that the utopia of smart fixing can counterbalance such a dystopia. Despite cautioning that 'the city is never a terminally ill patient in need of major surgery', even the most stubborn optimist would concede that Australia's major urban regions fast-tracking to megalopolitan development face significant challenges that could snowball into crises if not assertively addressed.[3] This chapter considers these challenges and presents the planning failures perpetuating them. It serves as a warning shot across the bows intended to increase public (and professional) awareness of the issues before they become so bad that they are virtually insoluble.[4]

1   The United Nations in Cheung, 12
2   Aurigi
3   Aurigi, 25
4   Aitken

URBAN CHALLENGES

Urban communities worldwide face daunting problems in repositioning growth, development and management for genuinely sustainable futures.[5] Here, we outline the principal challenges confronting Australia's cities and towns under two main categories: social and environmental issues.

SOCIETAL ISSUES

Despite half-hearted assurances that 'bigger does not have to be worse', the Lowy Institute Poll (2019) had 71% of Australians agreeing that Australian cities are too overcrowded.[6] Many Australians 'assume an unavoidable trade-off between quality of life and population growth'.[7] Unfortunately, many city problems (such as crushing congestion, escalating housing costs and diminishing access to public services) are directly or indirectly linked to population growth (and the 'problem' of immigration) by the media.[8] However, this tendency conveniently obscures the fact that many social issues are triggered by inadequate planning and funding (e.g., for public transport or housing) resulting from an expenditure-averse neo-liberal planning system, as opposed to population growth per se. Regardless, a series of recent surveys indicates that many Australians feel the benefits of population growth have already been achieved and that Australia will not benefit substantially from future population growth through immigration. Indeed, despite the considerable contributions of migrants to Australian society, some Australians regard population growth and, principally, immigration as a problem. For example, 31% of Australians feel 'if Australia is too open to people from all over the world, we risk losing our identity as a nation', although we note this percentage has declined since 2018.[9] Moreover, in a recent survey, 55% of respondents agreed or strongly agreed with the statement 'Australia is in danger of losing its culture and identity'.[10]

But is this fear overly melodramatic? Certainly, in Sydney and Melbourne, recent migrants are increasingly clustered together. One-quarter of Sydneysiders and nearly one-fifth of Melbournites live in a suburb where at least half the population was born overseas.[11] In the Sydney suburb of Auburn and the Melbourne suburb of Dandenong, people from a non-English-speaking background comprise 83% and 75% of the population, respectively.

5 Norman, Sustainable Pathways
6 Lowy Institute
7 Southphommasane, 147
8 Betts and Birrell
9 Lowy Institute
10 Betts and Birrell, 4
11 Button and Rizvi

Moreover, poor English speakers are contained within just 20 suburbs in the two big cities, predominantly in Sydney's west and Melbourne's outer southeast.[12] These historically high concentrations drove the Scanlon Foundation to ask in its 2017 Mapping Social Cohesion report 'whether past patterns of integration are continuing or whether new norms are being established'?[13] Indeed, from a baseline in 2007, social cohesion has been sliding downwards.[14] Rightly or wrongly, many voters are also worried about the consequences of escalating ethnic diversity. Forty-eight per cent supported a partial ban on Muslim immigration to Australia, with only 25% in opposition.[15]

Entrenched negative attitudes to immigration lead to the conclusion that Australia – and its major cities – are already 'full', echoing former NSW premier Bob Carr's 2000 famous proclamation that 'Sydney is full'.[16] Such opinions partly emerge from long-standing immigration destinations.[17] Indeed, before the COVID-19 pandemic, most new arrivals gravitated towards the bustling cities of Melbourne or Sydney. As a result, the populations of these cities swelled by over 100,000 people annually (Figure 2.1).[18]

Against this backdrop, residents perceived the impacts of escalating housing costs, infrastructure deficits and traffic congestion.[19] Indeed, home ownership among young people is declining precipitously, while renters and marginalised groups face worrying insecurity as housing affordability deteriorates. Despite Australia's 'liveability superpower' status, the Australian Dream of owner-occupied detached housing is increasingly out of reach for many citizens following in the wake of the baby boomers (born 1946–1964).[20] Moreover, traffic and public transport congestion cause economic and social stresses and strains; urban congestion costs across Australia are forecast to reach $39.8 billion by 2031.[21]

Nonetheless, these issues are also compounded by policy fractures, such as relative under-investment in public transport and, more indirectly, negative-gearing policies, which spur speculative property investment. Broader housing policies, such as negative gearing for housing investors and first homebuyers' grants allied to a lack of investment in public housing construction, have also been linked to increased housing costs and reduced affordability in different urban housing markets.[22] Population growth is undoubtedly essential, but its 'precise role requires viewing as part of the complex geography of housing markets, rather than being generalised as the major contributor to higher housing costs in all settings'.[23]

12 Button and Rizvi
13 Scanlon Foundation Research Institute
14 Chan
15 Betts and Birrell
16 Seamer, 16
17 Bolleter et al., 'Implications of the Covid-19 Pandemic'
18 Birrell and Healy
19 Benson and Brown; Seamer; Kelly and Donegan
20 The Economist
21 Hill et al.
22 Fincher
23 Fincher, 342

FIGURE 2.1: THE SUBURBAN FABRIC OF WESTERN SYDNEY'S DEVELOPMENT FRONTIER. IMAGE BY HARLEY KINGSTON COURTESY OF SHUTTERSTOCK (STOCK PHOTO ID: 1977700022).

CHAPTER 2

Density Wars

The intuitive understanding of the quality of life in urban Australia reflects a deeply sentimental ideal where, as Tim Southphommasane opines, 'children can play with abandon in sunshine. Not for us, those high-rise apartment blocks of dark, polluted metropolises in Asia and elsewhere.'[24] However, despite the allure of suburbia, since the 1980s, planning orthodoxy in Australia has advocated that a surging population should be accommodated through urban consolidation in existing urban areas.[25] Indeed, across the nation, state capital city policies propose that most new housing should be in established suburbs; for instance, Adelaide 85%, Melbourne 70%, Sydney 70%, Southeast Queensland 60%, and Perth 47%.[26] Nonetheless, achieving these targets is no small feat in the face of community hostility. Increasing density, resulting partly from population growth and the turn to multi-dwelling buildings, is also often regarded as a threat to quintessential suburban life (Figure 2.2).[27] Sarkissian tells us that a 'huge battle has been waging for more than two decades about this matter in Australia'[28] – and that a public 'sullenness' exists regarding urban infill in suburban neighbourhoods.[29] For example, in 2011, 52% of suburban residents of Australia's capital cities said they 'would not like' population increases in their neighbourhood; and only a miserly 11% responded favourably to this idea.[30]

While much of this change is driven by planning philosophies advocating '30-minute cities', mixed-use, urban villages, smart cities, and walkability – with supporters proudly endorsing the moniker of YIMBY (yes, in my backyard) – the resistance in established neighbourhoods is more entrenched. NIMBY (not in my backyard) supporters are typically active, strident and well-networked residents who protest new apartment development proposals in their community while often accepting these developments would benefit their city on a broader scale (just in someone else's backyard).[31] While not always acknowledged, NIMBY sentiments can swirl around preserving class status, excluding lower-income groups (particularly those in social housing), reducing competition for parking, protecting views and green spaces, resisting higher densities, and insulating much-coveted house prices.[32]

NIMBYism typically rises in tandem with gentrification and increased socioeconomic advantage,[33] and most immediate inner areas of Australia's capital cities have already been thoroughly gentrified.[34] This situation poses an issue as state government policies aim to encourage urban densification in these very areas where resistance is most strident.[35] As a result of entrenched resistance to densification in inner suburbs, cities often fall short of their infill targets,[36] further compounding housing affordability issues.[37]

24 Southphommasane, 148
25 McCrea and Walters
26 Department of Planning, Transport and Infrastructure; Victorian State Government; Urban Taskforce Australia; Department of Infrastructure, Local Government and Planning; Department of Planning, Lands and Heritage
27 Dovey and Woodcock; Bolleter et al., 'Delivering Medium-Density Infill Development'
28 Sarkissian
29 Kelly and Donegan, 129.
30 Productivity Commission
31 Bolleter et al., 'Long-term settlement scenarios for Australia'
32 Bolleter et al., 'Long-term settlement scenarios for Australia'
33 Einstein et al.
34 Pegler et al.
35 Pegler et al.
36 Bolleter and Weller; Newton; Randolph
37 McNee and Pojani

Societal Segregation and Stratification

A further effect of the resulting sprawling cities is a new urban divide, which is challenging long-held Australian ideals of a 'fair-go' for all and deepening socioeconomic divides within our cities.[38] The social harm caused by inequality cannot be quarantined to low-income people. Unequal societies generate morbidities, such as failing mental health, obesity and violence, that affect all social strata.[39]

The yawning gap between people who live near the centre of our cities and those who live near the outer fringes is of particular significance.[40] As city populations grow, housing close to jobs and public transport continues to appreciate more quickly than housing in outer areas. Wealthier households generally seek to live in these bastions of gentrified privilege in the inner cities[41] and, increasingly, are the only ones able to afford the requisite higher housing costs.[42] The price escalation in the inner and middle ring of our cities is resulting in significant property cost increases across the whole of the metropolitan area, which is reducing owner-occupation, putting pressure on rental accommodation and, worst of all, leaving many people homeless.[43]

Poorer households are increasingly locked out of these areas because of the more significant numbers of accessible jobs with higher incomes and greater security that the inner and middle suburbs offer.[44] For those exiled to the wrong side of the divide (known variously in Sydney as the 'Latte' or 'Red Rooster' line), poorer access to jobs affects their ability to maintain and build a career over time, and extensive commuting is expensive and exhausting.[45]

While long work journeys have been a facet of suburban life since the 1970s, the total distance and number of car trips in Australian cities are still growing.[46] Sadly, more than a quarter of all commuters in Australia's big cities spend more time commuting than with their children,[47] and unsurprisingly, longer commutes are linked to reduced time for social connection and lower overall well-being and life satisfaction.[48] The yawning gulf between the locations of our jobs and people also makes the economy much less productive than it should be.[49]

38 Bolleter et al., 'Long-term settlement
    scenarios for Australia'
39 Gleeson, Lifeboat Cities
40 Kelly and Donegan
41 Gleeson, 'Waking from the Dream'
42 Kelly and Donegan
43 Seamer
44 Kelly and Donegan
45 Kelly and Donegan, 48; Chrysanthos
    and Ding
46 Cities Commission; Kelly and Donegan
47 Kelly and Donegan
48 Kelly and Donegan
49 Kelly and Donegan

FIGURE 2.2: POOR QUALITY INFILL DEVELOPMENT COMPOUNDS ANTI-DENSITY SENTIMENT IN PERTH'S MIDDLE-RING SUBURBS. PHOTO BY DAVID PONTON.

ENVIRONMENTAL ISSUES

A further consequence of public contestation of infill development in established leafy suburbs is that these localities rarely meet their targets for urban densification and, in some cases, sprawl into biodiversity hotspots or high-value peri-urban agricultural areas with alarming consequences.[50] The bulldozing of biodiversity is particularly worrying in Brisbane, Perth and Sydney, which sit within two global biodiversity hotspots. Biodiversity hotspots are vital globally because 60% of threatened mammals, 63% of threatened birds and 79% of threatened amphibians are found exclusively within them.[51] Indeed, globally, if conservation efforts fail in the hotspots, we lose nearly half of all terrestrial species regardless of how successful we are everywhere else.[52]

Australia has a strong and well-resourced planning system, so we should lead the world in creating hotspot havens. Nevertheless, how are we tracking towards protecting the hotspots in Australia? Not well, unfortunately. Australia's biodiversity hotspots have been stripped of more than 70% of their native vegetation cover through development.[53] Indeed, Australian cities generally have a disproportionately high number of threatened species and are home to, on average, three times as many threatened species per hectare as rural environments.[54] Let's zoom into one of the hotspots for a closer look. The important south west Australia biodiversity hotspot encircling Perth is in a perilous state, with more species of threatened plants (c.2500) than other Australian states and most countries, and only 7% of the original vegetation intact (Figure 2.3).[55]

So how does urban development contribute to this sorry situation? Urban development tends to impact biodiversity in two main ways. Firstly, suburban expansion devastates remnant ecologies through the broad-scale clearing of sites for suburban developments (Figure 2.4). Land developers aim to create a tree-free tabula rasa upon which project homes can be easily plopped with minimum hassle and for maximum profit. Contorting layouts around complex ecological considerations is simply not feasible in many situations. In this mode, the endemic ecology of a site is mainly erased, with only hapless remnants tokenised to support the development's marketing. Secondly, the increasing ratio of building area relative to site area on lots in infill development and new compact suburbs means the space for trees, plants and outdoor recreation at both the front and rear of houses has decreased.[56] As a result, private sector residential development in the past 20 years has less tree cover than in previous decades.[57] This situation leaves planners in a predicament, simultaneously trying to put the brakes on sprawl through compact development and intertwining ecology through this consolidated development without abetting further sprawl – a highwire act.

50 Ramalho et al.; Hill et al.
51 Mittermeier et al.
52 Mittermeier et al.
53 Hill et al.
54 Hill et al.
55 Southwest Australia Ecoregion Initiative;
    Hopper and Gioa
56 Hill et al.
57 Hill et al.

Plant associations

Cleared land

FIGURE 2.3: MAPS SHOWING THE ENDEMIC PLANT ASSOCIATIONS OF THE SOUTH WEST AUSTRALIA BIODIVERSITY HOTSPOT BEFORE (LEFT) AND AFTER (RIGHT) 200 YEARS OF EUROPEAN SETTLEMENT. MAPPING COURTESY OF THE DEPARTMENT OF BIODIVERSITY, CONSERVATION AND ATTRACTIONS.

Climate Change Issues

Other looming threats to biodiversity stem from climate change. Nonetheless, Australia continues to have a stubborn reliance on fossil fuels. Despite the widespread plastering of solar panels on suburban roofs, coal, oil and natural gas accounted for 94% of Australia's primary energy mix in 2018–19.[58] This situation is worrying because, despite Australia's sluggish efforts in mitigating climate change, we have much to lose from a changing climate.[59] Indeed, in a recent major report, the authoritative International Panel on Climate Change (IPCC) warns that 'the region faces an extremely challenging future that will be highly disruptive for many human and natural systems' and that climate impacts are 'cascading and compounding across sectors, socioeconomic, and natural systems'.[60] Or as Brendan Gleeson puts it,

The wonderful climate – the envy of the world – seems to be turning on us. Terra Australis is becoming Terror Australis, a blast furnace of drought, heat and capricious tempests.[61]

Almost nine out of 10 Australians live in cities and towns, and they are already experiencing climate change impacts through the lens of an urban environment.[62] Indeed, since 2020, our urban environments have already experienced several one-in-100-year climate shocks and stresses.[63] Our progressively hotter global climate will trigger further environmental hazards, including bigger bushfires, floods, storms and temperature extremes, which are all increasingly urban issues.[64] Climate change will also damage urban biodiversity and ecosystems that support social well-being, provide services fundamental to our health, such as clean air and fresh water, and offer some protection from natural disasters.[65] So, what are the most severe threats caused by climate change in Australia's cities?

58 Hill et al.
59 O'Neil and Watts
60 IPCC, 3
61 Gleeson, 'Waking from the Dream', 15
62 Australian Academy of Science
63 Hill et al.
64 Norman, Climate Change; Kelly and Donegan; Seamer
65 Australian Government, 'National Climate Resilience and Adaptation Strategy'

Heat Stress

The year 2019 was Australia's hottest on record, with mean maximum temperatures across the continent over l.5°C above the long-term average (Figure 2.5).[66] Moreover, current global emission reduction policies are projected to allow a global warming of between 2.1°C and 3.9°C by 2100, leaving some of Australia's cities and towns at very high risk.[67] Periods of extreme heat increase human mortality and morbidity, especially among vulnerable members of the population: the socioeconomically disadvantaged, outdoor workers, those with medical conditions, children and older adults.[68] Indeed, heat stress contributes to the deaths of more than 1000 people over 65 across Australia annually, with excess heat contributing to as many as 1.7 million deaths between 2006 and 2017.[69] The ongoing vulnerability of older Australians is of particular significance, with a quarter of the Australian population estimated to be older than 65 by 2056.[70] Accordingly, the World Health Organization has identified extreme temperatures as a leading global health threat.[71] Heat stress is more than just an isolated health issue, though. Other correlations with heat stress are increased crime and negative impacts on labour productivity.[72]

The urban heat island effect compounds heat stress in urban areas. This is a night-time occurrence driven by heat stored in thermal mass in the urban landscape during the day (picture red-hot roads or roofs at the end of a summer day) and then slowly released at night while undeveloped areas cool uninhibited.[73] As a result, the excess heat load in urban areas can reach a colossal 10°C compared with greener peri-urban surroundings.[74] The urban heat island effect also increases air conditioning usage, requiring more energy, compounding climate change and adding anthropogenic heating to urban areas.[75]

So, which Australian cities might be most affected by heat stress? Quite possibly, it will be the cities and towns of northern Australia because the effects of the most lethal heat waves are elevated temperatures, urban heat island effects and humidity. Extremely high heat combined with high humidity diminishes the human body's ability to regulate its temperature by sweating. Put simply, when humidity is high, sweat is no longer evaporated off your skin; therefore, the cooling effect of sweating stops. Hence, hot and humid conditions can be more dangerous to human health than the equivalent hot but dry conditions (imagine a hot but dry summer day in Perth compared to the sweltering humidity of a hot summer day in Darwin).[76] As a result of this confluence of extreme heat and humidity, heat stress will impinge on the liveability, and to some degree even the viability, of northern Australian cities in this century.

66 IPCC; Flannery
67 IPCC
68 Australian Academy of Science
69 Hill et al.
70 Australian Academy of Science
71 Gubernot et al.
72 Hill et al.
73 Coutts et al.
74 Sharifi et al.
75 Hill et al.
76 Steadman

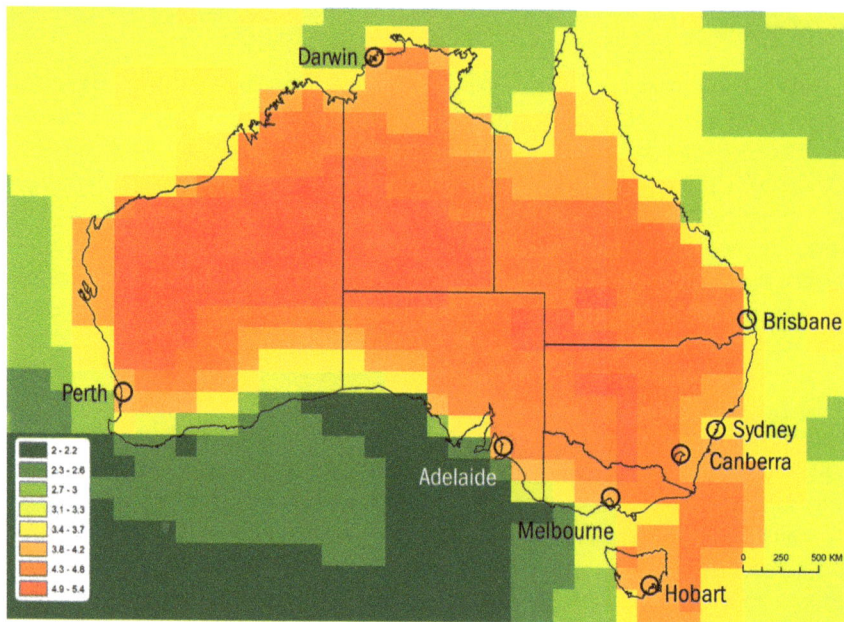

FIGURE 2.5: PROJECTED TEMPERATURE (CELSIUS) INCREASES BY 2090, RELATIVE TO 2005, UNDER AN RCP8.5 CLIMATE CHANGE SCENARIO. MAPPING COURTESY OF CLIMATE CHANGE IN AUSTRALIA/CSIRO.

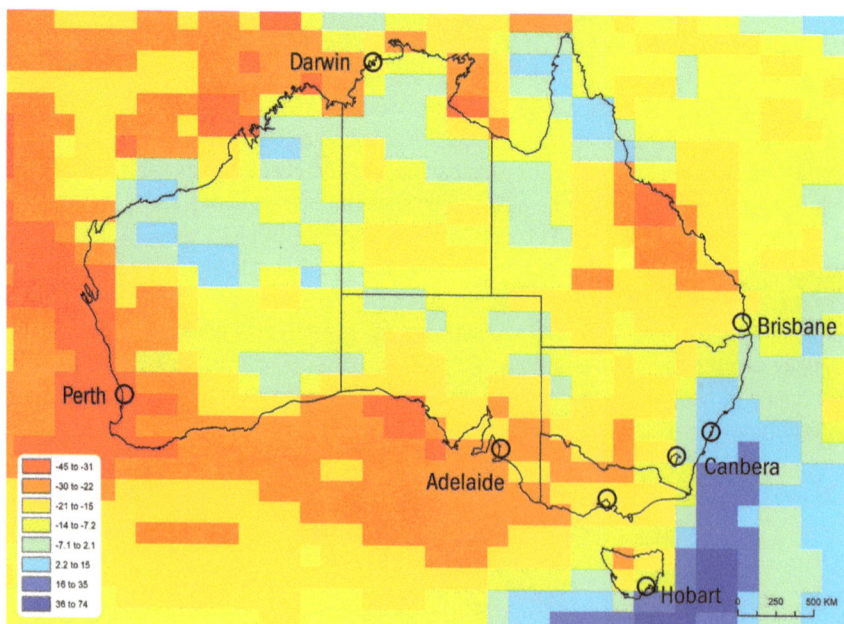

FIGURE 2.6: PROJECTED CHANGES IN ANNUAL RAINFALL C' BY 2090, RELATIVE TO 2005, UNDER AN RCP8.5 CLIMATE CHANGE SCENARIO. MAPPING COURTESY OF CLIMATE CHANGE IN AUSTRALIA/CSIRO

FIGURE 2.7: DROUGHT CONDITIONS IN WESTERN AUSTRALIA'S WHEATBELT REGION. IMAGE BY PBR IMAGES COURTESY OF SHUTTERSTOCK (STOCK PHOTO ID: 1655091541).

Drought

Australia is the driest inhabited continent, making its cities highly vulnerable to the impacts of global warming.[77] Indeed, 2019 was also Australia's driest year on record (Figure 2.6).[78] This situation is concerning because water availability is directly and indirectly linked to human health.[79] Water in many cities and towns across southern Australia is already in short supply due to prolonged droughts, and there will be increasing challenges in the coming years as temperatures rise. This situation occurs because, even if the rainfall stays the same, water availability will decline because of greater potential evaporation and increasing atmospheric dryness associated with increased temperatures.[80]

If global warming increases beyond 1.5°C as projected, many communities will be forced into what we would have considered 'last resort' alternatives only a few decades ago, such as a reluctant reliance on carbon-intensive desalination plants and the transportation of water into low-supply areas by truck or pipe.[81] Of course, big cities with big desalination plants can survive a prolonged drought because desalination ensures enough potable water for basic needs, and these cities source their agricultural produce

77 Australian Academy of Science
78 IPCC
79 Australian Academy of Science
80 Australian Academy of Science
81 Australian Academy of Science

from multiple catchment areas (some of which likely won't be in drought).[82] However, a drawn-out drought tends to wipe out smaller settlements, which may not be able to afford desalination plants, are stranded inland and are not big enough to economically source their food needs from multiple catchments (Figure 2.7).[83] In such cases, increased operating expenses associated with desalination or water transportation, health risks, declining agricultural productivity and negative impacts on local economies may trigger an exodus of people to areas where water is plentiful.[84]

Bushfires

Years of prolonged drought and an increase in the number of extreme fire weather days, especially in Australia's south and east,[85], have ignited a series of 'urban immolations', beginning with the Canberra fires of 2003 and then the Black Friday fires of 2009 (which came perilously close to the edge of Melbourne[86]) and the catastrophic Black Summer bushfires of the 2019–20 summer that destroyed 3094 houses in southeast Australia and blanketed Melbourne, Canberra and Sydney in a choking cloud of smoke (Figure 2.8). Undoubtedly, climate change will compound this situation, particularly at higher temperatures (beyond 1.5°C warming), where it is confidently predicted fire seasons will become more sustained and severe.[87]

Flooding and Storms

Climate change will, ironically, lead to differing contexts with either too little water (as already discussed) or too much water, where a rise in sea levels can lead to flooding. As a coast-hugging society, more than 85% of Australians live along the coast, with the majority in the coastal capital cities. As sea levels inevitably encroach, the risk of coastal flooding increases during high tides and storm surges. Accordingly, the Australian Academy of Science estimates that more than $226 billion in commercial, industrial, road, rail and residential assets are potentially subject to inundation from a projected 1.1-metre sea-level rise by 2100[88]; at risk are an estimated 160,000 to 250,000 properties.[89] Compounding flooding associated with sea-level rise will be cyclones and associated storm surges. While there are not projected to be more cyclones affecting Australia (some good news), there will likely be an increase in the frequency of 'whopper' (Category 4/5) cyclones with greater destructive power.[90]

82 Diamond
83 Diamond
84 Australian Academy of Science
85 IPCC
86 Gleeson, 'Lifeboat Cities'
87 IPCC
88 Australian Academy of Science
89 Australian Academy of Science
90 Dale

Many inland areas will also not be spared from flooding, as 2022, the year of what the Climate Council dubbed 'the Great Deluge', reminds us. The Great Deluge saw record-breaking rain and floods lashing large parts of eastern Australia; submerging whole towns; and causing muddy, heartbreaking devastation for both residents and, ultimately, the broader Australian economy.[91] While floods are a part of the fabric of Australian history, the untold destruction of the Great Deluge had the 'fingerprints of climate change' all over it.[92]

Cataclysmic cyclones, heartbreaking floods and ferocious mega-fires could mean that the insurance industry 'red-lines' parts of Australia to limit its exposure to massive pay-outs.[93] Indeed, such climate-related disasters could mean that one in every 19 property owners faces the prospect of unaffordable insurance premiums in just a few years. The looming possibility of a 3° warmer world would render many more properties and businesses uninsurable, leading to worrying insecurity, and residents and business owners 'pulling up stumps' and moving to safer ground.[94]

A GLOBAL CHALLENGE

Buckminster Fuller reminded us some time ago that the scale and innovation of solutions to global problems must match the problems.[95] As this chapter has set out, undeniable challenges lie in waiting for the planners of existing and future Australian cities. Given these considerable challenges, readers could be forgiven for feeling fearful or weary. However, we argue creative and coordinated planning on a national scale is required for future population growth to be of net benefit to Australia environmentally, economically and socially. Indeed, many of the problems discussed here find the clearest expression at a national scale (climate change being one example) and it makes sense to tackle them at the scale at which they manifest. An additional challenge lies therein: the current state of a national planning system that is jurisdictionally fragmented, generally uncoordinated and awaits more effective, sustained and democratic national leadership. In the closing chapter, we return to this issue, but ahead is the first of three tabling different scenarios that speak to this weighty ambition and point to the rationale for a national policy for population expansion and urban settlement.

91 Climate Council of Australia
92 Climate Council of Australia, 6
93 Dale
94 Australian Academy of Science
95 Fuller

FIGURE 2.8: THE BLACK SUMMER BUSHFIRES FROM SPACE. IMAGE BY ELROCE COURTESY OF SHUTTERSTOCK (STOCK PHOTO ID: 16089971).

CHALLENGES AHEAD

IMAGE BY ELIAS BITAR COURTESY OF SHUTTERSTOCK (STOCK PHOTO ID 2286666545).

3

CONQUERING
CAPITALS

On the whole,
Australians like
living in big cities.
They intend to
continue to live in
them, and it would be
futile and pointless
to deny that.[1]

BACKGROUND

Australia has one of the highest rates of urban primacy in the world.[2] Despite Australia's continental expanse, more than six out of 10 people live in the urban footprints of the six state capitals: Sydney, Melbourne, Adelaide, Perth, Brisbane and Hobart. This apparently 'unbalanced' system is nothing new; the fundamental structure of Australian settlement had already coalesced by the second half of the nineteenth century and, despite massive population growth being grafted on, the basic pattern of population distribution has remained steadfast.[3]

So why is Australia, with its bustling capitals, so exceptional in this respect? This situation is partly due to the pattern of colonial administration, which developed from the top down compared with other democracies, where it grew organically at the local level. Australia's capital cities had colonial origins; all were ports, with commercial and administrative functions relating more back to imperial London than to each other (much like small siblings ignoring each other and lavishing attention on a parent).[4] Smaller inland cities in Australia were never much more than local service centres.

The emergence of the Australian colonies differed distinctly from the frontier tradition of the United States, which led to a much more decentralised settlement pattern aided by a more fertile agricultural interior. Political control was also much more centralised in the Australian colonies, with less personal initiative and self-determination. Moreover, as

1   Aitken, 56
2   Wilkinson et al.
3   Hugo, 'Population Distribution, Migration and Climate Change in Australia'
4   Bolleter, The Ghost Cities of Australia

early as the 1870s, decades ahead of the United States, employment in Australia was dominated by 'services', the most typical trait of an urban, city-centric society.

Federation in 1901 confirmed strong and competitive metropolitan growth in each state without considering any sense of a balanced or integrated national urban system.[5] The continued concentrated development in the state capitals resulted from centralised power and infrastructure investment, reinforcing state and regional primacy.[6] Powerful commercial interests and the metropolitan press also compounded this centralising dynamic.[7]

Climatic conditions also help to explain the exceptional distribution of population. The bareness of the interior and a pitiless desert that Indigenous peoples understood, but European explorers were bewildered by, led to development along the littoral. Large swathes of central and western Australia were (and are) arid and regarded as suitable only for extensive forms of grazing.[8] As a result of these intertwined factors, by the late colonial era, the 'path dependency' of metropolitan dominance was firmly established.[9]

So, given the distinctive dominance of Australia's coastal capital cities, why would policymakers seek to perpetuate this extreme situation further?

AGGLOMERATION ECONOMIES

Lively cities are the engine rooms of economic growth in most countries. Indeed, what economists term 'urbanisation economies' are conducive to booming economic development.[10] So, what are urbanisation economies? Take the example of big service industries, such as IT, finance, design, media, management, higher education, hospitality and entertainment. They want to cluster in big, bustling cities where they can exchange ideas and people.[11] Advantages of such an economy include a critical mass of workers and infrastructure, and interwoven networks of suppliers and collaborators.[12] Locating in the city clusters gives businesses access to the most potential employees, even with a sizeable working-from-home contingent. It narrows the gap between the skills required for a role and the skills of the worker who undertakes it; put simply, the better the match, the more productive the employee and the business will be.[13] City clusters also germinate new ideas that flow between firms and workers so each can learn from the other.[14] Indeed, knowledge production remains closely tied with locational clustering despite technological innovation and improvement in digital connectivity, and dense urban areas continue to be good at generating creative ideas through competition and serendipitous interaction.[15]

In part, because of these factors associated with urbanisation economies, Australia's economy is highly concentrated. Indeed, a weighty 80% of economic activity occurs in a tiny

5   Paris
6   Wilkinson et al.
7   Potts
8   Lonsdale, 'Manufacturing decentralization'
9   Freestone, 'Back to the Future'
10 Laquian
11 Button and Rizvi
12 Nathan and Overman, 'Agglomeration, Clusters, and Industrial Policy'
13 Kelly and Donegan
14 Nathan and Overman, 'Agglomeration, Clusters, and Industrial Policy'
15 Nathan and Overman, 'Will Coronavirus Cause a Big City Exodus?'; Tuli and Hu

0.2% of Australia's continental landmass in our large cities. [16] Therefore, large cities are the backbone of our economy and their central business districts and inner-city areas are critical to the nation's prosperity. [17] With this in mind, concentrating further growth in the capital cities will fuel the engine rooms of Australian economic growth to all our mutual benefit.

COSMOPOLITANISM

Beyond their economic zing, the cosmopolitanism and urban amenities (such as major entertainment venues, educational and cultural institutions, and health centres) of Australia's major capital cities make them honey pots for migrant knowledge workers, who, in turn, contribute to the cities' economic development and cosmopolitanism. [18] The concept of cosmopolitanism evokes the dynamic intermingling of diverse cultures through migration and travel and the resulting shifting social formations, attitudes and politics. [19] Ideally, these shifts include valuing difference (or at least indifference to difference), a desire for greater social equality and justice, and recognising different aspirations amongst people of divergent backgrounds. [20] Cosmopolitanism embodies the old German adage, *stadtluft macht frei* (city air makes you free). [21] And, for the most part, Australia's vibrant capitals do. Sydney, Australia's genuinely global city, is one example. Across Sydney, diverse neighbourhoods are home to people of 230 different cultural and linguistic backgrounds with a polyglot array of languages and cultures. [22] This cultural diversity manifests in a seemingly endless parade of events such as NAIDOC (National Aborigines and Islanders Day Observance Committee) Week and Reconciliation Week, Parramasala Indian festival in Parramatta, Multicultural Eid Festival in Fairfield, Norton Street Italian Festa, and the Sydney Gay and Lesbian Mardi Gras. [23] Despite the strains our multicultural model is under (discussed in Chapter 2), Sydney still manifests sociologist Richard Sennett's deceptively simple definition of a city as 'a human settlement where strangers are likely to meet'. [24]

If Australia retains its current geographic settlement patterns, most of our future population will reside in our major capital cities, further driving their economic and cultural dynamism. Given the readily apparent virtues of Australia's state capital cities, this chapter's pair of scenarios explores their potential to accommodate sustained population growth and the consequences of that 'business as usual' pathway.

16 Kelly and Donegan
17 Kelly and Donegan
18 Tuli and Hu
19 Schech
20 Schech
21 McGuirk
22 Greater Sydney Commission, 'City-Shaping Impacts of Covid-19'
23 Greater Sydney Commission, 'City-Shaping Impacts of Covid-19'
24 Sennett

MEGACITIES

FIGURE 3.1 IMAGE BY NUR MOHD ROZLAN

MEGACITIES SCENARIO

In 1950, New York, with a population of just over 12 million, was the world's only megacity (city with a population of 10 million or more). By 2000, the number of world megacities had surged to 18,[25] a figure that has now swollen to 32, mostly in developing countries (Figure 3.3).[26] Despite a crop of Asian megacities in our region (Figure 3.4), Australia has yet to contribute any megacities to this global mix.

However, by 2066, Melbourne and Sydney will be entering megacity status, according to ABS projections, based on them continuing to attract the most migrants (and generate the bulk of Australia's gross domestic product). Accordingly, the Victorian and New South Wales state governments have tabled plans for Melbourne and Sydney[27] to accommodate population surges to almost 8 million each by the middle of the century (Figure 3.2). Of the two, Melbourne is projected to be firmly entrenched as the largest city in Australia, surpassing Sydney sometime between 2031 and 2057.[28] Rather than megacities emerging organically, what if we consciously cultivated a crop of Australian megacities for the end of this century?

25 Laquian
26 World Population Review
27 Victorian State Government; Greater Sydney Commission, *Greater Sydney Region Plan*
28 Australian Bureau of Statistics, 'Population Projections, Australia, 2017 (Base) - 2066'

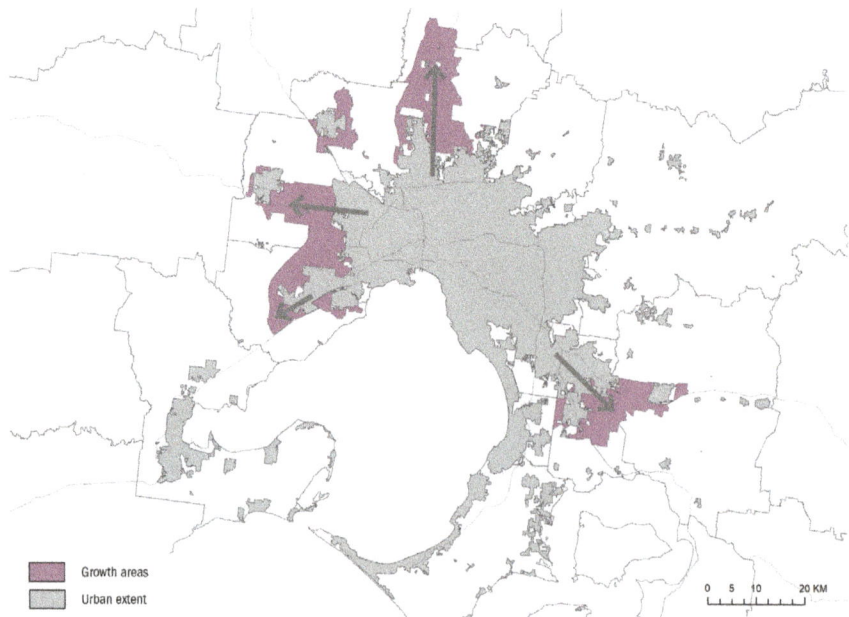

FIGURE 3.2: SIGNIFICANT PLANNED GROWTH AREAS ON MELBOURNE'S URBAN PERIPHERY. MAPPING COURTESY OF THE VICTORIAN DEPARTMENT OF TRANSPORT AND PLANNING.

Growth areas

Urban extent

0   5   10   20 KM

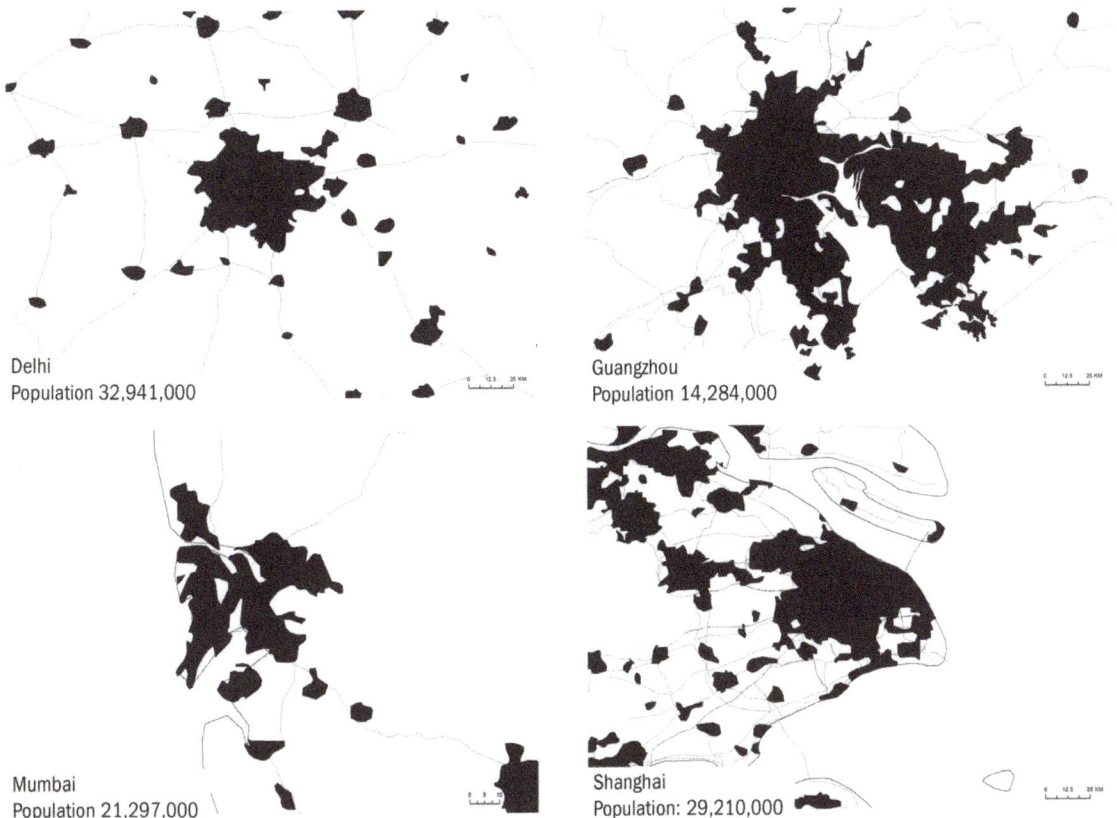

Delhi
Population 32,941,000

Guangzhou
Population 14,284,000

Mumbai
Population 21,297,000

Shanghai
Population: 29,210,000

FIGURE 3.3: EXAMPLES OF GLOBAL MEGACITIES.

FIGURE 3.4: THE METROPOLITAN POPULATION OF GUANGZHOU IS PREDICTED TO GROW TO NEARLY 17 MILLION BY 2035.
IMAGE BY LZF COURTESY OF SHUTTERSTOCK (STOCK PHOTO ID: 2350831453).

SCENARIO DESCRIPTION

Our megacities scenario used official projections to hypothesise that, by 2101, Melbourne and Sydney will increase by almost 7 million people each (to 12.2 and 12.1 million people, respectively) and comfortably reach megacity status (Figures 3.5, 3.6, 3.7). Such a surge in population could potentially be achieved through unmanaged growth, if not by impeding population growth elsewhere and luring immigration flows to Melbourne and Sydney through visa concessions for immigrants and aggressive high-rise apartment building programs.

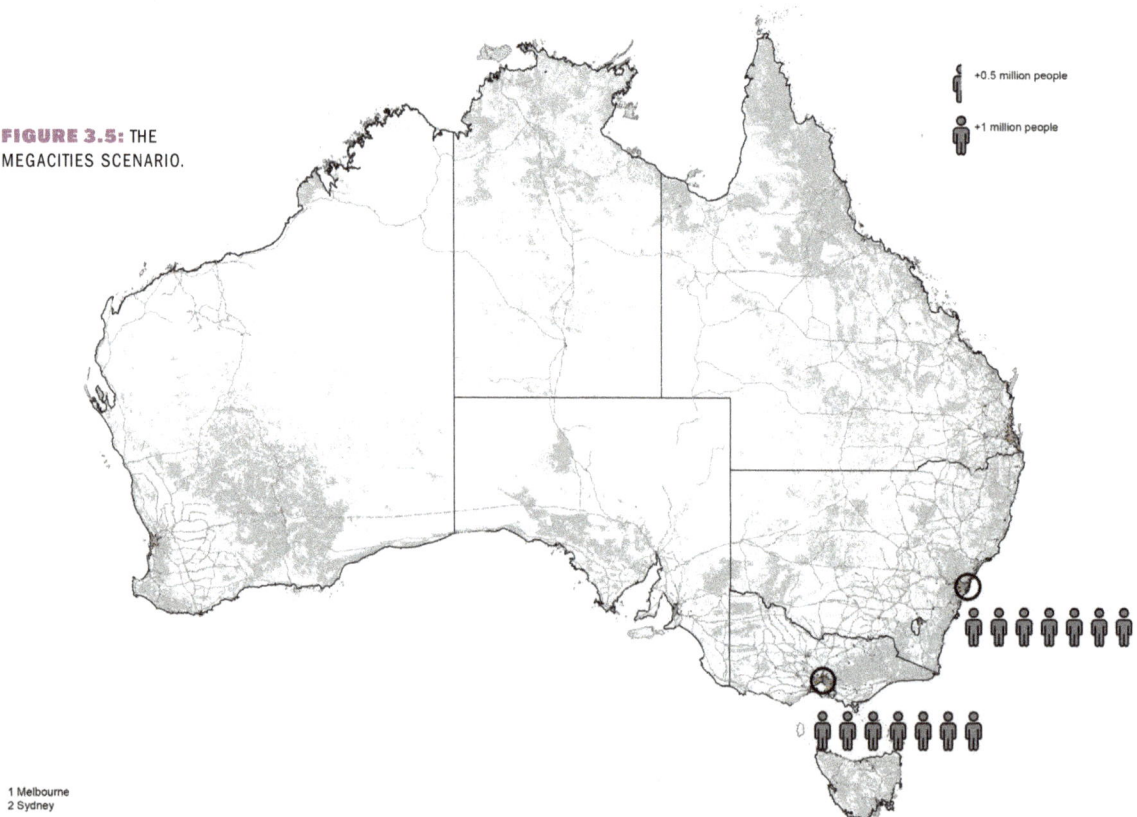

FIGURE 3.5: THE MEGACITIES SCENARIO.

+0.5 million people

+1 million people

1 Melbourne
2 Sydney

MEGACITIES

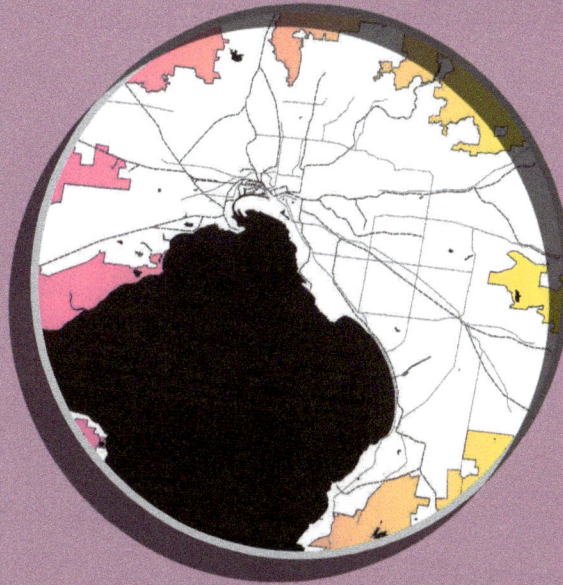

Melbourne

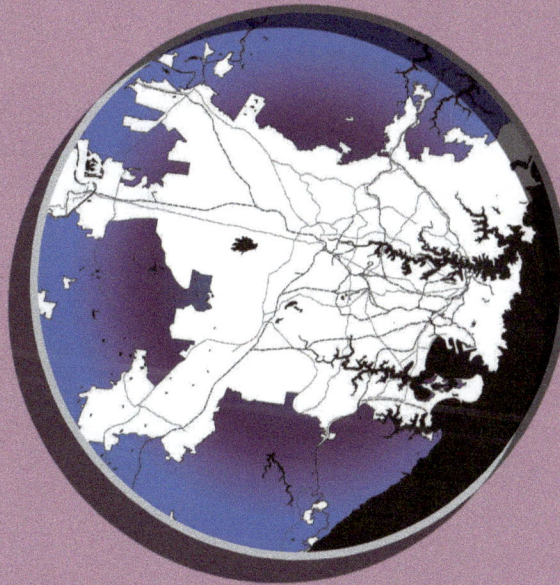

Sydney

FIGURE 3.6: THE EXISTING CORES OF THE TWO PROPOSED MEGACITIES.

FIGURE 3.7: A FUTURE MEGACITY – SYDNEY'S FOREST OF TOWERS IN 2101. SELECT BUILDINGS PHOTOGRAPHED BY JOHN GOLLINGS PHOTOGRAPHY. IMAGE BASED ON A PHOTO BY STEVE MINOR COURTESY OF FLICKR (HTTPS://WWW.FLICKR.COM/PHOTOS/SMINOR/12329392655).

CONQUERING CAPITALS

SCENARIO SENTIMENT

While megacities may be fascinating from afar, the Megacities scenario was almost universally loathed by laypeople and expert respondents to both our Plan *My* Australia surveys. It was ranked last and second-last, respectively.[29] However, while the bulk of people were hostile, some hardy optimists enthused that, if developed appropriately, the Megacities scenario could result in 'sustainable, compact, high-density cities and effective use of existing infrastructure'. They envisaged 'world-class megacities with cultural diversity, infrastructure investment, commercial and economic growth'.

The dominant theme in the avalanche of negative commentary was that megacity growth would critically diminish Melbourne and Sydney's liveability due to congestion, social conflicts, crime, poverty, resource shortages, pressure on community services and erosion of community character (to name just a few).[30] As one respondent exhorted:

Yuk. Overcrowding, expensive property, people living in high rises, outlier ghetto suburbs, increasing crime, and long commute times. Honestly, though, this is probably what will happen (but without any mindful planning) because the government seems incapable of planning ahead of its election cycle.

Alternatively, as another neatly surmised:

Melbourne and Sydney are already third-world ghettos; better to keep them shit and leave the rest of Australia pristine.

29 Bolleter et al., 'Long-Term Settlement Scenarios;' Bolleter et al., 'Evaluating Scenarios'

30 The respondent quotations below come from Bolleter et al., 'Long-Term Settlement Scenarios.'

Similarly, others were feeling the pain of living in Sydney with 'just' 5 million people.

Sydney is such a painful place to live – commute times are terrible, and costs are astronomical. Another few million people would make it impossible to live there.

Others expressed concern that Sydney and Melbourne 'will turn into dirty, concrete jungles like megacities in Asia', which might be a buzz to visit but are hardly somewhere you would want to live.

Many people drew a direct line between declining liveability and increasing population size, stating, 'the most liveable cities in the world have single-digit million populations and generally less than 5 million' and 'Australian cities are among the most liveable due to their size, keep them that way!'

Immune to the charms of 'cosmopolitanism', some people perceived that intensifying immigration in Melbourne and Sydney could create a cultural divide between the cities (mainly 'new settlers') and the outer suburbs and near regional towns ('Australians and past generation migrant settlers who were more integrated to the Australian norms'). As this commentator explained, 'the city centres would be abandoned by the [local Australian] residents and left to foreign students, tourists and office workers'.

For this scenario to not erode liveability and ensure integration, it was perceived that it required unprecedented (and frankly unlikely) government planning accompanied by investment in infrastructure, housing and services needed to keep up with extreme population pressures. One person reasoned: 'I do not think the people in charge of planning are capable of making the right decisions for this to be successful.'

Another significant theme was that the Megacities scenario would lead to 'uneven economic investment and growth, uneven distribution of political power, and would be detrimental to Australia's remaining capital cities and regions'. Some people worried that the Megacities scenario would lead to 'mega-sprawl', pressure on the natural environment, biodiversity loss and encroachment on food-producing lands. As one warned, 'the destruction of the surrounding environment would be unavoidable and devastating' and a 'recipe for social and environmental disaster'.

Conversely, others felt that 'high-density living is at odds with Australians' preference for lower density' and would result in 'slums and ghettos'. As one proclaimed, 'Megacities with a population of 7 million would be un-Australian and against all Australia represents'. Finally, people fretted that 'lessons learnt from COVID-19, that high density equals disease' were being forgotten and that 'megacity economy and prosperity is vulnerable in the event of a citywide lockdown'.

SCENARIO SUITABILITY

Given the tide of damning assessments, how does the Megacities scenario rate in terms of our suitability mapping (Figure 3.9)? Both Sydney and Melbourne rate well as the economic powerhouses of the national economy and providing abundant employment opportunities. Two centuries of investment means both cities are complex knots of interwoven infrastructure with ready access to major ports, international airports, metropolitan and regional rail lines, (tolled) motorways and NBN. Melbourne's chilly winters aside, the future megacities also have a generally temperate climate with moderate rainfall, boosting their scores.[31] However, biodiversity and topography constrain Sydney with its encircling national parks and World Heritage areas, which comprise part of the globally significant South Eastern Australia biodiversity hotspot (Figure 3.8).[32] Biodiversity hotspots are the planet's life support systems; any development compromising such globally important ecosystems is unquestionably unsuitable. For this reason, Melbourne has more capacity for growth, given the broad expanses of cleared land to the city's west.

Despite a comparatively positive assessment via our mapping analysis, all but the hardiest optimists regarded the Megacities scenario as a 'stinker'. Given that the populace reviled population growth in the major capitals, what about a scenario that flips the logic and turbo-charges Australia's secondary capital cities into significant cities in their own right?

31 Bolleter et al., 'Informing future Australian settlement planning'.
32 Mittermeier et al.

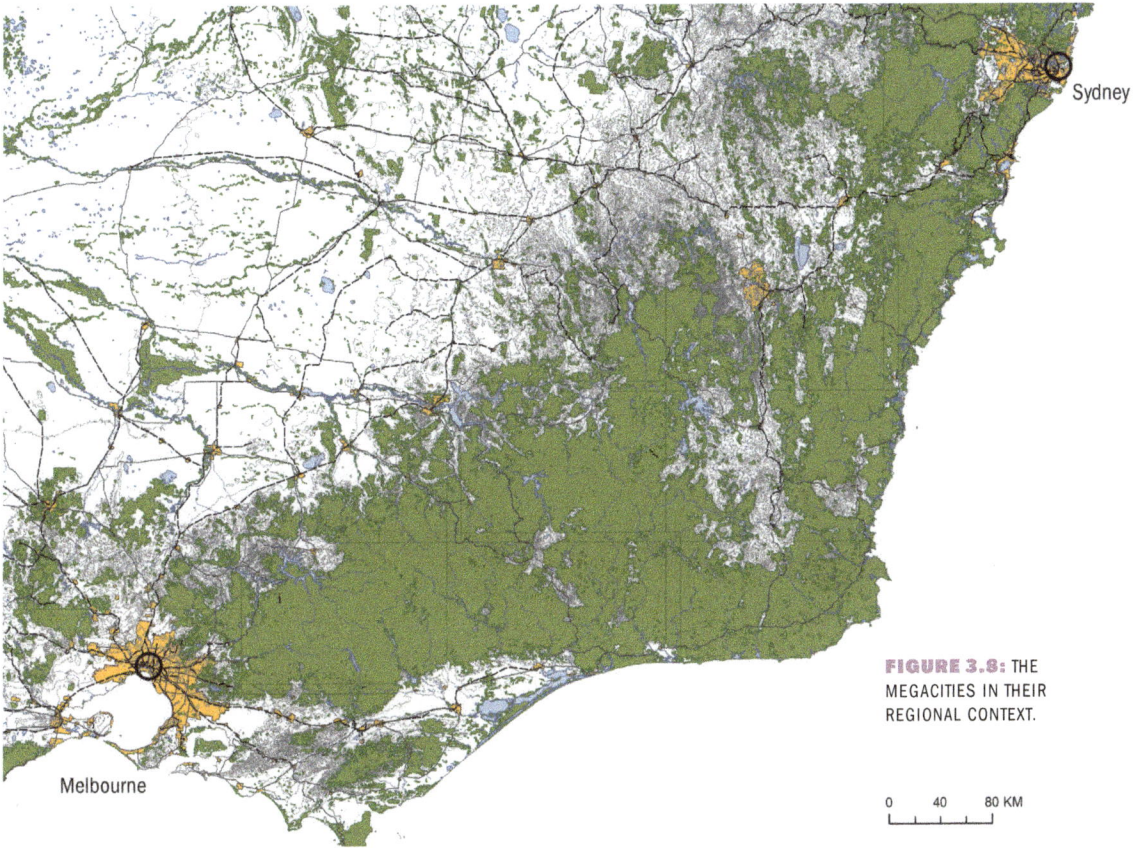

FIGURE 3.8: THE MEGACITIES IN THEIR REGIONAL CONTEXT.

0   40   80 KM

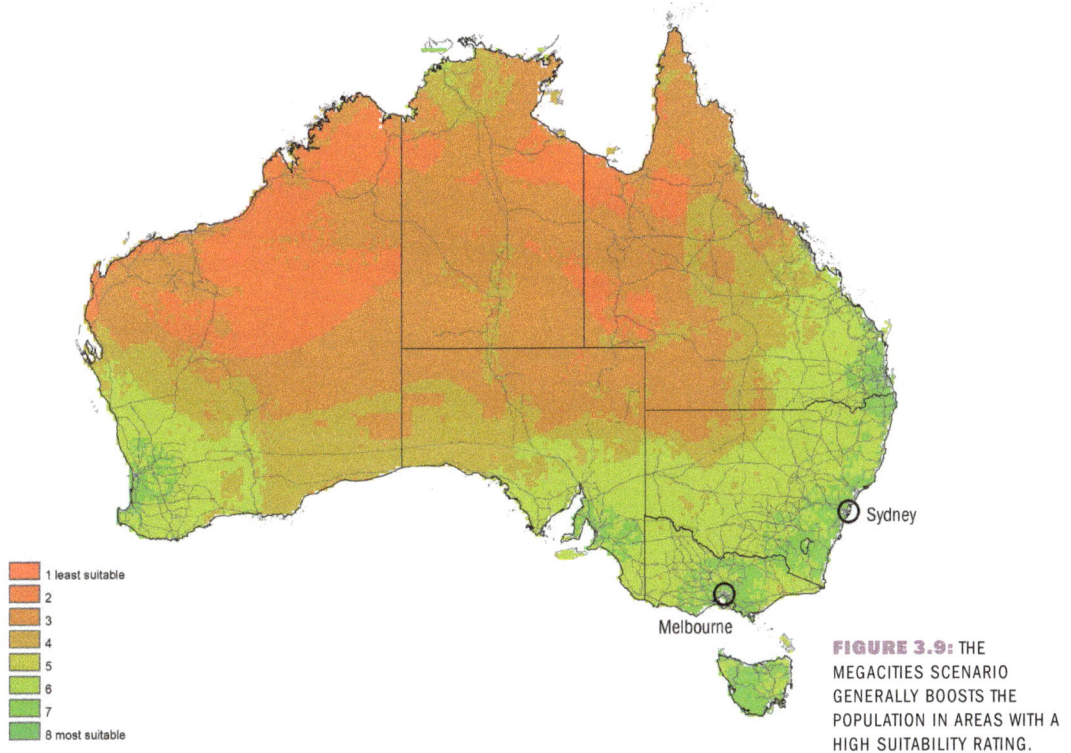

1 least suitable
2
3
4
5
6
7
8 most suitable

FIGURE 3.9: THE MEGACITIES SCENARIO GENERALLY BOOSTS THE POPULATION IN AREAS WITH A HIGH SUITABILITY RATING.

SECONDARY CAPITAL CITIES

FIGURE 3.10 IMAGE BY THE AUTHORS.

FIGURE 3.11: THE LEAFY SUBURBS OF BRISBANE REVEAL CONSIDERABLE POTENTIAL FOR ACCOMMODATING POPULATION GROWTH THROUGH CAREFULLY PLANNED INFILL DEVELOPMENT. PHOTO BY MAKE 2 DIGITAL COURTESY OF SHUTTERSTOCK (STOCK PHOTO ID: 142363255).

SECONDARY CAPITAL CITIES SCENARIO

Surging population growth in Melbourne and Sydney for nearly 200 years, combined with a smattering of policy failures, have resulted in two congested and costly conurbations.[33] Conversely, the smaller state and territory capitals – Perth, Adelaide, Brisbane, Darwin and Hobart – may have a reasonable capacity for hoovering up population growth into either urban infill (Figure 3.11) or suburban expansion on the fringe (typically the latter).[34] To some degree, this is reflected in their overarching planning documents, which seek to house an additional 1,886,600 people in Brisbane (and Southeast Queensland more generally), 1,500,000 in Perth, 540,000 in Adelaide, 177,000 in Canberra, 60,000 in Hobart and 61,697 in Darwin by the middle of the century and beyond. Combined with these projections, the 'boosted' Secondary Capital Cities scenario also stems from the previous federal government's attempt to 'encourage migrants to settle outside Sydney and Melbourne' to ease population growth pressures.[35] Such aspirations reside in immigration programs, such as those allowing extensions on graduate visas for international student graduates who have studied in smaller cities, such as Perth, Adelaide, the Gold Coast, Canberra and Hobart.[36]

33 Kelly and Donegan
34 Archer et al.
35 Australian Government, 'Planning for Australia's Future Population,' 6
36 Department of Home Affairs

FIGURE 3.12: THE SECONDARY CAPITAL CITIES SCENARIO.

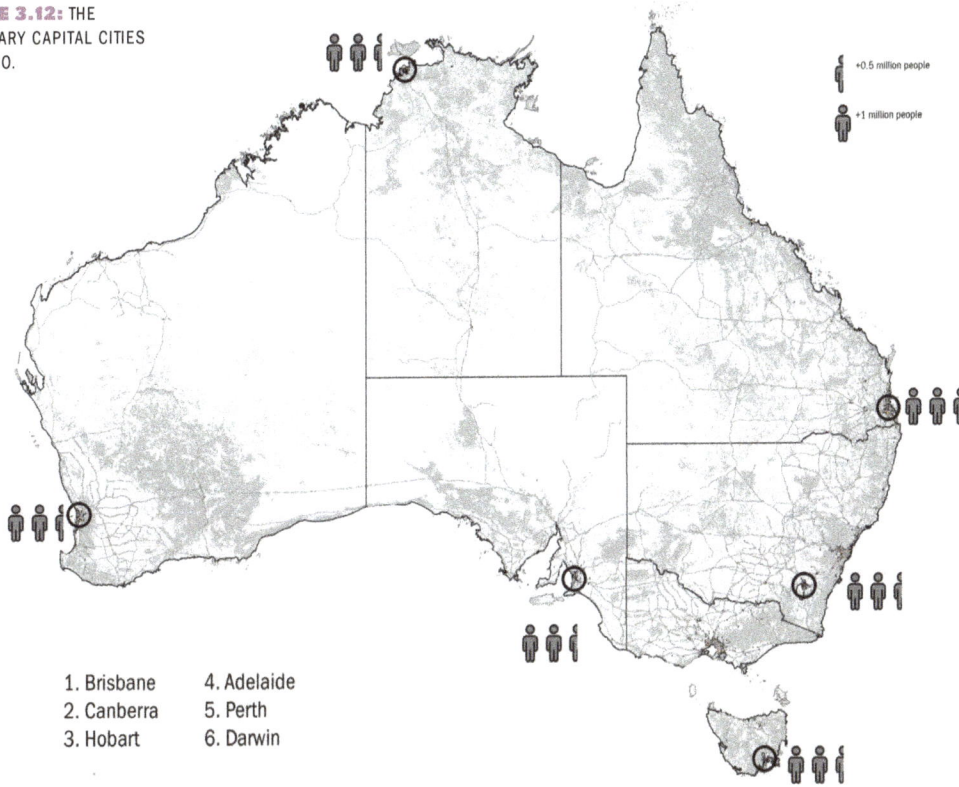

+0.5 million people

+1 million people

1. Brisbane
2. Canberra
3. Hobart
4. Adelaide
5. Perth
6. Darwin

SECONDARY CAPITAL CITIES

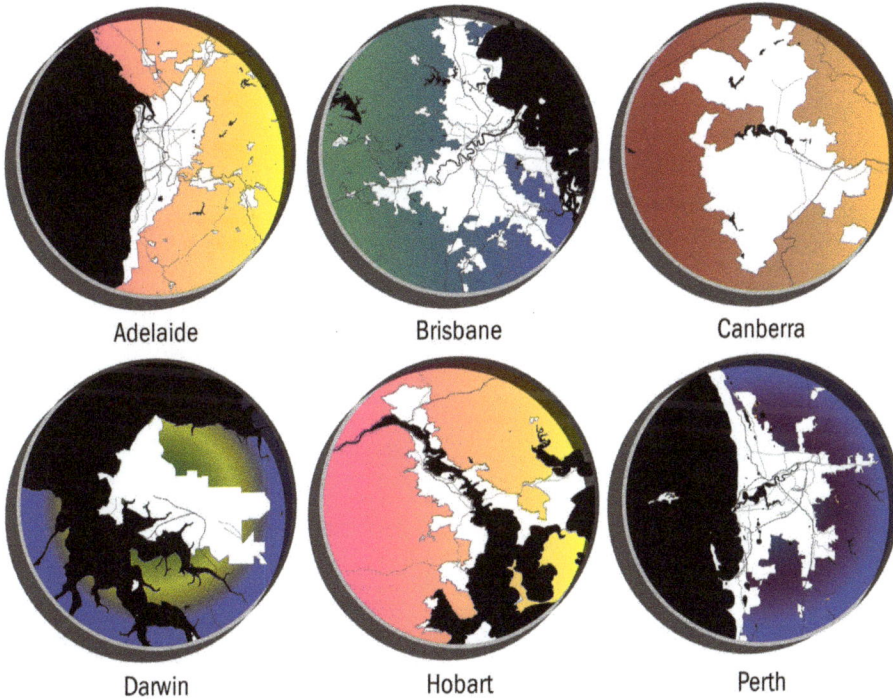

Adelaide

Brisbane

Canberra

Darwin

Hobart

Perth

FIGURE 3.13: THE SECONDARY CAPITAL CITIES.

SCENARIO DESCRIPTION

The boosted Secondary Capital Cities scenario responds to pressures in Sydney and Melbourne by redirecting population growth to the remaining six state and territory capitals, projecting population increases by over 2 million people in each by 2101 (Figures 3.12, 3.13, 3.14, 3.15).[37] To some degree, this will happen organically, as the availability of jobs and existing community connections are major drawcards for migrants. However, delivering the Secondary Capital Cities scenario would also require proactive planning. Such strategies could include policies incentivising immigrants to reside in the smaller state and territory capitals through generous visa concessions. Furthermore, policymakers could lock down the urban growth boundaries for Sydney and Melbourne to block further waves of suburban expansion and build impetus for the secondary capitals.

SCENARIO SENTIMENT

So, how did the Secondary Cities scenario rate with Australians? In our Plan *My* Australia community survey, this scenario was also profoundly unpopular with laypeople, ranking seventh out of the eight scenarios.[38] Conversely, the experts rated the scenario highly in the second position.[39] These divergent results highlight a complete disconnect between the layperson and expert opinion, probably based on diverging assessments of the planning profession's ability to manage growth to positive ends.

Nonetheless, the positive commentary from lay people reflected the thinking that an 'even population distribution among capital cities is a generally good idea' and that 'Brisbane, Perth and Darwin can benefit from expansion'. Conversely, others sympathised with harried Sydneysiders and Melbournites, stating that 'Melbourne and Sydney should not have to carry all of the burdens alone'. Another theme in the commentary was that uplifting the secondary capital cities' population would provide an economic shot in the arm because 'larger cities increase productivity and economic diversity, producing greater economic growth'.[40]

37 Bolleter et al., 'Long-Term Settlement Scenarios'
38 Bolleter et al., 'Long-Term Settlement Scenarios'
39 Bolleter et al., 'Evaluating Scenarios'
40 Bolleter et al., 'Long-Term Settlement Scenarios'

The tide of negative commentary focused primarily on perceptions that further growth in these cities would erode their liveability, as one person implored:

> *Why repeat the mistakes of Melbourne and Sydney? Overpopulation leads to congestion, an unaffordable housing market, loss of community, unique character, resource scarcity and crime.*[41]

Some people questioned whether some secondary cities could even accommodate this scale of growth. One respondent cautioned:

> *The even distribution growth scenario is unlikely, and smaller cities of Hobart, Darwin, and Canberra will struggle with an extra 2 million people.*

Constraints of site and situation were highlighted. Hobart was depicted as 'trapped inside a hilly landscape, and it would be difficult to increase .... population tenfold' without suburbia sprawling into the hinterland. Darwin was also said to lack the capacity for the proposed scale of growth:

> *Darwin does not have the space to accommodate a further 2 million people without essentially building a new inland city to the south well beyond current urban boundaries.*

41 Bolleter et al., 'Long-Term Settlement Scenarios'

FIGURE 3.14: THE SECONDARY CAPITAL CITY OF ADELAIDE IN 2101. IMAGE BY SHUBHAM GAUTAM BASED ON A PHOTO BY GOOGLE (HTTPS://MAPS.APP.GOO.GL/DMPTX2QAVAXT5UM96?G_ST=IC).

LOCATION: ADELAIDE, SA
INDIGENOUS REGION: KAURNA
YEAR: 2101
COORD: 34.9285°S, 138.6007°E
POPULATION: 3,745,623

CONQUERING CAPITALS

LOCATION: PERTH, WA
INDIGENOUS REGION: WAJUK
YEAR: 2101
COORD: 31.9523°S, 115.8613°E
POPULATION: 4,582,808

CONQUERING CAPITALS

Other themes in the negative commentaries were a preference for growth in regional centres over secondary cities and, frankly, understandable scepticism about the necessary infrastructure investment eventuating. Further concerns were that the scenario would irrigate more suburban sprawl, bulldoze fringing biodiversity, entomb valuable agricultural lands under housing developments, and diminish dwindling water supplies.[42]

SCENARIO SUITABILITY

So, what does the mapping analysis say about the suitability of such a scenario? The analysis map reveals five broad regions of suitability, within which the southern and eastern secondary capital cities are nested (Figure 3.17).[43] The secondary cities within these regions are relative economic powerhouses and provide abundant employment opportunities and strong networks of existing infrastructure. Canberra is close to rail and road corridors connecting Melbourne and Sydney and is well-placed for future urban development (Figure 3.16). Moreover, a typically temperate climate and reasonable rainfall characterise these regions. The southern secondary capitals generally have reserves of cleared land awaiting suburban expansion, although Perth and Brisbane are constrained by globally significant biodiversity hotspots and, in the latter, steep hillsides.[44] The exception to the rule is the northern secondary city of Darwin, which rates poorly due to a damning mix of wet season heat stress, cyclones and a mosaic of mangroves constricting concentric expansion.

42 Bolleter et al., 'Long-Term Settlement Scenarios'
43 Bolleter et al., 'Informing Future Australian Settlement Planning'
44 Bolleter et al., 'Informing Future Australian Settlement Planning'

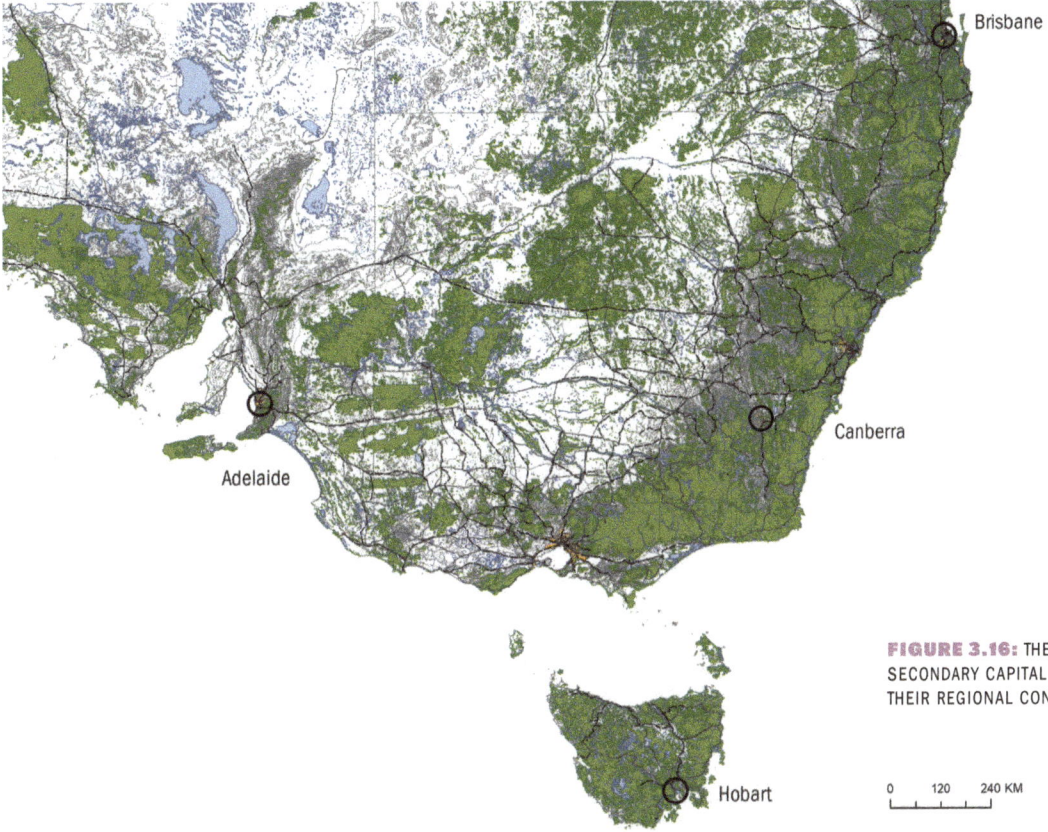

FIGURE 3.16: THE EASTERN
SECONDARY CAPITAL CITIES IN
THEIR REGIONAL CONTEXT.

0   120   240 KM

FIGURE 3.17: THE REGIONAL
SUITABILITY OF THE SECONDARY
CITIES DIFFERS MARKEDLY,
FAVOURING SITES IN THE SOUTH
OF THE CONTINENT.

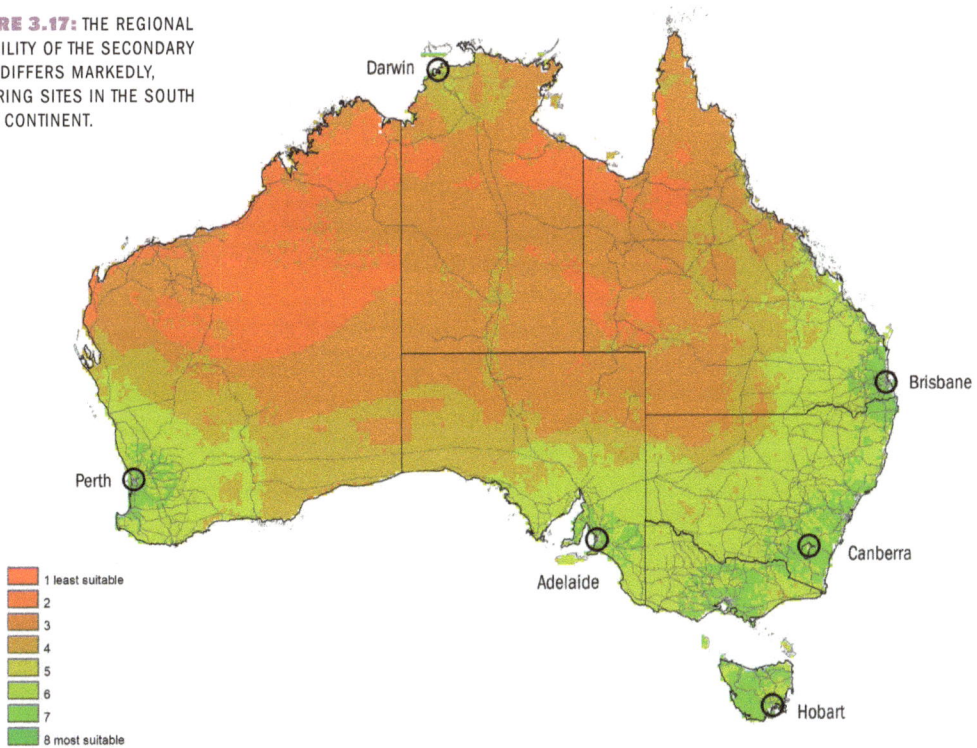

1 least suitable
2
3
4
5
6
7
8 most suitable

DISCUSSION

While Australia's urban development has been characterised by a distinctive pattern of 'metropolitan dominance',[45] evidently, laypeople have little appetite for this pattern to be further compounded. Indeed, both the Megacities and Secondary Capital Cities scenarios were consigned last and second-last by our Plan *My* Australia community survey respondents.

Given that the supremacy of capital cities is a particularly Australian characteristic, why is it so loathed by Australians? One hypothesis is that there could also be a national-scale NIMBYism at work, given that 50% of our survey respondents were from major cities.[46] Shlomo Angel identifies that many cities are already disturbingly large for their residents. Therefore, allowing them to expand further is 'nonsensical and unacceptable'.[47] Hence, newcomers and immigrants from overseas (or even Aussies from other parts of the country) are unwelcome and are seen as 'nuisances rather than as assets'.[48] This assessment undoubtedly stems from the urban challenges that bedevil our cities (as discussed in Chapter 2). However, other factors in this mix could be a 'Malthusian view' that further population growth would outstrip the available resources, triggering a messy collapse.[49] This pessimistic view was widely accepted by most politicians, demographers and the general public, and remained popular until relatively recently.[50] Perhaps it still lingers in the collective unconscious. So, what other headwinds could the capital city-centric scenarios confront?

THE ERODING LIVEABILITY OF MAJOR CITIES

As the survey responses made crystal clear, concerns swirl around the issue of urban liveability, particularly in relation to the Megacities scenario. Indeed, more than two-thirds of people believe Sydney is *already* full, with a population of 'just' 5 million (Figure 3.18).[51]

Despite their fascination for tourists, megacities typically receive rotten ratings in liveability indices.[52] For example, Los Angeles is a city that bears many similarities to Australian cities such as Perth, albeit on a larger scale. It is currently ranked a lowly 37th in The Economist's 2022 'World's Most Liveable Cities Index'.[53] Other 'great' (mega) cities struggle, such as London, which staggers over the line in 33rd position. In contrast, the average population of the top 10 most liveable cities in 2022 is a modest and manageable 1.58 million.[54] Although the rankings can be disputed and the variables are many, size, it seems, is important.[55]

45 Freestone, 'Back to the Future', 236
46 Bolleter et al., 'Long-Term Settlement Scenarios'
47 Angel, 4
48 Angel, 4
49 Butler
50 Butler
51 Farrelly
52 Bolleter and Weller
53 Economist Intelligence Unit
54 Economist Intelligence Unit
55 Bolleter and Weller

Of course, estimations of when a city's size becomes problematic are varied. Nonetheless, the urban economist Max Neutze offered the most rigorous analyses in the 1960s and 1970s. He reasoned that when a city reaches a population of 2 million, most of the advantages derived from sheer size have been exhausted.[56] While some offerings were generally only available in cities larger than 2 million, like international opera houses and stock exchanges, it was felt that these were the exception to the rule.[57] Then again, other commentators point out that the ideal size for a typical city is 1 million people. Beyond that number, pollution, health problems and the overloading of housing begin to negatively impact the environment.[58] Clearly, back-of-an-envelope estimations of an ideal city size for urban liveability are all over the place and vary by the criteria applied. Nonetheless, megacities of 10 million or more people are well above all estimations we have uncovered.

FIGURE 3.18: MORE THAN TWO-THIRDS OF PEOPLE BELIEVE SYDNEY IS *ALREADY* FULL, WITH A POPULATION OF 5.1 MILLION. PHOTO BY HDC CREATIVE COURTESY OF SHUTTERSTOCK (STOCK PHOTO ID: 225714192).

56 Neutze
57 Bolleter et al., 'Informing future Australian settlement planning' Neutze
58 Wennersten and Robbins

LIMITS TO AGGLOMERATION ECONOMIES

As we discussed on page 54, all-powerful agglomeration economies have driven the dominance of Australia's major cities. However, research shows that there can be diminishing marginal returns for agglomeration benefits as cities grow ever bigger, potentially kicking in at just 2 million people.[59] Diminishing returns occur because the costs of being big (congestion and high living costs) undermine the benefits of having additional skilled workers nearby.[60] As a result, as a city grows, costs will begin to outweigh benefits and workers and firms will be better off relocating elsewhere.[61] Indeed, optimists, such as the Regional Australia Institute, believe smaller cities, with over 70,000 people and without congestion and high living costs, can experience the benefits of agglomeration economies.[62] If such assessments are believed (and the jury is still out), Australia could have more noteworthy net economic gains as smaller cities grow and capture further agglomeration economies than from boosting the growth of our largest cities.[63] Such claims are reinforced, to some degree, by Organisation for Economic Co-operation and Development (OECD) research, which also shows that nations with many cities rather than one or two dominant cities (such as in Melbourne and Sydney) tend to have higher gross domestic product (GDP) levels.[64]

SUSTAINABILITY ISSUES OF MAJOR CITIES

While megacities may experience diminishing agglomeration economies, concerns about their enduring sustainability also linger.[65] Indeed, some commentators see vast urbanisation as ecologically, economically and socially unsustainable. Rees and Wackernagel, for example, have argued that big cities are ecologically unsustainable by their very nature.[66] To them, conspicuous consumption levels, as exemplified in Western cities, do not allow megacities and hinterlands to regenerate resources or dissipate their wastes fast enough to keep up with growth. Because these cities lack essential resources in their immediate hinterlands, they must draw on an ever-expanding 'ecological footprint' to maintain viability.[67] Indeed, 'however brilliant its economic star, every city is an ecological black

59 Archer et al.; Haratsis
60 Archer et al.
61 Nathan and Overman, 'Agglomeration, clusters, and industrial policy
62 Regional Australia Institute
63 Archer et al.
64 Archer et al.
65 Laquian
66 Laquian
67 Laquian

hole drawing on the material resources and productivity of a vast and scattered hinterland many times the size of the city itself.'[68] Therefore, allowing a monocentric settlement to endlessly sprawl is 'a recipe for disaster'. As Laquian explains:

> *In a sprawling city region, it becomes extremely expensive to extend basic urban services to all urban residents in the peri-urban area. Waterworks systems have to go farther to tap new sources for raw water supply. Getting rid of sewage and gray water becomes difficult. Appropriate sites for solid waste disposal will be hard to find. Moving people, goods, and services will be extremely costly as roads and other transport networks stretch to the agglomeration's outer limits. Such a settlement may find it extremely difficult to feed itself as more and more agricultural land is converted to urban uses.*[69]

Clearly, these challenges would manifest in the Megacities, if not the Secondary Cities, scenario. While we celebrate the wealth and success of our globally connected inner cities, the Conquering Capitals scenarios would see most future population growth grafted onto the urban periphery of our capitals, and it would likely be dogged by the urban problems (canvassed in Chapter 2) and depicted by Laquian.

Despite state government planning for the capital cities to house the overwhelming majority of Australia's projected twenty-first-century population growth, it is evident that this planning runs counter to the view of the Australian community and, in some cases, the experts. As such, pursuing such approaches will likely be an unrewarding, uphill push over the longer term. Given the white-hot hostility of our respondents towards the Conquering Capitals scenarios, in Chapter 4 we canvass visionary and ambitious plans that seek to siphon population growth to regional centres at a substantial scale.

68 Laquian, 20
69 Laquian, 383

IMAGE BY JAMES LYON, COURTESY OF KENT LYON.

4

DECENTRALISATION DREAMING

The overgrown
urban complex
must be selectively
dismantled and
dispersed if we are
to cure the ills of the
megalopolis.[1]

BACKGROUND

Since the early years of European annexation, grave concerns have been held about the concentration of the population in the colonial administrative centres.[2] Indeed, a mere two years after Adelaide's establishment in 1836, Governor George Gawler railed against the overconcentration of people.[3] Since such times, commentators have expressed disquiet about the dramatic growth of the earliest coastal townships into dominant capital cities, which they perceived as an 'unhealthy departure from the European ideal of villages and small proprietorship'.[4]

The need to decentralise population and industry became Australia's recurring theme of national development thinking.[5] A critical turning point from the late 1960s was to link decentralisation to more selective programs focused on expanded and new regional centres rather than ineffectively sprinkling incentives across numerous, and sometimes marginal, rural centres.[6] Between 1970 and 1975, there was a genuine chance that Australia would 'embark on a large-scale process of new city building' in regional areas.[7] Under Gough Whitlam's federal Labor government (1972–1975), the Department of Urban and Regional Development (DURD) was forged to institutionally control the built environment, especially with regard to problems plaguing the major cities and the development of prospective regional growth centres.[8] This was a dramatic shift in that it came after many years of the federal government washing its hands of city matters, apart from the national capital of Canberra, which became the poster child for modern new town planning in the 1960s and '70s.[9] Traditionally, such issues were left to state governments.[10] According to the Whitlam government, fragmented state government responses to city planning and management (when viewed through a federal lens) were partly responsible for Australia's entrenched urban problems.[11]

1   Spilhaus, 710
2   Bolleter, The Ghost Cities of Australia
3   Rushman
4   Davison, 'Fatal Attraction?', 45
5   Neutze
6   Bolleter, 'The Ghost Cities of Australia'
7   Nichols et al, 2
8   Rushman
9   Bolleter, 'The Ghost Cities of Australia'
10 Rushman
11 Oakley

DURD had a brief, but momentous, life – the dismissal of the Whitlam government in 1975 heralding its downfall.[12] Nonetheless, it is unequalled in terms of the federal government machinery deployed to achieve decentralisation outcomes through both boosting selected towns to city status, such as Albury-Wodonga and Bathurst-Orange, and proposing shiny new cities, such as Monarto, southeast of Adelaide. At the same time, it never produced a coherent national urban strategy, being defeated by the task's scale, complexity and politics when conceived on continental lines. There was a movement to focus on the overall goals of efficiency, equity and proto-sustainability to make sense of scattergun programs, but with no breakthrough to a foundation of genuine national urban system thinking promoted by its own conscripted experts, such as American geographer Allan Pred.[13] Despite failing to live up to its rhetoric, the DURD was a critical juncture in Australian national decentralisation programs.

As Brendan Gleeson wonderfully evokes, 'When a big ship sinks, it takes everything around it with it'.[14] And so it was with DURD, which was denounced in the years following the Whitlam dismissal.[15] Subsequent federal government programs for cities stepped away from the decentralisation dreams of the Whitlam era, preferring to facilitate, rather than radically rethink, the processes of urban development in the Building Better Cities Program (1991–96) under the Hawke/Keating Labor governments. The drafting of a national urban policy in the 2010s outlined a cohesive set of principles for urban design and planning, but, disappointingly, omitted any spatial propositions for settlement patterns.

Clearly, the 1970s was the high-water mark for decentralisation dreaming in Australia. So, what were the underlying factors driving these radical attempts to address our lopsided, capital city–centric settlement patterns? And do these factors still exist?

CITIES IN CRISIS

Dreams of decentralisation emerged from enduring perceptions of the capital cities in crisis, especially the two biggest cities, Sydney and Melbourne.[16] In the 1970s, decentralisation proponents won critical political and thought leader support for the case that Australian cities were oversized, overcrowded and overcome by diseconomies, social pathologies and environmental deterioration.[17] Sharp-tongued critics such as Robin Boyd, who penned *The Australian Ugliness*, and Donald Gazzard, author of *Australian Outrage*, portrayed ugly, low-density, car-oriented strip development and problematic fringe suburbs as symptomatic of serious issues afflicting the capital

12 Bolleter, 'The Ghost Cities of Australia'
13 Pred; Wilmoth et al.
14 Gleeson, 'The greatest spoiler: Salvation in the cities'
15 Gleeson, 'The greatest spoiler: Salvation in the cities'
16 Bolleter, 'The Ghost Cities of Australia'
17 Cities Commission

cities.[18] Moreover, critics believed this form of decay was insidiously spreading. The crisis encompassed suburban sprawl, urban ugliness, overcrowding, pathology, congestion, pollution, environmental degradation and social inequality.[19] Notably, such gloomy assessments have contemporary relevance given the 'widespread perception that the quality of life in urban areas is deteriorating', especially in outer suburban areas of Australia's major cities.[20] Sound familiar? Interestingly, these perceptions have lingered, as evidenced by a spate of recent books cataloguing the precipitous decline of our cities, with evocative titles such as *Breaking Point: The Future of Australian Cities*,[21] *City Limits: Why Australian Cities are Broken and How We Can Fix Them*[22] and *Killing Sydney: The Fight for a City's Soul*,[23] to name just a few.

While contemporary thinking (logically) seeks to address the problems of our cities, in the 1970s, responses to the perceived crisis were more extreme. Indeed, one drastic school of thought suggested it necessary to continue to concentrate population in the major cities 'since they are already such a mess ... they might as well be written off altogether to save the rest of Australia'.[24] Another held that structure was more the problem than size alone. The third diagnosis, which gained ground, tapped into longstanding hopes for boosting decentralised settlement to ease growth pressures on the big cities.

CITY OVERCONCENTRATION

Critiques of overconcentration stemmed from the belief that Australia experienced the most significant 'territorial imbalance in population and economic opportunity' between urban and rural areas of all modern industrialised countries.[25] The idea was that Australia's primate cities were growing too large at the expense of the rural areas and country towns. Among the reasons for this belief, which were appealing but lacked robust research evidence, was an argument for 'balanced development'.[26] Influenced by this thinking, the Cities Commission, a companion entity to the DURD charged with devising a new cities program, declared that significant advantages of a large city, with a minimum of disadvantages, could exist with a population of between approximately 100,000 and 500,000 people.[27] Therefore, so-called 'balanced development' would ideally require superfluous populations (above 500,000) to be siphoned to underpopulated centres and regions. One reason for this was the imagined or real pathologies associated with big cities.

18 Boyd; Gazzard
19 Bolleter, 'The Ghost Cities of Australia'
20 Southphommasane, 143
21 Seamer
22 Kelly and Donegan
23 Farrelly
24 Neutze, 263
25 Lonsdale, 'Manufacturing Decentralization', 321
26 Neutze, 259
27 Cities Commission

CITY CONTAGION

By the nineteenth century, polluted and crowded industrial cities were regarded as deadly, and linking large cities to various forms of pathology was common.[28] By the 1840s, British doctors had confirmed that the life expectancy of the average English city dweller was barely half that of a resident of rural areas.[29] British statistician William Farr even devised a formula to describe it: death rates varied according to the sixth root of density.[30] Density not only incubated disease, but moral contagion. As Reverend John Montgomery thundered in 1860:

If human beings are crowded together moral corruption takes place, as certainly as fermentation or putrefaction in a heap of organic matter.[31]

Writing in the post-war reconstruction era, Australian war historian Charles Bean captured a similar tone in his *War Aims of a Plain Australian* (1945), stating that 'people evenly distributed in small or medium size towns tend to be stronger, morally and mentally as well as physically, than one concentrated in a few big cities'.[32] The question of morality stemmed from the fear of the 'moral contagion that they associated with the communalism and promiscuity of tenements and apartments, compared with the privacy and decorum of the cottage and the villa'.[33]

Conversely, the country, being good for moral improvement and physical health, washed away the wickedness in city folk, or at least provided an opportunity to hide it.[34] Accordingly, sanatoriums were built 'among the mountain ash and clematis in the hinterlands of cities'.[35] Country people, so the theory ran, were morally and physically superior to their weedy and consumptive city cousins.[36]

During the 1930s, when there was widespread fear of Australia's population declining, it was noted that birth rates were higher in rural areas. As such, it was regarded that hearty country folk were better suited to wage the looming struggle for national survival. 'The best crop on our farms is the annual crop of babies', a 1920 New South Wales Committee on Agricultural Industry observed.[37] This belief reflected a 'ruralist' view of society: as well as producing greater numbers of healthy children, rural areas generated most of Australia's exports, and politically, they provided a bulwark against the (imagined or real)

28 Bolleter, 'The Ghost Cities of Australia'
29 Davison, 'City Dreamers'
30 Davison, 'City Dreamers'
31 In Davison, 'City Dreamers', 81
32 Bean, 118
33 Davison, 'City Dreamers', 245.
34 Bolleter, 'The Ghost Cities of Australia'
35 Watson, 111
36 Davison, 'City Dreamers'
37 Davison, 'City Dreamers', 147

revolutionary threats from the subversive urban proletariat. In these imaginings, healthy and bountiful rural areas were flatteringly contrasted against the cities' moral decadence, disease, vice and poverty.[38]

Mid-twentieth-century arguments railing against population overconcentration stemmed partly from research on the perturbing effects of overcrowding on rats.[39] Moreover, mirroring the exposes of inner-city slumdom in the early days of the town planning movement, the Cities Commission tabled health data that confirmed the dangers cities posed.[40] Data on psychiatric patients in Victoria revealed that a person living in a city was three times more likely to be admitted for alcoholism and more than two times more likely to have a personality disorder than those residing in rural areas. The commission determined that per capita physiological and mental illness rates, crime, and juvenile delinquency, and social stress in big cities were also well above the national incidence.[41]

Evidently, these ideas linger in the public consciousness, and the COVID-19 pandemic reignited notions of a linear correlation between the density of humans and the prevalence of disease. Mournful imagery of COVID-rife, locked-down Melbourne public housing towers certainly fuelled this fire, despite inconvenient evidence to the contrary. Conversely, a general perception was that detached suburban housing allowed for safe quarantining in a trifecta of spacious surroundings, privacy and nature.[42]

CITY CONGESTION

Yet another critique of our overconcentrated capitals in the 1970s was that they were mired in inefficiency.[43] Evidence of this decline was sclerotic traffic congestion and punishing commutes from outer suburbs that had become 'part of life' in Australia's capital cities (Figure 4.1).[44] Arguably, the traffic congestion was disproportionately affecting residents of far-flung fringe suburbs. Accordingly, Hugh Stretton ventured that the poor are more disadvantaged, relative to the wealthy, in large cities than in smaller, more easily traversed towns and cities.[45]

Recent data suggest that congestion and its disproportionate effect on fringe communities have compounded in recent decades, with far-flung workers forced to endure extended commutes. Indeed, the average commute time in the mainland state capitals had surged from 55 minutes per day in 2002 to an infuriating 66 minutes in 2017.[46] Against this backdrop, decentralisation spruikers argued that modest-sized regional cities would have considerably less congested and time-consuming commutes than the sprawling capital cities.

38 Neutze
39 Alonso
40 Bolleter, 'The Ghost Cities of Australia'
41 Cities Commission
42 Bolleter et al., 'Implications of the Covid-19 Pandemic'
43 Alonso
44 Lonsdale, 'Decentralization '
45 Stretton
46 Ye and Ma

FIGURE 4.1: A TRAFFIC JAM IN MURRAY STREET, PERTH, 1967. IMAGE COURTESY OF THE STATE LIBRARY OF WESTERN AUSTRALIA (118051PD HTTPS://PURL.SLWA.WA.GOV. AU/SLWA_B3597899_1).

Decentralisation proponents also foresaw opportunities presented by mass telecommuting as early as the 1970s.[47] Like the automobile and the telephone before it, they reasoned that computer communication was a potential force for decentralisation.[48] As the American Association for the Advancement of Science exhorted:

Why can't people live wherever they wish and congregate electronically? Sight, sound, the sense of touch, and, in the near future, even the sense of smell, can be transmitted anywhere in the world. Many of the business and cultural advantages of the city can be re-created equally in a study high in the Rocky Mountains or in an artist's studio out of Washington on Cape Cod.[49]

47 Bolleter, The Ghost Cities of Australia
48 Davison, 'Fatal Attraction?'

While premature, such assessments were borne out during the pandemic, when office workers feared contracting the coronavirus while commuting or working in shared offices.[50] Catalysed by the pandemic, the image of office workers in rural idylls dialling into high-paying, big-city jobs, promised since the 1970s, finally materialised.[51]

DECENTRALISATION AS THE CURE

While pragmatists argued that the problems of major cities should be dealt with in situ, advocates believed decentralisation was the only effective cure.[52] Indeed, the American Association for the Advancement of Science, adding another metaphor capturing the long-held view of urban planning as akin to a medical intervention on a growing organism,[53] conceptualised urban renewal of slum-like urban areas in the existing major cities to eradicate sinkholes of inequality as akin to aspirin, which 'may relieve a headache and bring down a fever' but will still leave the patient sick.[54] A more transformative intervention was required.

These drastic diagnoses influenced and fuelled Australia's population overconcentration and decentralisation debate.[55] Thus, 1970s Australian decentralisation spruikers believed siphoning people from the major cities into new or boosted cities in regional areas could act as a cure-all for the crushing problems of Australia's cities, lessening societal segregation, sprawl, congestion and pollution, while boosting housing affordability and generating jobs.[56] As a result, in the 1970s, even though the kind of watertight business case demanded today was lacking, decentralisation emerged as a top-down program fuelled by rhetoric and supported by many key expert policymakers and commentators.

This chapter tables three scenarios that emerge from this vein of thought: Satellite Cities, Rail Cities and Sea Change Cities. Each of these scenarios explores different decentralisation manifestations.

49 American Association for the Advancement of Science, 709
50 Whitaker
51 Nathan and Overman, 'Will Coronavirus Cause a Big City Exodus?'
52 Bolleter, 'The Ghost Cities of Australia'
53 Amati
54 American Association for the Advancement of Science, 709
55 Bolleter, 'The Ghost Cities of Australia'
56 Neutze

SATELLITE
CITIES

FIGURE 4.2 IMAGE BY NUR MOHD ROZLAN.

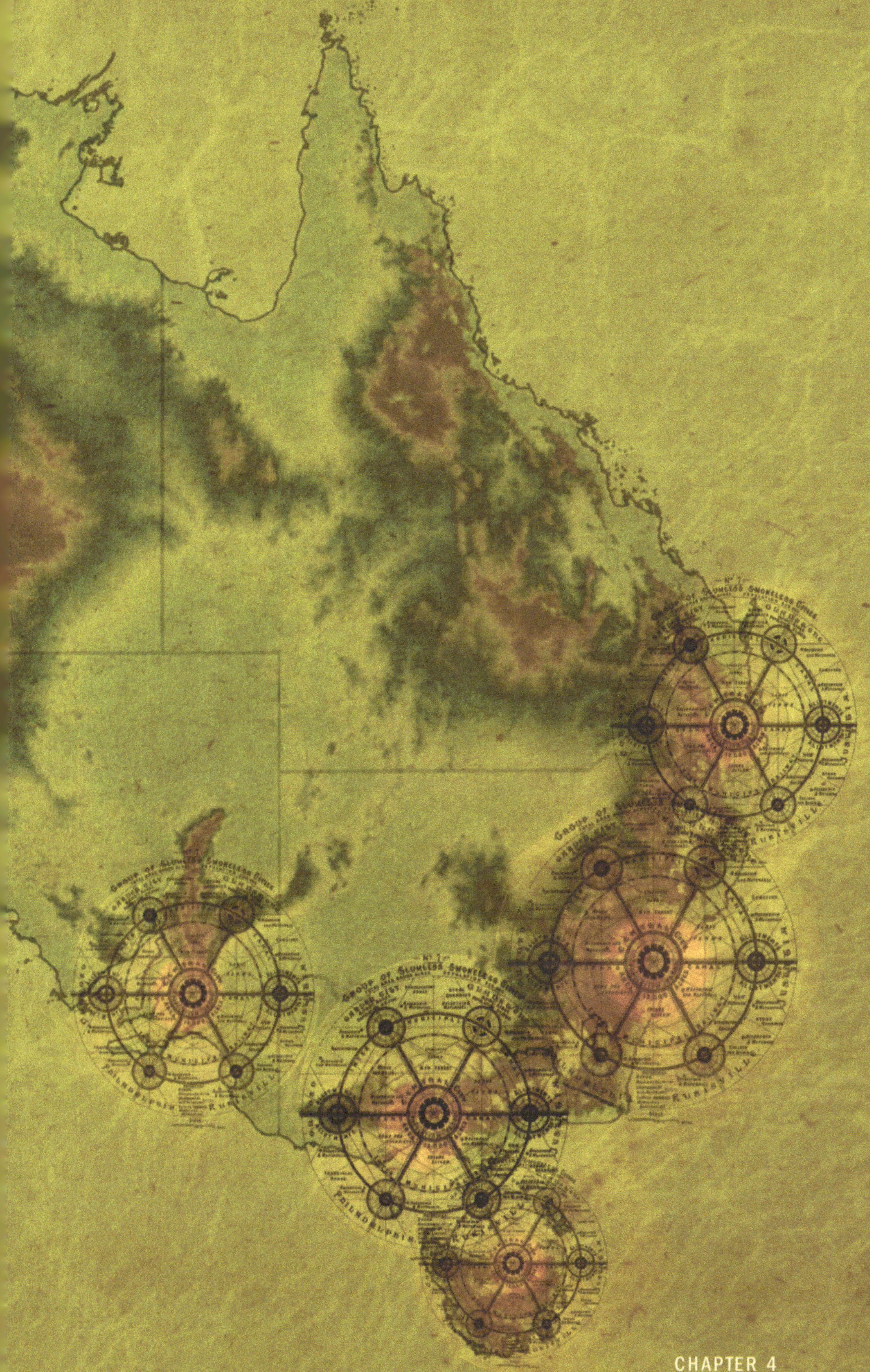

DECENTRALISATION DREAMING

SATELLITE CITIES SCENARIO

Satellite cities have been a recurring trope in Australian planning that emerged from the garden city tradition in the early twentieth century. One of the most vocal satellite city proponents was Alfred Brown, who had worked on the design of Welwyn Garden City in the United Kingdom.[57] In the late 1930s, he prepared a grand plan for Sydney, advocating a halo of new satellite towns around Sydney 'because of a passionate conviction that herein lies the hope for the survival of urban life' (Figure 4.3).[58] There was a spate of proposals for satellite towns in the 1940s, including a 1945 development plan for St Mary's near Sydney envisaging the area as an industrial satellite, and Benko and Lloyd's 1949 vision of the Adelaide region studded with satellites, each with 10,000 to 20,000 people and 'surrounded by their own green belts and recreation areas'.[59] The 'classic' satellite towns from the early 1950s were Elizabeth, built by the South Australian Housing Trust, and Kwinana, south of Perth – both required adjuncts to major industrial expansion.[60]

In 1972, DURD identified a series of sites for a national Growth Centres Program in response to the alleged crisis in Australia's capital cities and a projected surge in the population (Figure 4.4).[61] The dominant type of growth centre was the satellite city, which was to be developed within the 'influence of an existing metropolitan area but as a self-contained entity rather than a metropolitan dormitory area'.[62] Urban design thinking mandated cellular urban forms reminiscent of Ebenezer Howard's polycentric garden city networks[63] adapted to the linear forms of city planning favoured in the 1970s.[64] Areas of interest included Holsworthy-Campbelltown, Gosford-Wyong, Geelong (Figure 4.5) and the Salvado corridor north of Perth – all sites also under investigation by state governments at the time. The more contemporary use of the term 'satellite city' embraces the extension of existing centres physically distant from, but connected to, the metropolis and not just ab initio new towns in the historic garden city tradition.

57 Freestone and Pullan
58 Brown quoted in Freestone, 'The Garden City Idea in Australia', 40
59 Freestone, 'The Garden City Idea in Australia', 40
60 Freestone ,The Garden City Idea in Australia'
61 Bolleter, 'The Ghost Cities of Australia'
62 Rushman
63 Bolleter, 'The Ghost Cities of Australia'
64 Freestone, 'The Garden City Idea in Australia'

FIGURE 4.3: A.J. BROWN'S PLAN FOR SYDNEY, *SYDNEY MORNING HERALD,* 4 SEPTEMBER 1937. TRACED BY SHUBHAM GAUTAM.

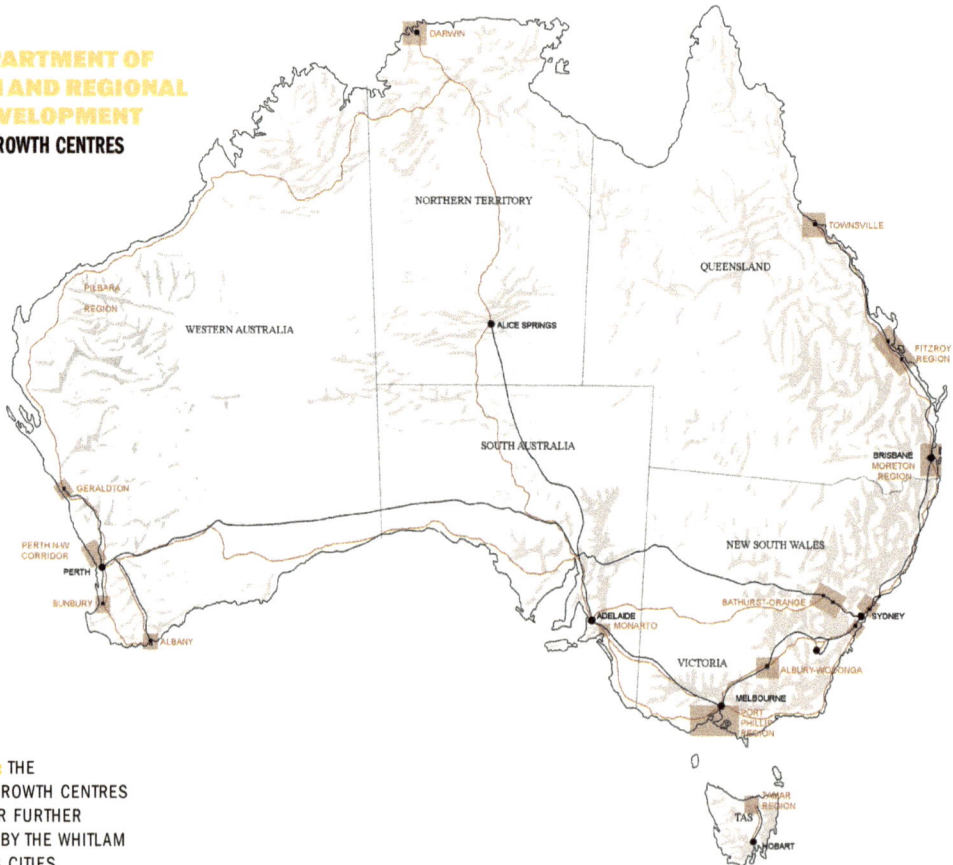

DEPARTMENT OF
URBAN AND REGIONAL
DEVELOPMENT
GROWTH CENTRES

DARWIN

NORTHERN TERRITORY

QUEENSLAND

TOWNSVILLE

PILBARA
REGION

WESTERN AUSTRALIA

ALICE SPRINGS

FITZROY
REGION

SOUTH AUSTRALIA

BRISBANE
MORETON
REGION

GERALDTON

NEW SOUTH WALES

PERTH N.W.
CORRIDOR

PERTH

BATHURST-ORANGE

SYDNEY

ADELAIDE
MONARTO

SUNBURY

ALBURY-WODONGA

ALBANY

VICTORIA

MELBOURNE
PORT
PHILLIP
REGION

TAMAR
REGION

TAS

HOBART

FIGURE 4.4: THE
PROSPECTIVE GROWTH CENTRES
NOMINATED FOR FURTHER
INVESTIGATION BY THE WHITLAM
GOVERNMENT'S CITIES
COMMISSION. MAP BY THE
CITIES COMMISSION. TRACED BY
SHUBHAM GAUTAM.

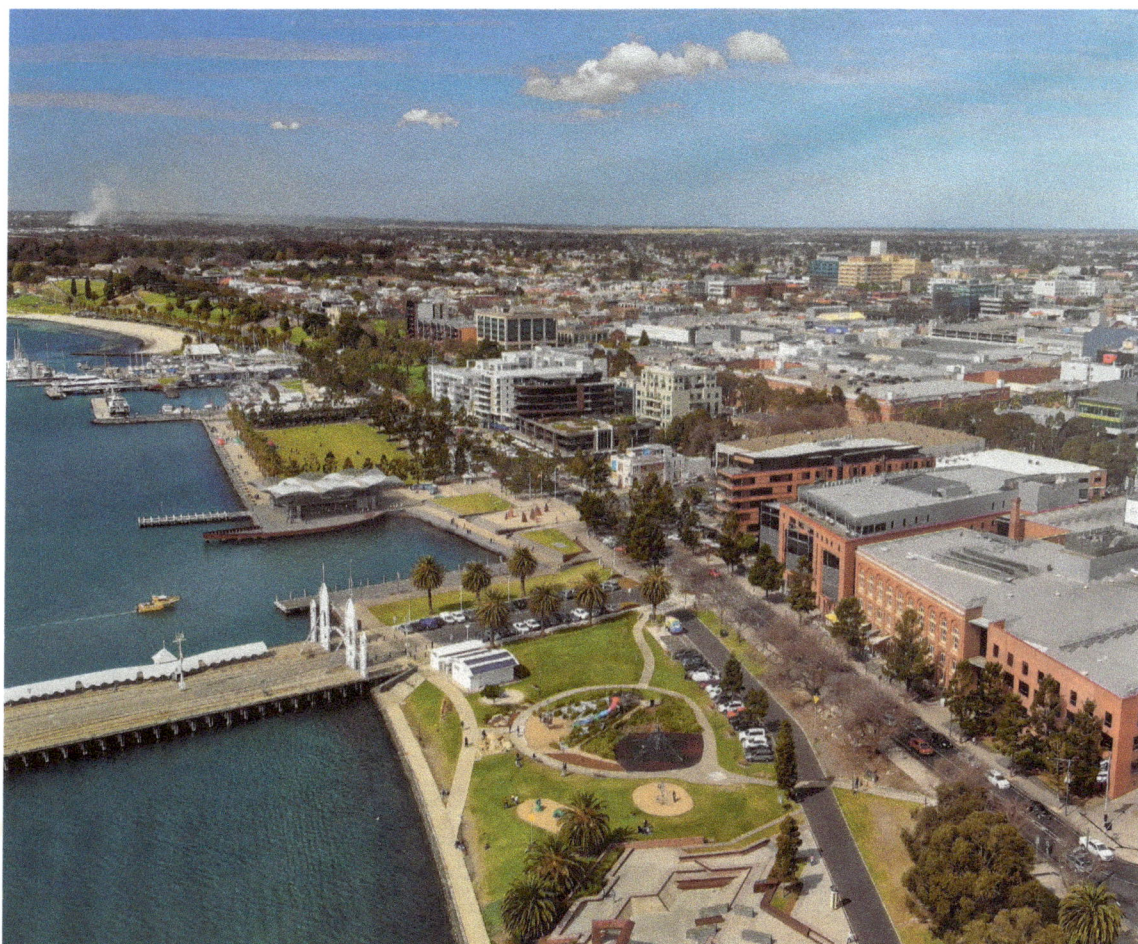

FIGURE 4.5: GEELONG, A LONG-TIME SATELLITE CITY OF MELBOURNE. IMAGE BY GAGLIARDIPHOTOGRAPHY COURTESY OF SHUTTERSTOCK (STOCK PHOTO ID: 1924577564).

SCENARIO DESCRIPTION

Building on the lineage of satellite city planning in Australia, and responding to growth pressures in the state capital cities, the Satellite Cities scenario siphons population growth to 14 satellite cities. Within commuting distance of state capital cities, these orbiting satellites increase by over 1 million people by 2101 (Figure 4.6, 4.7, 4.8, 4.9). These satellites are not the planned new towns envisaged in the 1940s, but serious existing centres capable of absorbing a more significant share of national population growth.

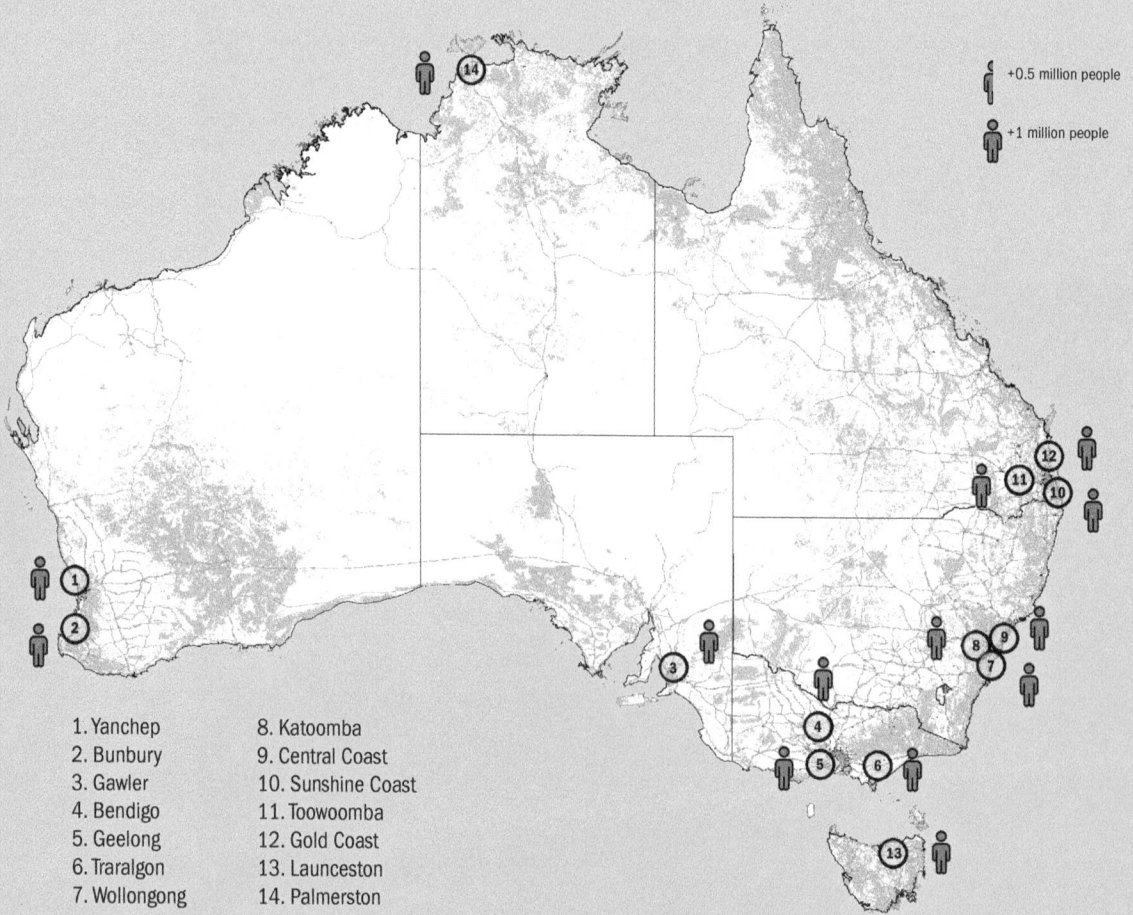

+0.5 million people

+1 million people

1. Yanchep
2. Bunbury
3. Gawler
4. Bendigo
5. Geelong
6. Traralgon
7. Wollongong
8. Katoomba
9. Central Coast
10. Sunshine Coast
11. Toowoomba
12. Gold Coast
13. Launceston
14. Palmerston

FIGURE 4.6: THE SATELLITE CITIES SCENARIO.

SATELLITE CITIES

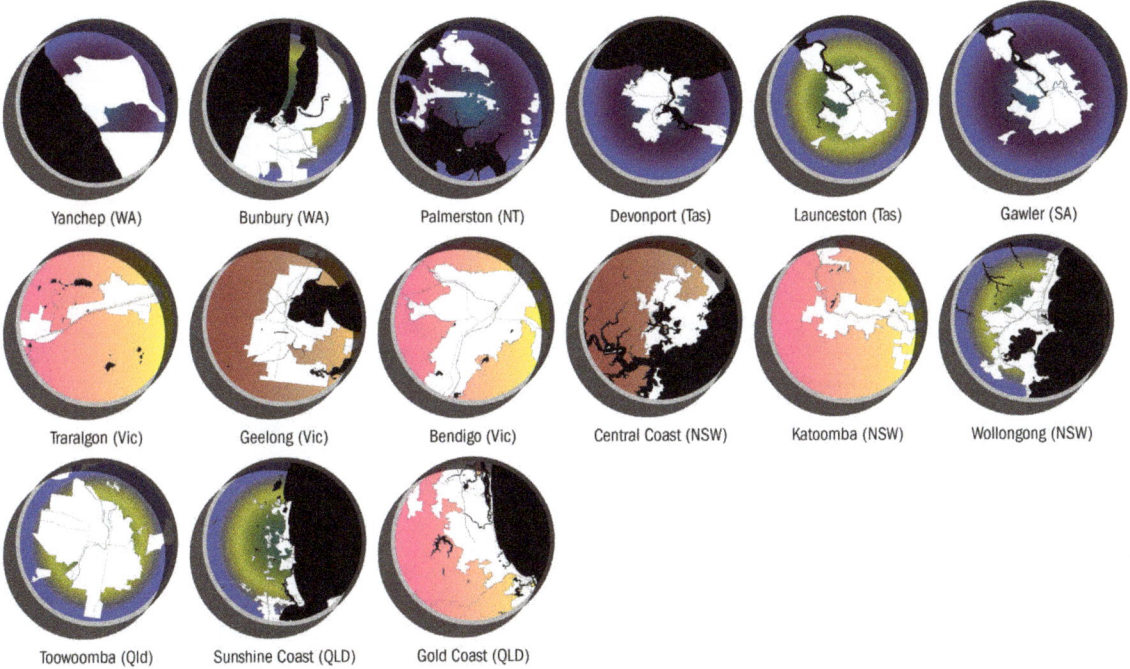

Yanchep (WA)　　Bunbury (WA)　　Palmerston (NT)　　Devonport (Tas)　　Launceston (Tas)　　Gawler (SA)

Traralgon (Vic)　　Geelong (Vic)　　Bendigo (Vic)　　Central Coast (NSW)　　Katoomba (NSW)　　Wollongong (NSW)

Toowoomba (Qld)　　Sunshine Coast (QLD)　　Gold Coast (QLD)

FIGURE 4.7:
SATELLITE CITIES.

LOCATION: GOLD COAST, QLD
INDIGENOUS REGION: BUNDJALUNG
YEAR: 2101
COORDINATES:
28.0167°S, 53.4000°E
POPULATION: 1,713,549

DECENTRALISATION DREAMING

LOCATION: WOLLONGONG, NSW
INDIGENOUS REGION: THARAWAL
YEAR: 2101
COORD: 34.4248°S, 150.8931°E
POPULATION: 780,564

FIGURE 4.9: WOLLONGONG SOUTH OF SYDNEY: FROM REGIONAL INDUSTRIAL CITY TO LIFESTYLE SATELLITE BY 2101. IMAGE BASED ON A PHOTO BY FRANK AND DONNIS (HTTPS://FRANKEEG.WORDPRESS.COM/2015/08/). SELECT BUILDINGS PHOTOGRAPHED BY JOHN GOLLINGS PHOTOGRAPHY COURTESY OF IVAN RIJAVEC.

DECENTRALISATION DREAMING

SCENARIO SENTIMENT

In a revealing convergence of expert and layperson opinion at the top of the Plan *My* Australia ratings, the Satellite Cities scenario was voted into first place as a preferred national approach to long-term absorption of future urban populations. The dominant theme of the slew of positive commentary was that this scenario would realistically relieve growth pressures on the capital cities. One person elucidated, 'Satellite cities are a sensible and practical approach to spreading population'. Another explained that the scenario would 'distribute the population to areas with more room to establish growth, start manufacturing and businesses, and become liveable and prosperous in the long term'. A further theme was that the scenario would allow for 'effective use of existing infrastructure and act as a catalyst for infrastructure investment'. People also felt the Satellite Cities scenario would effectively catalyse the surrounding region's economic growth.[65]

While generally well received, concerns existed. Some worried the Satellite Cities scenario would 'just result in sprawl and degradation of the natural environment and agricultural hinterland' as the 'satellite cities will become sprawling extensions of the capital cities' (i.e. mega-sprawl). Furthermore, one person explained that the scenario lacks ambition because it is 'still technically centralisation if you consider that these satellite cities are close to major cities'. Pragmatists also doubted that the satellite cities would receive the necessary injection of investment – for rail and road infrastructure, health services and education – and that they needed to be more than dormitory suburbs. An informed history buff cautioned that:

History is littered with failed satellite experiments; those that made it off the drawing board were characterised by poor urban design and unrealised expectations of growth resulting from the reality that people would rather live and work in thriving, established metropolitan regions.

65 The respondent quotations below come from Bolleter et al., 'Long-Term Settlement Scenarios.'

Others were anxious that sustained population growth would threaten the liveability of the existing towns and cities designated for satellite city status. As one reasoned:

'Difficulty increases exponentially with size/congestion/people.' Said another: 'By stuffing an extra million people into these cities, you will transform them beyond recognition and destroy their character.' Clearly, even the most popular scenarios were not above critique, highlighting the variability and vitality of opinion running right through our community and expert sample groups.

SCENARIO SUITABILITY

By way of a reminder, our suitability analysis of the Satellite Cities scenario focused on climatic factors (such as heat stress, annual rainfall and cyclone risk) and natural and cultural heritage in the form of significant native vegetation, hydrological features, slope, conservation reserves and native title determinations. Our analysis also included infrastructure in the form of major ports, airports, regional railway lines, water pipelines, major power lines, telecommunications (NBN) and principal roads. So, how did the satellite city locations rate in terms of suitability? Again, the scenario locations in the south are all positively rated (Figures 4.10, 4.11, 4.12). These satellites are in reasonable proximity to the capital cities and their abundance of employment opportunities. As pre-existing urban centres, they benefit from extant infrastructure investments, including (in many cases) regional rail, NBN and major roads that provide an umbilical cord to the primate capitals. Moreover, they are close to the capital city's major ports and international airports. They generally have a temperate climate with moderate rainfall. However, perceived constraints related to the presence of biodiversity and topography, such as at Palmerston, the satellite city of Darwin, which is hemmed in by mangroves and seasonally exposed to extreme heat, humidity and cyclonic conditions. Nonetheless, the general high suitability of the satellite sites helps underpin the judgement of Australians on their most preferred urbanisation scenario, which effectively trades off metropolitan orientation and regional identity.

Despite the wellspring of support for the Satellite Cities scenario and its evident suitability, perhaps it doesn't go far enough – the subservient satellite cities are still firmly locked in the orbit of the predominant primate cities. With this in mind, the following scenario (Rail Cities) cuts the umbilical cord and stretches deeper into the regions.

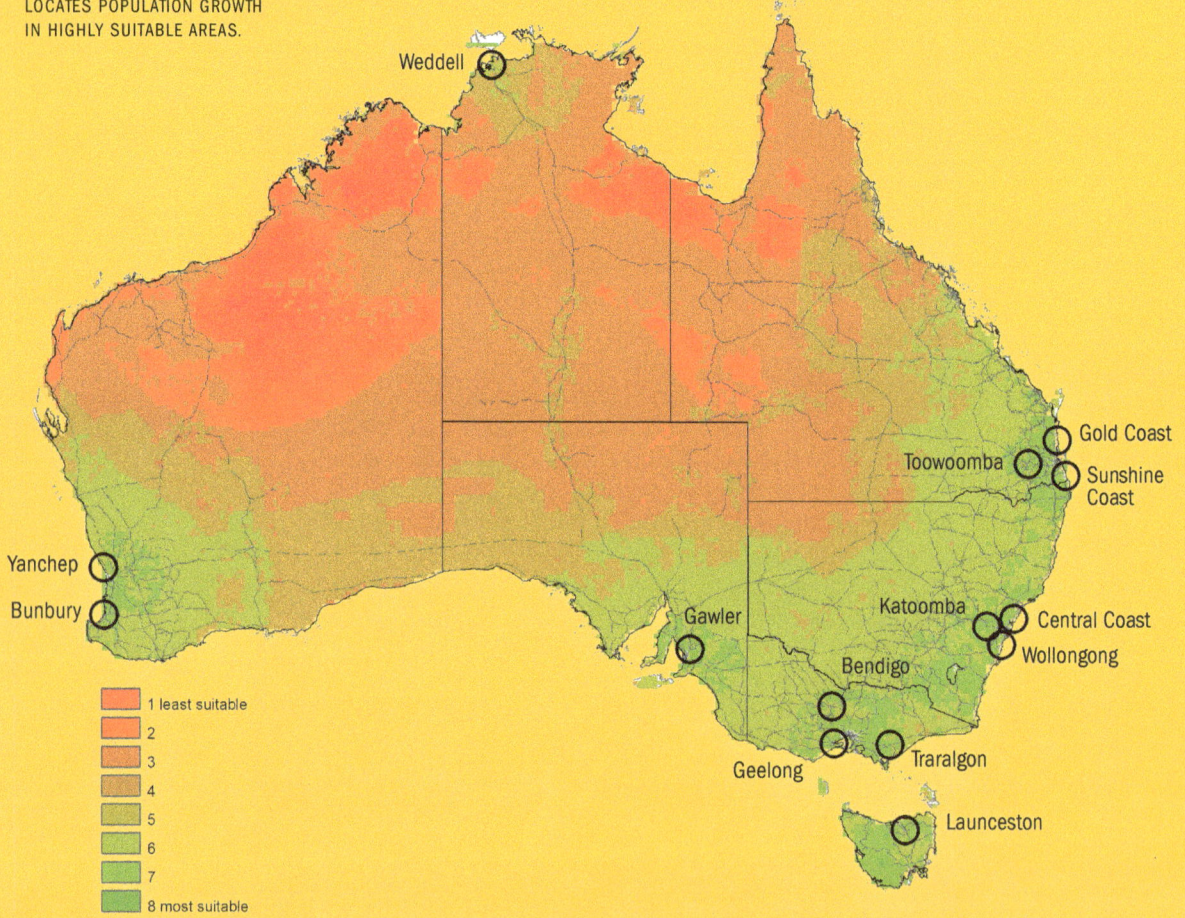

FIGURE 4.10: THE SATELLITE CITIES SCENARIO GENERALLY LOCATES POPULATION GROWTH IN HIGHLY SUITABLE AREAS.

Weddell

Gold Coast

Toowoomba

Sunshine Coast

Yanchep

Bunbury

Katoomba

Gawler

Central Coast

Bendigo

Wollongong

Geelong

Traralgon

Launceston

1 least suitable
2
3
4
5
6
7
8 most suitable

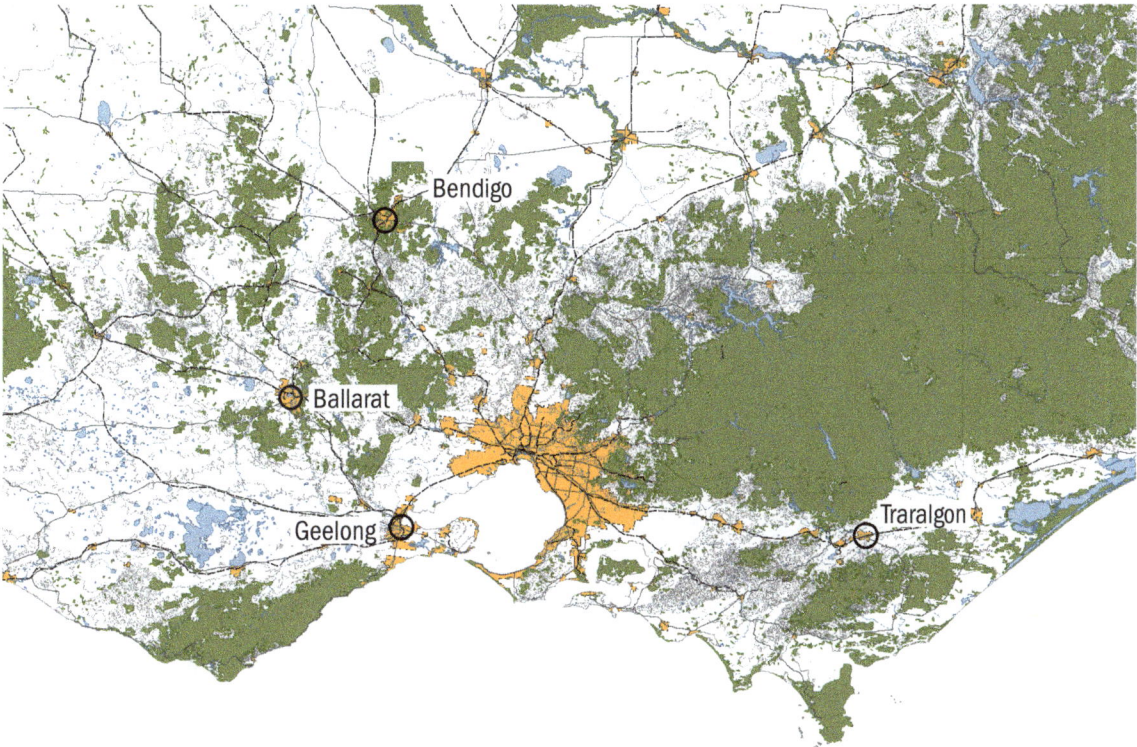

FIGURE 4.11: VICTORIA'S SATELLITE CITIES OFFER PROXIMITY TO MELBOURNE'S EMPLOYMENT OPPORTUNITIES, INFRASTRUCTURE AND GENERALLY CLEARED LAND.

FIGURE 4.12: PROSPECTIVE SATELLITE CITIES NORTH AND SOUTH OF PERTH.

RAIL CITIES

Departures

TIME	TO
12:00	ORANGE
12:04	SYDNEY
12:09	WAGGA GAGG...
12:15	YANCHEP
12:19	CANBERRA
12:21	ADELAIDE
12:23	MANJIMUP
12:26	SYDNEY
12:09	ALBURY
12:15	DUBBO
12:19	PERTH
12:21	PERTH
12:23	
12:26	
12:26	

FIGURE 4.13 IMAGE BY NUR MOHD ROZLAN.

GATE   REMARK

RAIL CITIES SCENARIO

The Rail Cities scenario emerges from a wellspring of thought around regional scales of networked urbanity, upscaling the prospect of satellite cities into mega-regions connected by high-speed rail. So, what are mega-regions? First identified by geographer Jean Gottman in his 1961 study of the urban corridor from Boston to Washington (referred to as Bos-Wash),[66] mega-regions consist of a regional system of cities linked economically and socially in a coherently integrated network (Figure 4.14).[67] In more evocative terms, Richard Florida defined mega-regions as contiguous lit areas when viewed from a satellite at night, with networks of major cities that produce more than $100 billion in annual economic productivity.[68] Contemporary examples of mega-regions include Japan's Tokyo, Osaka, Kyoto, and Nagoya Keihanshin region, or China's bustling Hong Kong, Guangzhou, Macao, and Shenzhen development triangle.[69]

Ideally, the constituent cities are physically separate but networked, and draw economic strength from a functional division of labour.[70] In this sense, the centres concomitantly exist both as separate entities, in which most residents work locally, and as parts of a wider mega-region connected by dense flows of people and information conveyed along freeways, high-speed rail lines and telecommunication networks: the 'space of flows'.[71]

More than just a geographic curiosity, mega-regions such as Bos-Wash are economic powerhouses leading to Richard Florida describing them as the 'fundamental economic unit of our world' and have been predicted to become the 'dominant forms of settlements' in the new millennium.[72] Carried forward by other futurist planners like Constantine Doxiadis, by the 1970s, poly-centred mega-regions became a *de rigueur* spatial planning imaginary for continuous long-term growth.

Most mega-region examples cited have emerged organically over time and without conscientious planning, but how could you proactively precipitate an Australian mega-region? International experience has explored the extent to which infrastructure, particularly high-speed rail, could be instrumental. Research concludes that high-speed rail can decentralise settlement patterns by reducing the time it takes to connect primate cities to each other and networks of surrounding regional centres.[73] Greater connectivity can attract business investment to regional centres; attract more students to regional tertiary institutions; significantly grow regional tourism; improve regional access to health, educational and employment services; and enhance the broader competitiveness, liveability and investment appeal of newly connected regional areas.[74] Despite its transformative potential, Australia has been among the slowest of the developed nations in

66 Gottman
67 Laquian
68 Florida, 'Megaregions'
69 Laquian
70 Hall and Pain, 3
71 Hall and Pain, 3
72 Florida, 'Megaregions'
73 Archer et al.
74 Archer et al.

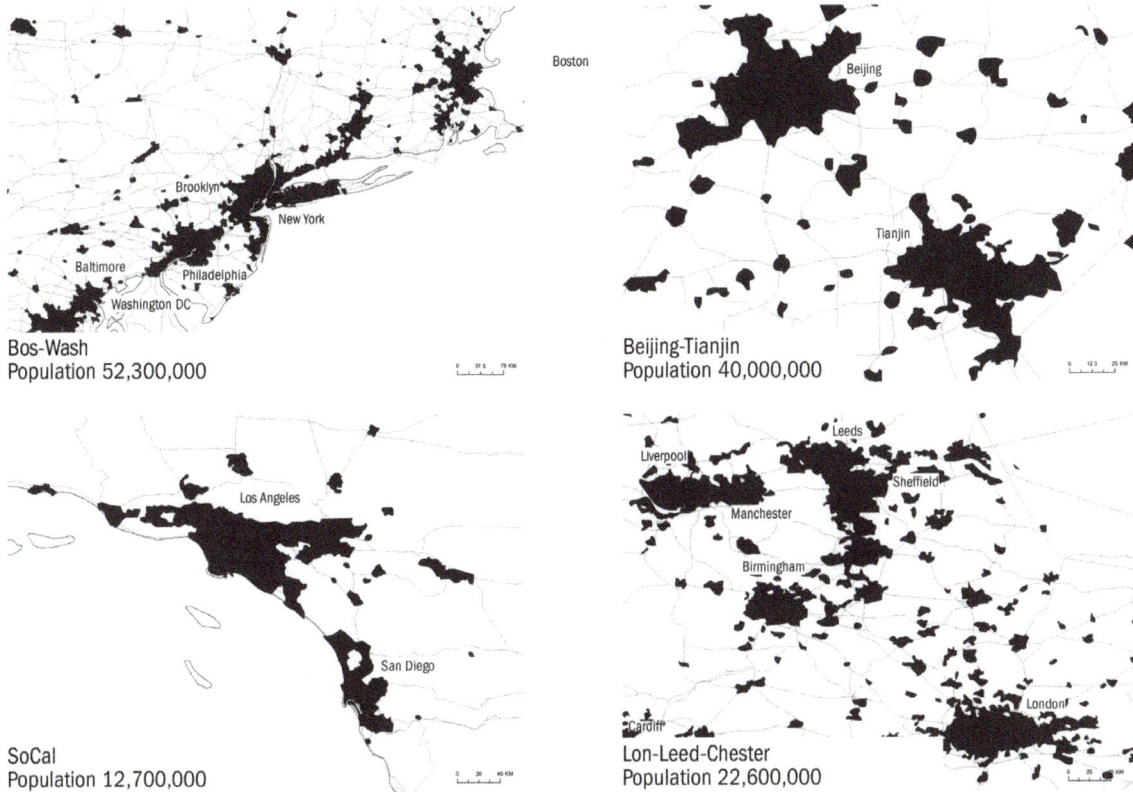

Bos-Wash
Population 52,300,000

Beijing-Tianjin
Population 40,000,000

SoCal
Population 12,700,000

Lon-Leed-Chester
Population 22,600,000

FIGURE 4.14: GLOBAL MEGA-REGIONS.

adopting high-speed rail compared with the European Union, Taiwan, China, South Korea, Russia and Turkey, to name a few. This sorry situation is despite many false starts and failed business cases.[75] Consequently, air transport remains Australia's dominant intercity transport regime, which tends to reinforce the primacy of the capital cities rather than open up opportunities for boosted cities and towns threaded along the route.

Private enterprise has already flagged interest in venturing down this path. The CLARA (Consolidated Land and Rail Australia) Plan proposes building up to eight new regional smart cities plugged into a high-speed rail system connecting Sydney and Melbourne via Canberra. CLARA has outlined a 'value capture' business model based on recouping costs from private land development in the new cities, not government handouts.[76] That said, in late 2022, the Albanese Labor government established a new High-Speed Rail Authority to investigate the possibilities for southeastern Australia with a priority focus on connecting Sydney and Newcastle, and a longer-term, aspirational vision to link Brisbane to Melbourne, with stops in Canberra, Sydney and regional centres (Figure 4.15).[77]

75 Charles et al.
76 Steele
77 Ittimani; King, 'High Speed Rail Gathers Speed.'

FIGURE 4.15: IN 2023 THE COMMONWEALTH GOVERNMENT COMMENCED INVESTIGATION OF THE FEASIBILITY OF HIGH-SPEED RAIL CONNECTING SYDNEY TO NEWCASTLE (PICTURED) RECAST BY THE NSW GOVERNMENT AS PART OF A 'SIX CITIES' METROPOLITAN REGION CENTRED ON SYDNEY. PHOTO BY SNAPSHOTSFP COURTESY OF SHUTTERSTOCK (STOCK PHOTO ID: 2006023589).

DECENTRALISATION DREAMING

SCENARIO DESCRIPTION

A mega-region can potentially be orchestrated in anticipation of population growth. For example, high-speed rail, in combination with the NBN, could allow large numbers of Australians to maintain productive lives in attractive regional settings.[78] Accordingly, the Rail Cities scenario proposes to distribute population growth to 18 regional cities connected to the state capital cities by significant rail links to catalyse not one, but two Australian mega-regions (Figures 4.16, 4.17, 4.18). Each of these regional city's populations is nominally boosted by over 750,000 people by 2101.[79] This scenario replayed a previously developed scenario in 2013[80] and a federal government–funded investigation for 'High-Speed Rail' in 2010–2011, commissioned by then Minister for Infrastructure and Transport, Anthony Albanese.[81]

SCENARIO SENTIMENT

So, were people ready for such an ambitious and transformative scheme? To our surprise, generally, yes. In a broadly favourable appraisal, laypeople ranked this scenario second highest[82] and experts third.[83] Dominant themes in the positive comments were that rail would make regional areas more attractive and 'close the gap' between capital cities and the regions, as one fan enthused:

> *Yes! The perfect model. Every state needs high-speed rail to link all its cities. It encourages the redistribution of people, wealth, and energy across more land areas instead of most of the state's resources being directed to one city. This scenario will increase the dynamics of the entire region.*

Others gushed:

> *High-speed regional rail offers an incredible opportunity to reimagine Australia's pattern of settlement and deliver new forms of urbanisation and ways of living through the founding of compact, sustainable rail-connected city developments.*

78 Bolleter and Weller
79 Bolleter et al., 'Long-Term Settlement Scenarios'
80 Bolleter and Weller
81 AECOM
82 The respondent quotations below come from Bolleter et al., 'Long-Term Settlement Scenarios.'
83 Bolleter et al., 'Evaluating Scenarios'

Another positive theme was that the Rail Cities scenario would stimulate the social, cultural and economic revitalisation of regional centres and surrounding regions and relieve growth pressures in the capital cities. Finally, people felt that the scenario could lead to safer, more convenient travel options within regions.

The negative comments understandably focused on the pricey infrastructure investment required, including water pipelines, high-speed rail, broadband internet, education, medical and essential services in the high-growth regional areas. As one pragmatist cautioned: 'The thousands of kilometres of track laid between cities' will be 'prohibitively expensive and impractical – they will never happen'. Others, with some cause, worried about supplying water to inland rail cities:

> *What pray tell, will these people drink? There is an ongoing and worsening drought in regional Australia. What happens if you add millions more people? Where is the water going to come from?*

With an eye to equity, several people felt that the scheme discriminated against other options for population distribution and, in particular, the scenario ignored the Northern Territory, Tasmania and South Australia.

Other respondents were anxious that population pressures would erode regional centres' liveability. As one proclaimed, 'It will destroy those regional areas', including 'irreplaceable farmland and wilderness areas' and 'make them wannabe capital cities'. Other regional voices echoed this sentiment, 'Being a country girl, there is much charm about relaxed regional areas that the locals love; they may be scared their serenity will be affected.' Finally, other themes were that the scenario would merely result in urban sprawl, not deliver employment opportunities, and settle unattractive lands; as one person stated: 'the inland is dry and boring'.

SCENARIO SUITABILITY

Indeed, the suitability of the scenario's far-flung inland cities was diminished by the aridity of some inland areas and a dearth of infrastructure relative to the capital cities (Figures 4.19, 4.20, 4.21). Nonetheless, high-speed rail and the NBN could be transformative in stretching the economic opportunities of the capital cities deep into regional areas. In addition, the vitality of most existing centres, a relatively comfortable climate and large reserves of cleared, developable land boosted suitability scores.

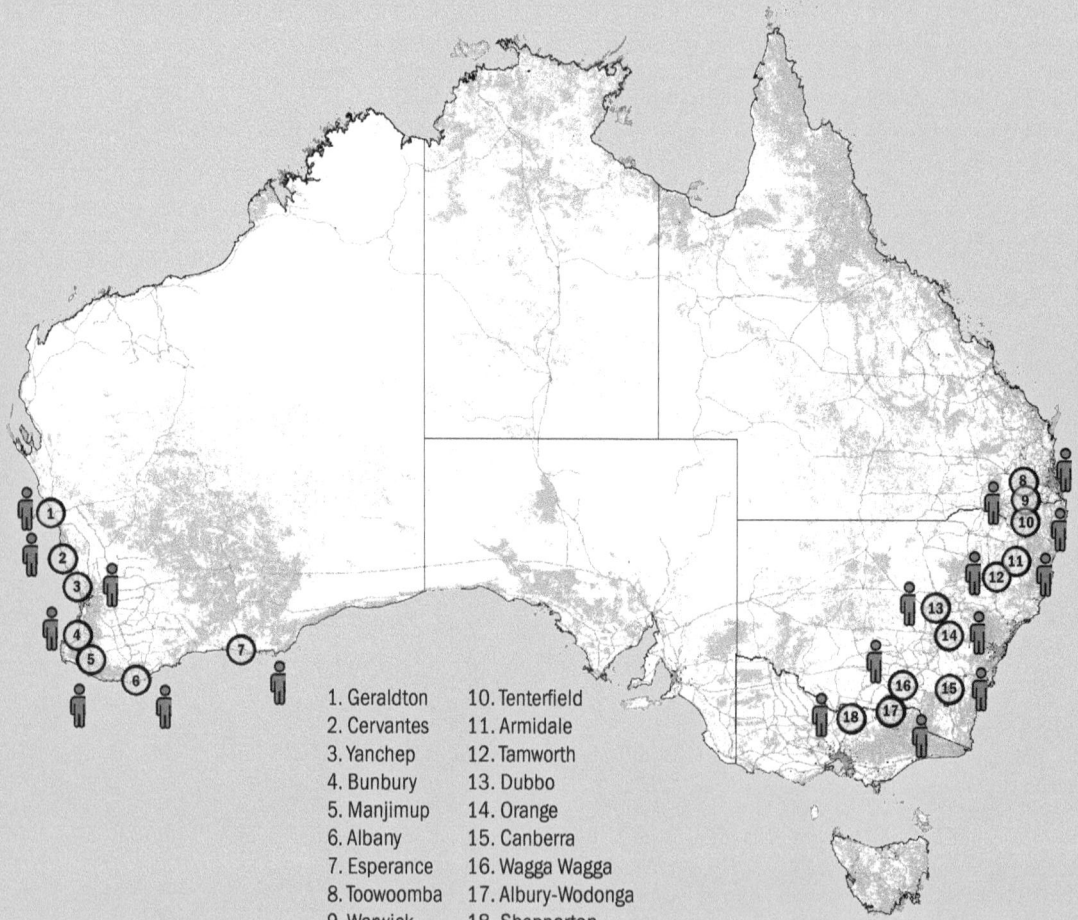

1. Geraldton   10. Tenterfield
2. Cervantes   11. Armidale
3. Yanchep   12. Tamworth
4. Bunbury   13. Dubbo
5. Manjimup   14. Orange
6. Albany   15. Canberra
7. Esperance   16. Wagga Wagga
8. Toowoomba   17. Albury-Wodonga
9. Warwick   18. Shepparton

FIGURE 4.16: THE RAIL
CITIES SCENARIO SIPHONS
POPULATION GROWTH TO NEW
AND BOOSTED CENTRES ALONG
REGIONAL FAST RAIL LINKS.

RAIL CITIES

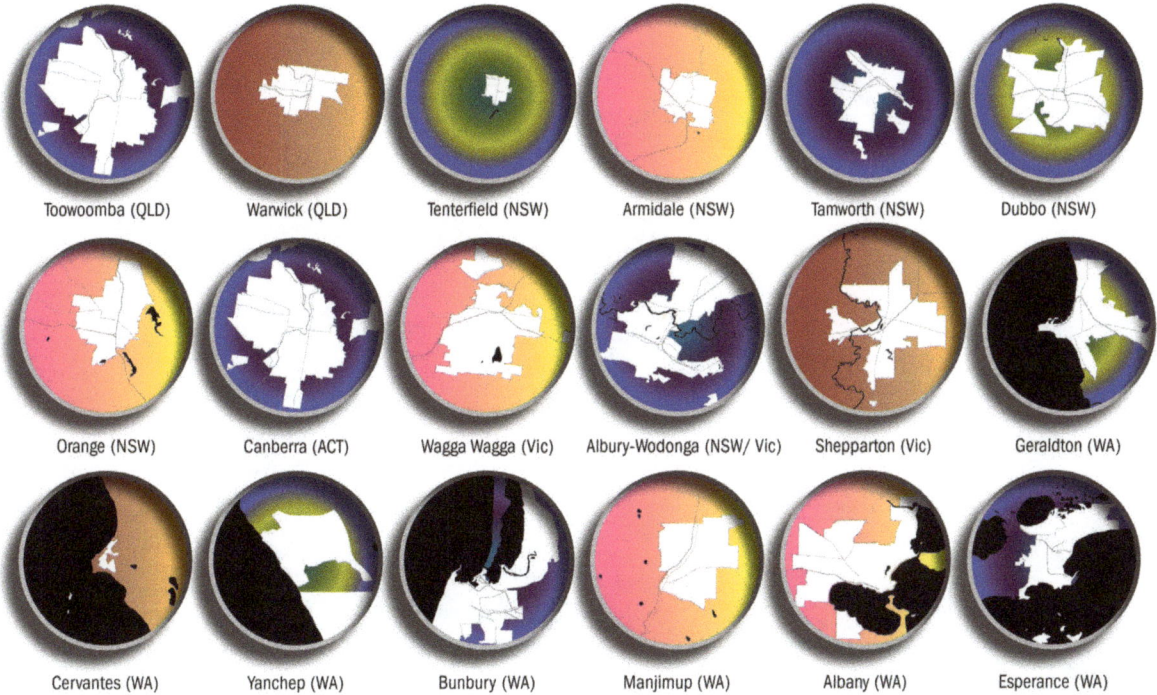

Toowoomba (QLD) Warwick (QLD) Tenterfield (NSW) Armidale (NSW) Tamworth (NSW) Dubbo (NSW)

Orange (NSW) Canberra (ACT) Wagga Wagga (Vic) Albury-Wodonga (NSW/ Vic) Shepparton (Vic) Geraldton (WA)

Cervantes (WA) Yanchep (WA) Bunbury (WA) Manjimup (WA) Albany (WA) Esperance (WA)

FIGURE 4.17: RAIL CITIES.

LOCATION: CANBERRA, ACT
INDIGENOUS REGION: NGUNAWAL
YEAR: 2101
COORD: 35.2802°S, 149.1310°E
POPULATION: 1,248,111

FIGURE 4.18: CANBERRA'S GROWTH STIMULATED BY HIGH-SPEED RAIL CONNECTIVITY. IMAGE BASED ON A PHOTO BY BIDGEE COURTESY OF WIKIPEDIA COMMONS (HTTPS://SV.M.WIKIPEDIA.ORG/WIKI/FIL:CITY_CENTRE_VIEWED_FROM_MOUNT_AINSLIE_LOOKOUT.JPG) SELECT BUILDINGS PHOTOGRAPHED BY JOHN GOLLINGS PHOTOGRAPHY COURTESY OF IVAN RIJAVEC.

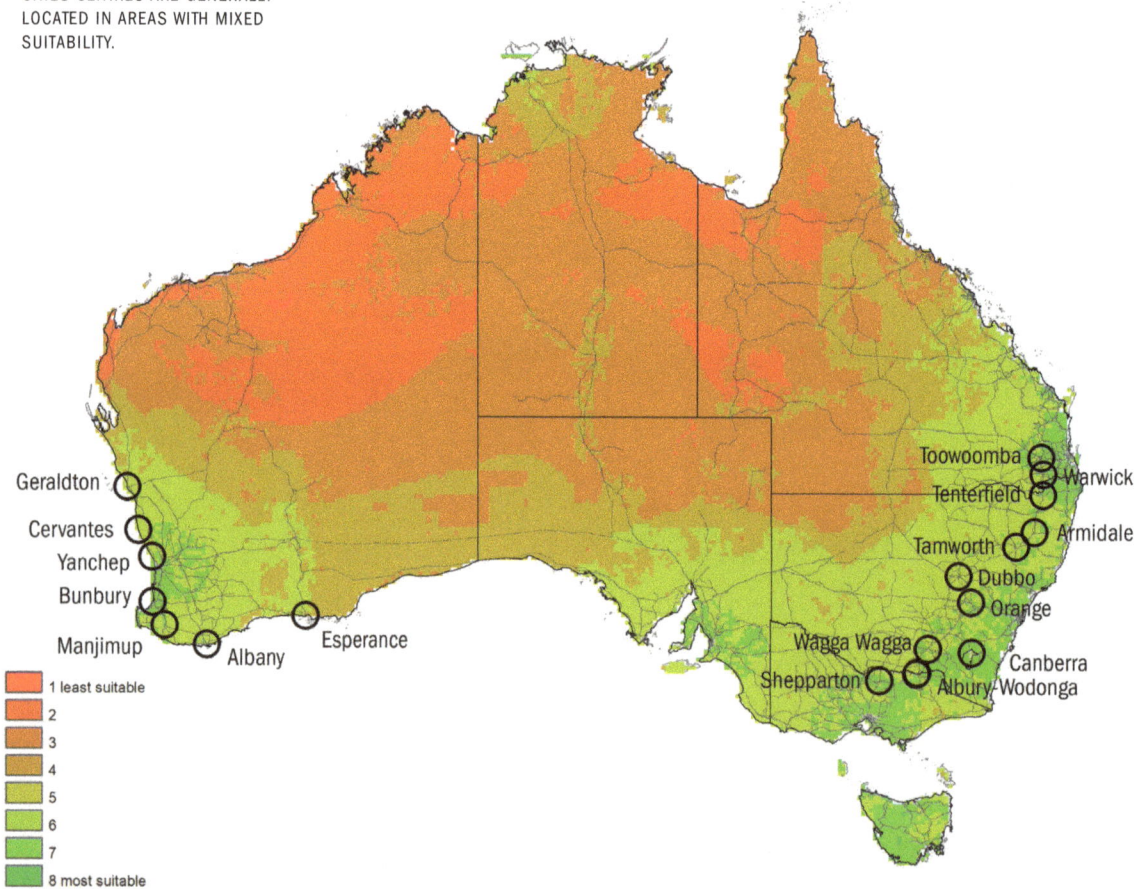

FIGURE 4.19: THE RAIL CITIES CENTRES ARE GENERALLY LOCATED IN AREAS WITH MIXED SUITABILITY.

Geraldton

Cervantes

Yanchep

Bunbury

Manjimup

Albany

Esperance

Toowoomba

Tenterfield

Warwick

Tamworth

Armidale

Dubbo

Orange

Wagga Wagga

Shepparton

Albury-Wodonga

Canberra

1 least suitable
2
3
4
5
6
7
8 most suitable

Toowoomba

Warwick

Tenterfield

Armidale

Tamworth

Dubbo

Orange

Wagga Wagga

Canberra

Shepparton

Albury-Wodonga

0   95   190 KM

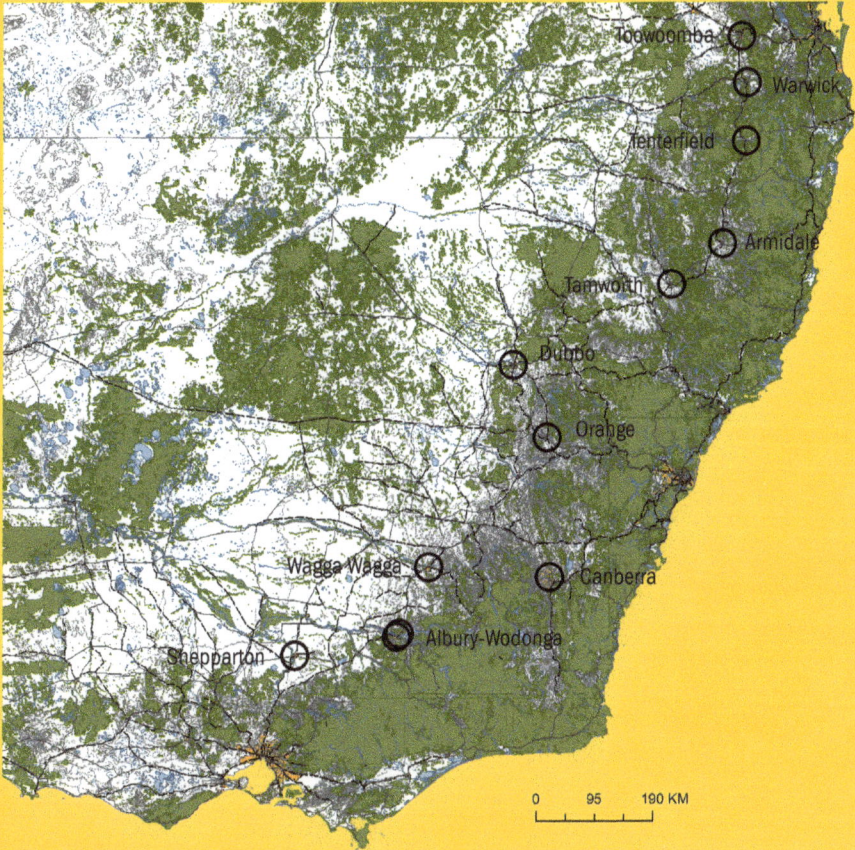

FIGURE 4.21: RAIL CITIES CORRIDOR BETWEEN GERALDTON AND ESPERANCE VIA PERTH.

Geraldton

Cervantes

Yanchep

Bunbury

Manjimup

Esperance

Albany

0   50   100 KM

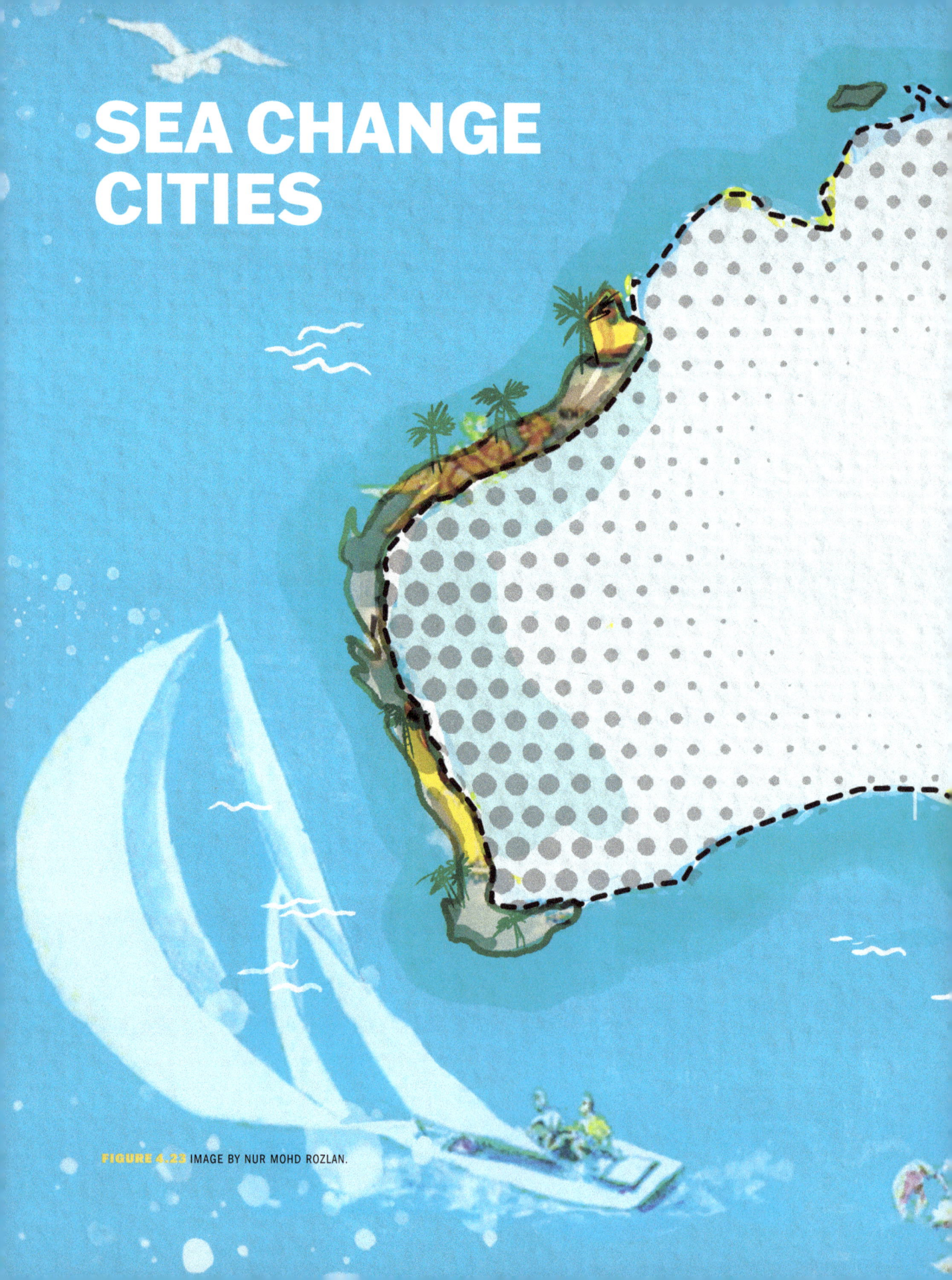

SEA CHANGE CITIES

FIGURE 4.23 IMAGE BY NUR MOHD ROZLAN.

DECENTRALISATION DREAMING

The result was still a mixed assessment of the suitability of the rail cities locations, particularly for inland and far-flung centres.[84] Given the evident impediments to forging inland, the final decentralisation scenario sought to consolidate the coast-hugging tendencies of Australians in chains of coastal cities.

SEA CHANGE CITIES SCENARIO

In contrast to the inland cities mooted in the Rail Cities scenario, Australia's populace tends to cling to the fertile edges of the continent, where population growth has responded to market forces outside any serious urban public policy initiatives.[85] In time, the government-fostered internal migration for the Growth Centre programs in the 1970s was far outstripped by the population explosion in coastal areas in Southeast Queensland and northern New South Wales. Indeed, the real growth in the Australian non-metropolitan population came through spontaneous and speculative coastal urbanisation, not areas for which there were official government targets. If Canberra was the pin-up story of the 1960s and 1970s, then the Gold Coast–Tweed corridor, developed by a very different paradigm, took over this mantle in the 1980s, on its way to becoming Australia's sixth-most-extensive urban complex.[86] Subsequently, urban growth has continued unabated along the vast Australian coastline, often driven by tourism and leisure industries, as part of the 'sea change' phenomenon.[87]

As the terms imply, sea changers and amenity migrants move primarily for lifestyle rather than to improve their financial situation.[88] Reflecting this, 'sea changers' often move to 'lifestyle cities' in retirement.[89] This trend, occurring since the 1970s in affluent societies where people can afford to move for lifestyle reasons, is driving population growth in, and urbanisation of, coastal areas that, in the past, have been low-key holiday destinations.[90]

Burgeoning coastal cities, such as Queensland's Gold Coast and the Sunshine Coast, dramatically manifest this coastalisation process. This lifestyle-driven urbanism has been developed as narrow bands of urban stretches along the region's sandy beaches (Figure 4.24).[91] The Gold Coast and its daring high-rise buildings 'exude images of confidence, vibrancy, colour, sparkle, profit, dynamism', creating a honey trap for prospective tourists and residents.[92] The Gold Coast and Sunshine Coast differ from other Australian cities in their demography, economy, politics and, most of all, because they have large numbers of 'sun belt' tourists who flock to their bars and beaches yearly.[93] By the 1990s, the Gold

84 Bolleter et al., 'Informing future Australian settlement planning'
85 Potts, 140
86 Freestone, 'Back to the Future'
87 Burnley and Murphy; Bohnet and Pert; Beer and Clower
88 Bohnet and Pert
89 Salt
90 Bohnet and Pert
91 Cooper and Lemckert, 8
92 Mullins, 'Tourist Cities as New Cities', 41
93 Bolleter, 'The Ghost Cities of Australia'

Coast and the Sunshine Coast were the largest cities in Australia dedicated to tourism and the fastest-growing of the nation's big cities.[94]

The coastalisation process is predicated on migration from capital cities and inland agricultural regions, creating what demographer Bernard Salt tagged the 'empty-island syndrome'.[95] While the aridity of Australia's interior has always curtailed inhabitation, the population differential between urbanised coastal areas and inland rural areas widened dramatically in recent decades.[96] As a result, there are two regional Australias: the coastal regions benefitting from dynamism and growth, and inland Australia experiencing slow incremental growth – at best.[97]

Given the groundswell behind coastalisation, the Sea Change Cities scenario abandons the hot and dusty inland, runs to the beach and plunges in for a refreshing swim.

SCENARIO DESCRIPTION

Related research highlights the attractiveness of mid-sized coastal cities in reasonable proximity to a major metropolitan centre.[98] Accordingly, the Sea Change Cities scenario distributes population growth to 25 regional yet coastal cities and, in doing so, boosts the population in these cities by over 500,000 people each (Figures 4.25, 4.26, 4.27).[99] High-speed ferries, regional rail, freeway and NBN networks connect these necklaces of coastal cities.

SCENARIO SENTIMENT

Despite its seeming populist appeal, laypeople in the Plan *My* Australia survey relegated the Sea Change Cities scenario to a lowly sixth place,[100] below that of the experts who had it in fourth.[101] Nonetheless, the dominant theme in the limited positive commentary was that the Coastal Cities scenario enshrines the Australian preference for coastal living and, as such, is inherently appealing.[102] One endorser explained:

'These cities are already attractive and are becoming more populated anyway. The coast is a wonderful place to live and should be promoted as such.'

94 Mullins, 'Cities for Pleasure '
95 In Kullmann, 243
96 Kullmann
97 Hugo, 'Population Distribution, Migration and Climate Change'
98 Vij et al.
99 Bolleter et al., 'Long-Term Settlement Scenarios'
100 Bolleter et al., 'Long-Term Settlement Scenarios'
101 Bolleter et al., 'Projected Extreme Heat Stress'
102 Bolleter et al., 'Long-Term Settlement Scenarios'

FIGURE 4.24: THE GOLD COAST EXUDES IMAGES OF CONFIDENCE, VIBRANCY, COLOUR, SPARKLE, PROFIT AND DYNAMISM. PHOTOGRAPH BY BLAZE PRO COURTESY OF SHUTTERSTOCK (STOCK PHOTO ID: 2006023589).

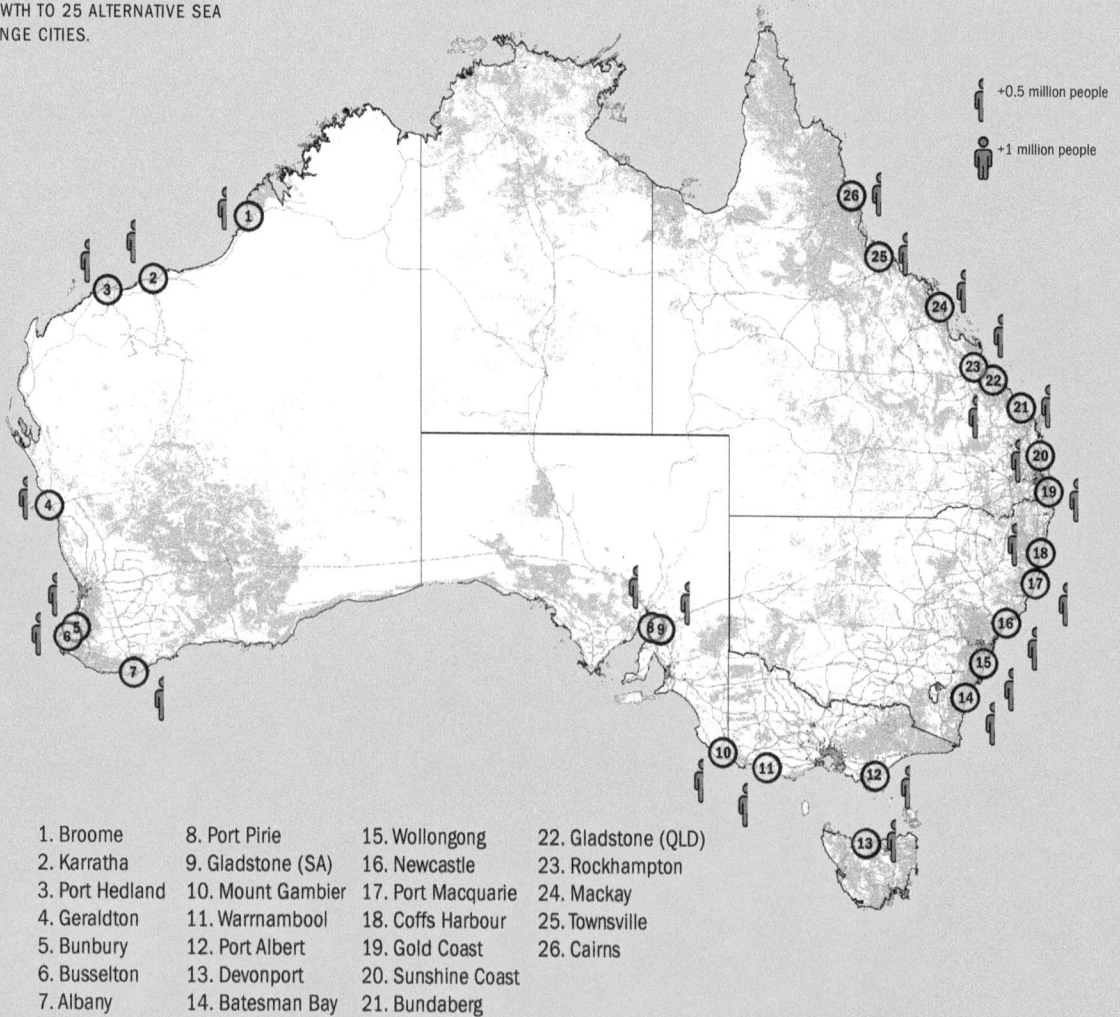

FIGURE 4.25: THE SEA CHANGE CITIES SCENARIO DISTRIBUTES POPULATION GROWTH TO 25 ALTERNATIVE SEA CHANGE CITIES.

+0.5 million people

+1 million people

1. Broome	8. Port Pirie	15. Wollongong	22. Gladstone (QLD)
2. Karratha	9. Gladstone (SA)	16. Newcastle	23. Rockhampton
3. Port Hedland	10. Mount Gambier	17. Port Macquarie	24. Mackay
4. Geraldton	11. Warrnambool	18. Coffs Harbour	25. Townsville
5. Bunbury	12. Port Albert	19. Gold Coast	26. Cairns
6. Busselton	13. Devonport	20. Sunshine Coast	
7. Albany	14. Batesman Bay	21. Bundaberg	

SEACHANGE CITIES

Cairns (QLD)

Townsville (QLD)

Mackay (QLD)

Rockhampton (QLD)

Gladstone (QLD)

Bundaberg (QLD)

Sunshine Coast (QLD)

Gold Coast (QLD)

Coffs Harbour (NSW)

Port Macquarie (NSW)

Newcastle (NSW)

Wollongong (NSW)

Bastemans Bay (NSW)

Port Albert (VIC)

Davenport (TAS)

Warrnambol (VIC)

Mt Gambier (SA)

Port Pirie (SA)

Albany (WA)

Bunbury (WA)

Busselton (WA)

Geraldton (WA)

Karratha (WA)

Port Hedland (WA)

Broome (WA)

FIGURE 4.26:
SEA CHANGE CITIES.

FIGURE 4.27: THE SEA CHANGE CITY OF BROOME IN 2101. IMAGE BASED ON A PHOTO BY CATHERINE LAWSON (HTTPS://WWW.WELLBEING.COM.AU/ ESCAPE/TRAVEL/WE-TRAVEL-WEST-TO-SUNNY-BROOME.HTML). IMAGE BY SHUBHAM GAUTAM.

DECENTRALISATION DREAMING

LOCATION: BROOME, WA
INDIGENOUS REGION: JUKUN
YEAR: 2101
COORDINATES:17.9618°S,
122.2370°E
POPULATION: 582,959

Other optimists foresaw that population growth in regional coastal cities would have 'much needed economic benefits' and catalyse 'infrastructure investment and greater regional connectivity'.[103]

The dominant theme in the wave of negative commentary was that extreme growth in existing coastal towns and cities would imperil fragile coastal ecosystems. As one aghast respondent explained, 'I sympathise with anyone who wants to live near the coast but am appalled at the prospect of one endless Gold Coast development, which will destroy what we most value about our coastline'. Other horrified observers worried that the scenario would place the 'liveability of coastal cities under threat', resulting in the loss of the 'Australian coastal lifestyle': 'How much of this nation's unique character will be destroyed in this mad, endless quest for false growth?' Other longer-term thinkers fretted that the scenario does not consider climate change impacts on coastal cities (e.g. sea-level rise, storm surges and coastal erosion) and, as such, 'is not a long-term solution'.[104]

Other damning commentaries were that, as a national scenario, it is too 'coastal centric', shuns inland areas, and requires 'costly' infrastructure investment to support population increases. One person reasoned, 'Parts of the coast are already straining under the weight of a lack of infrastructure and large populations'. People also worried about climate change effects on northern sea change cities, including extreme cyclones and rising temperatures. Finally, economic realists were concerned about the lack of employment opportunities in regional coastal towns – as work is primarily seasonal and relies heavily on the fluctuating tourist trade.

SCENARIO SUITABILITY

Reflecting the tide of negative survey commentary, the suitability analysis revealed the poor suitability of many sea change cities locations (Figure 4.28).[105] Indeed, such urbanisation would (in many cases) need to be hacked out of fragile and biodiverse ecosystems (Figure 4.29). In addition, many remote regions lack infrastructure and connectivity to the capital cities and confront challenging climatic constraints in the north and northwest. Conversely, positives relate to the proximity of a handful of the sea change cities to capital cities and the economic opportunities they offer.[106] All in all, the analysis presents a mixed bag of suitability scores, with many locations appealing but certainly challenging.

103 Bolleter et al., 'Long-Term Settlement Scenarios'
104 Bolleter et al., 'Long-Term Settlement Scenarios'
105 Bolleter et al., 'Informing Future Australian Settlement Planning'
106 Bolleter et al., 'Informing Future Australian Settlement Planning'

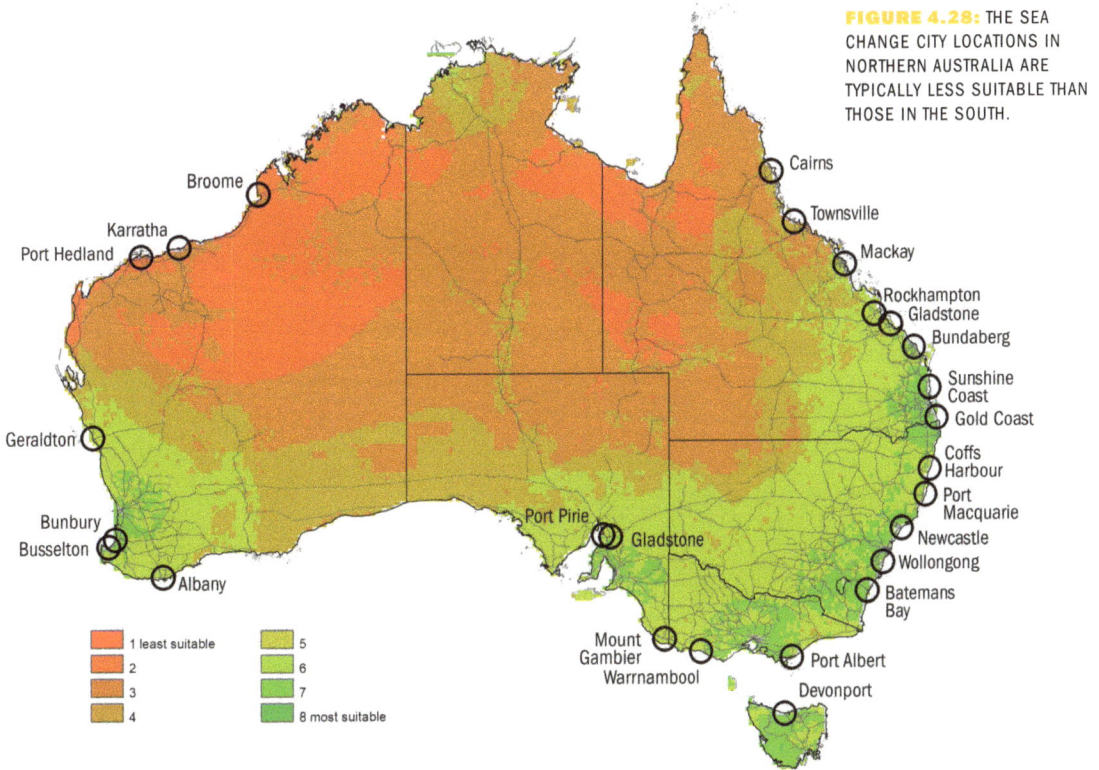

FIGURE 4.28: THE SEA CHANGE CITY LOCATIONS IN NORTHERN AUSTRALIA ARE TYPICALLY LESS SUITABLE THAN THOSE IN THE SOUTH.

Map labels (Figure 4.28): Broome, Karratha, Port Hedland, Geraldton, Bunbury, Busselton, Albany, Port Pirie, Gladstone, Mount Gambier, Warrnambool, Cairns, Townsville, Mackay, Rockhampton, Gladstone, Bundaberg, Sunshine Coast, Gold Coast, Coffs Harbour, Port Macquarie, Newcastle, Wollongong, Batemans Bay, Port Albert, Devonport

Legend:
1 least suitable
2
3
4
5
6
7
8 most suitable

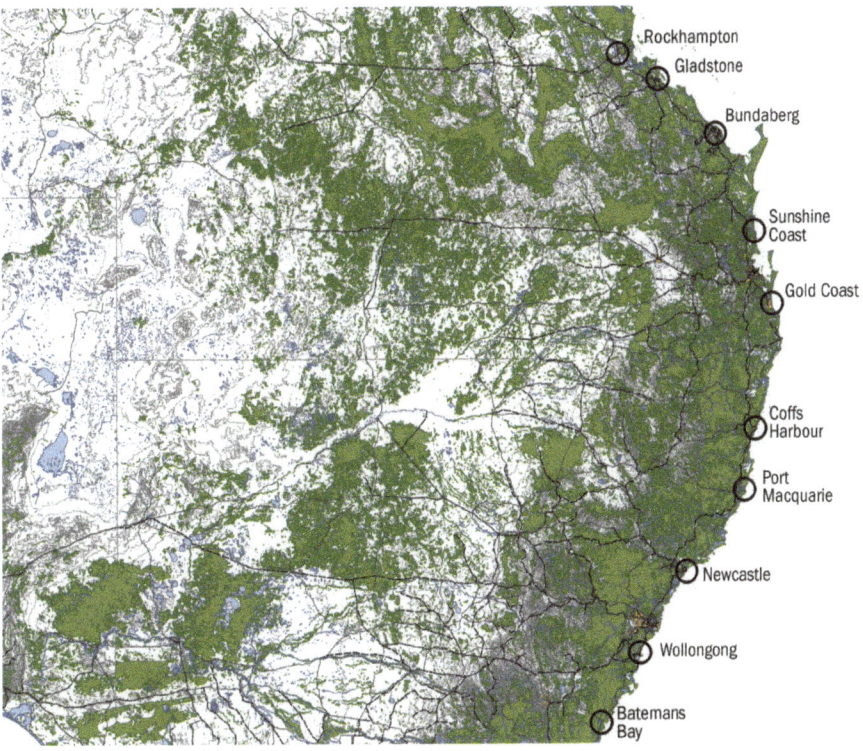

FIGURE 4.29: SEA CHANGE CITIES FROM CENTRAL QUEENSLAND TO SOUTHERN NEW SOUTH WALES.

Map labels (Figure 4.29): Rockhampton, Gladstone, Bundaberg, Sunshine Coast, Gold Coast, Coffs Harbour, Port Macquarie, Newcastle, Wollongong, Batemans Bay

DISCUSSION

Visionary planning documents can age rather swiftly. As Lloyd and Anderton caution us:

> *The documents of Federal and State Growth Centre, new town and decentralisation programs moulder on the shelves: design philosophies and studies, draft social plans, environmental impact statements, city centre designs, approaches to landscape, structure plans, recreation facilities, conservation of old buildings, and many more. The documentation, indeed, provides an often ironic counterpoint to what has actually happened on the ground.*[107]

So, given this chequered history, could these contemporary decentralisation dreams be wrestled into reality? History offers a wealth of lessons – mainly reality checks – for those who propose large-scale decentralisation in Australia, generally stemming from the Whitlam era, which we catalogue in the coming pages. The challenges are formidable: shifting the path-dependence empowering centuries of metropolitanisation on the one hand to the fiscal, political, psychological and environmental impediments to population turnaround on the other.

107 Lloyd and Anderton, 6

PSYCHOLOGICAL BARRIERS

Hampering decentralisation programs in Australia has been a poor image of country areas.[108] Urbanites in the 1970s often viewed such towns as 'dull, lacking in amenities, possessing poorer educational opportunities, and providing more limited social contacts'.[109] As one city writer (of course) said, 'There is nothing (for people) to do in the country town once the pubs shut'.[110] Even newcomers who arrived in the early decades of Canberra's construction recall enduring the difficulties of being suburban pioneers in the under-serviced new estates.[111] Indeed, challenges included lacking supportive friendship networks, boredom, isolation, scarce job opportunities, caring for small children[112] and a prevailing feeling that 'there is nowhere to go and nothing to do'.[113] All of these could see residents sink into a depression aptly known as the 'new town blues'.[114]

Moreover, Jean Craig, a sociologist who studied the country towns of New South Wales in the early 1940s, found that the most considerable challenge was not the remoteness, but the perceived homogeneity of traditional rural life. She explained: 'The rural community is unrelenting in its demands for conformity, whereas the urban community displays mere indifference to the eccentricities of its members.'[115] Such attitudes were probably prejudiced, but they express an important psychological dimension of the problem of large-scale decentralisation,[116] at the very least historically.[117]

Several DURD-nominated growth centres in the 1970s were inland areas. In nominating inland centres, the program bravely (or naively) ran counter to the preference of Australians for lifestyle locations on the coast.[118] Despite grudgingly being regarded as a success by the 1960s, even Canberra was often considered to suffer from fly plagues in summer, high winds in winter, and extremes of heat and cold greater than those experienced in coastal cities (Figure 4.30).[119] Trying to induce many people to venture inland, distant from major urban areas, was, and will likely remain, a considerable challenge.[120]

So, what does this catalogue of psychological barriers tell us about the likely success of our decentralisation dreams? Indeed, the pandemic altered perceptions of regional living and has prompted many Australians to rethink their urban living options, especially regarding the cost of living in the big cities.[121] The notion of bush cities as dull and dormant now seems somewhat stereotypical, given the attractors of lifestyle shifts, housing affordability, well-being and NBN connectivity. Some regional towns offer an alluring alternative lifestyle, with more time and space to pursue hobbies, grow food and have time with the family out of the rat race of capital city living. This shift in sentiment was reflected in data concerning internal migration, whereby in the March 2021 quarter, there was a net loss of 11,800

108 Bolleter, 'The Ghost Cities of Australia'
109 Lonsdale, 'Manufacturing Decentralization ', 327
110 Quoted in Lonsdale, 'Manufacturing Decentralization', 327
111 Pennay
112 Danaher and Williamson
113 Berkley, 484
114 Berkley, 484
115 Davison, 'City Dreamers', 155
116 Lonsdale, 'Manufacturing Decentralization '
117 Bolleter, 'The Ghost Cities of Australia'
118 Bolleter, 'The Ghost Cities of Australia'
119 Rushman
120 Rushman
121 Guaralda et al.; Bolleter et al., 'Implications of the Covid-19 Pandemic'

FIGURE 4.30: CANBERRA AS AUSTRALIA'S LARGEST INLAND CITY WAS GRUDGINGLY REGARDED AS A SUCCESS BY THE 1960S AND INFLUENCED THE PLANNING FOR NEW GROWTH CENTRES IN THE 1970S. PHOTO BY SF PHOTO COURTESY OF SHUTTERSTOCK (STOCK PHOTO ID: 52450786).

people from Australia's greater capital cities through internal migration. This migration was the most significant net loss on record since the series started in 2001. Melbourne lost the most people (–8,300), closely followed by Sydney (–8,200).[122] Significant as these outflows were, they were only a drop in the ocean compared with much longer and larger trends of regional areas draining population to the major cities.

Clearly, not all regional towns are the same. The inland location of some proposed cities in the rail cities centres would presumably present a formidable psychological barrier to population decentralisation. In contrast, populating the satellite city centres would not confront major psychological barriers because of proximity to the capital cities. Centres within the Sea Change Cities scenario could soften psychological impediments by promoting an enticing image of coastal liveability that could be marketed to harried, overworked capital city residents and sun-seeking tourists.[123]

However, one of the challenges of such lifestyle cities is not allowing population growth and attendant urban development to despoil the very amenity that drew migrants in the first place. Indeed, where people migrate primarily for 'lifestyle' reasons, poorly managed growth processes can trigger a transformation of the landscapes that sea changers sought to escape into the places they initially sought to leave.[124] Take Cairns and Townsville, for example, which nestle in dramatic settings close to Wet Tropics rainforest.[125] How large-scale development (such as in the Sea Change Cities scenario) would occur without significant destruction of biodiversity – and the destruction of the natural amenity that would draw migrants in the first place – is unclear (Figure 4.31). Moreover, regional cities in the Rail Cities scenario could lose their 'country town' feel under the scale of growth modelled in the scenarios.[126]

Clearly, the centres proposed for city status in the Satellite Cities, Rail Cities and Sea Change Cities scenarios have some appeal in this post-pandemic world. The issue remains more about the scale of the appeal and whether it could substantiate the ambitious population figures we have suggested.[127]

122 Australian Bureau of Statistics, 'Regional Internal Migration Estimates'
123 Florida, Rise of the Creative Class
124 Bohnet and Pert
125 Bohnet and Pert
126 Archer et al., 11
127 Vij et al.
128 Bolleter, 'The Ghost Cities of Australia'

CONSTRAINING GROWTH IN THE CAPITAL CITIES

Another historic barrier to population decentralisation is the lack of a 'push factor' on the population away from the capital cities.[128] As Don Aitken explained in the context of the Whitlam government Growth Centre Program:

FIGURE 4.31: ONE OF THE CHALLENGES OF LIFESTYLE CITIES, SUCH AS CAIRNS, IS NOT ALLOWING DEVELOPMENT TO DESPOIL THE AMENITY THAT DRAWS NEWCOMERS IN THE FIRST PLACE. PHOTO BY DOUBLELEE. COURTESY OF SHUTTERSTOCK (STOCK PHOTO ID: 2096306962).

I do not think it is any use at all talking in vague phrases like the quality of life or man's ideal role or the environment because it just washes straight off people's backs. The people in Sydney, like being in Sydney, cannot really imagine that it is going to be more pleasant living anywhere else and have no intention of moving.[129]

129 Aitken, 59

While contemporary Sydney and Melbourne have become populated and painful enough to generate centrifugal forces to fling residents into the regions, it is not clear this can be said of secondary state capitals, such as Perth or Adelaide. The resulting lack of dispersal forces pushing out from the smaller capital cities could create headwinds for national decentralisation programs. Would proactive planning be required to generate such centrifugal forces? Undoubtedly. Delivering the decentralisation scenarios canvassed here would require locking down population growth and urban development in the existing capital cities (Figure 4.33).[130] Such approaches fall under the rubric of 'negative planning' and include restrictive policy instruments, such as urban growth boundaries or greenbelts that can be unappealing when the constant cry is for less planning-induced brakes on creating new housing opportunities.[131] The curly issue is that if greenbelts (or similar) are to work, such planning policies need solid political support to withstand the pressures for development from potent land development lobby groups.[132] Sydney's famous green belt of the 1940s and 1950s was envisaged as ensuring a compact city, but collapsed under such pressures.[133] The failure of the Whitlam government's Growth Centres Program can be partly attributed to the lack of restrictive controls placed on capital city sprawl to fully support the Growth Centre plans.[134]

In all the capital cities today, there remains a continued commitment to housing growing populations on substantial swathes of fringing metropolitan land already earmarked for suburban development, as well as through higher-density redevelopment in inner suburbs (Figure 4.32).[135] There is considerable momentum in these existing development processes, which could take years to redirect towards large-scale decentralisation.

ECONOMIC FORCES COMPOUNDING CENTRALISATION

The 1970s Whitlam government's Growth Centres Program also battled against centralising economic forces,[136] which were 'too powerful and too fundamental' to be overcome.[137] Indeed, DURD's satellite and regional cities faced the geographic inertia of historic investments, such as manufacturing plants and other infrastructural networks in the capital cities.[138] Moving anywhere was prohibitively expensive for many firms and inconvenient for company staff, to say the least.[139] In addition, a patchy supply of existing workers, particularly professional and technical, in rural regions meant that employers who might have considered relocating to the regions would have confronted challenges coordinating the necessary labour.[140]

Boosted regional cities in the twenty-first century could confront similar headwinds. Overcoming such centralising constraints requires considerable investment in transformative infrastructure in ground transportation and telecommunications to link regional centres with speed and efficiency to the capital cities. Access to economic opportunity, cultural

130 Archer et al.; Newman
131 Siedentop et al.
132 Neutze
133 Neutze
134 Birrell
135 Bolleter et al., 'Delivering Medium-Density Infil Development'
136 Bolleter, 'The Ghost Cities of Australia'
137 Lonsdale, 'Manufacturing Decentralization', 328
138 Bolleter, 'The Ghost Cities of Australia'
139 Lonsdale, 'Manufacturing Decentralization'
140 Lonsdale, 'Manufacturing Decentralization'

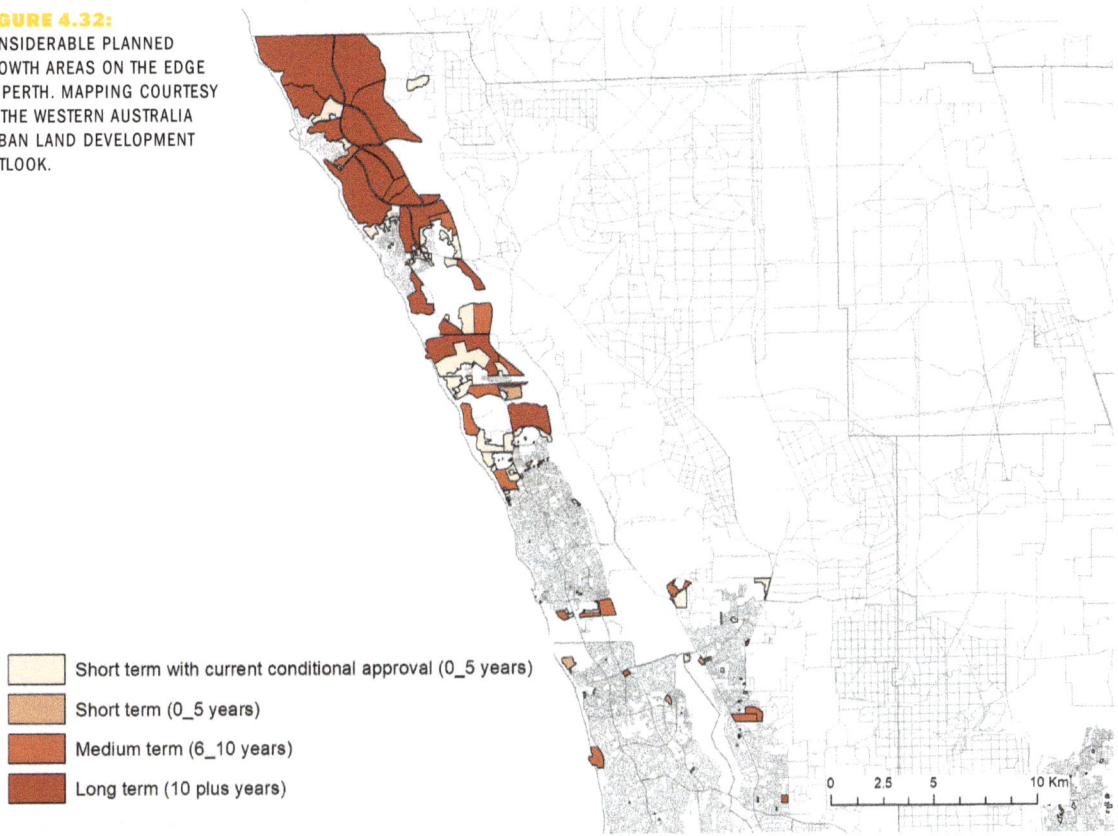

FIGURE 4.32:
CONSIDERABLE PLANNED
GROWTH AREAS ON THE EDGE
OF PERTH. MAPPING COURTESY
OF THE WESTERN AUSTRALIA
URBAN LAND DEVELOPMENT
OUTLOOK.

Short term with current conditional approval (0_5 years)

Short term (0_5 years)

Medium term (6_10 years)

Long term (10 plus years)

0   2.5   5   10 Km

amenities and existing social connections could be stretched into regional areas through the umbilical cords of high-speed rail and extensive broadband networks.

Regardless, the tyranny of distance is not to be underestimated. Urban scholars have long recognised that transportation costs are a fundamental determinant of cities' population size and land-use patterns.[141] Therefore, the Satellite City scenario is probably the most feasible of the three decentralisation scenarios. The satellites would thrive due to access to the agglomeration economies of larger cities, while far-flung rail cities or sea change cities centres might whither on the vine.[142]

141 Duranton and Puga, 'Agglomeration,
    Clusters, and Industrial Policy'
142 Duranton and Puga, 'Agglomeration,
    Clusters, and Industrial Policy'

FIGURE 4.33: DELIVERING ANY DECENTRALISATION SCENARIOS WOULD REQUIRE LOCKING DOWN POPULATION GROWTH IN THE EXISTING CAPITAL CITIES. NONETHELESS, A PLANNED SPRAWL CONTINUES TO VARYING DEGREES IN ALL CAPITAL CITIES (MELBOURNE PICTURED). PHOTO BY DOUBLELEE COURTESY OF SHUTTERSTOCK (STOCK PHOTO ID: 2096306962).

POLITICAL REALITIES

Political realities were another stumbling block for the Whitlam-era Growth Centres Program. From a political point of view, decentralisation programs are a tough sell for politicians, who are dependent on the votes of capital city electorates.[143] For large numbers of people to migrate to regional cities, incentives must be generously bestowed. At the same time, disincentives need to be imposed on the existing capital cities.[144] Because the bulk of voters live in the capital cities, this raises the question: What politician would willingly push the barrow of anti-capital city policies?[145] The answer is a daring or foolhardy one. The underlying problem is that Australia's political structure is not geared toward such changes. It is not politically or economically realistic to consider the 'rundown' of existing capital cities regardless of the lure of the decentralisation policy.[146]

Moreover, boosting regional towns into cities involves considerable upfront capital while the population is still tiny.[147] This capital must be diverted from other expectant beneficiaries who are likely to object.[148] All these impediments, real and perceived, begin to add up. As a result, it is challenging for democratic governments to radically change the geographic pattern of development without jeopardising their electoral fortunes.[149]

DURD's attempts to boost regional towns into cities also received angst from the many towns not chosen for growth.[150] Since a decentralisation policy involves choosing a necessarily limited number of centres, it inevitably entails a political problem.[151] Although voters in the selected regions might support the policy, more areas are inevitably not nominated and may feel excluded.[152] Historically, the Country/National Party, reading the mood of its core rural electorates, has been circumspect about picking winners and has long favoured distributing government largesse more widely.

So, what does this history tell us about contemporary political hurdles that modern-day decentralisation dreams would confront? The Rail Cities scenario, in particular, is likely to face political impediments. Indeed, the delivery of this scenario would hinge on the ability of governments to fund construction. For example, high-speed rail along the east coast under the Rudd government was costed at well over $100 billion for a very long-term construction program. It is unclear if this could be afforded and, if so, what other causes funds would be diverted from. Perhaps international investment would need to be sought to enable its construction, but this would have its own problems (funding from the Chinese government, anyone?). Challenges also stem from the overlapping role of federal and state governments in developing the scenario. Who manages and pays for the high-speed rail and which centres it connects would undoubtedly be deeply contested.

143 Bolleter, 'The Ghost Cities of Australia'
144 Bolleter, 'The Ghost Cities of Australia'
145 Llewellyn-Smith
146 Bolleter
147 Bolleter
148 Neutze
149 Neutze
150 Rushman
151 Bolleter
152 Neutze

A lack of federal and state government coordination could also hamper a contemporary decentralisation program.[153] For example, while a dictatorial governance model could be more effective in delivering the restructuring required to accomplish boosted regional cities in Australia, it must be negotiated through the often messy democratic processes of a political federation.[154] Delivering scenarios like rail cities, which transcend state borders, would require federal government oversight and drawn-out negotiations with state governments that may not share the federal government's priorities concerning decentralisation.[155] Indeed, in the Growth Centres era, some recalcitrant state governments (notably Queensland) were reluctant to cede power to the federal level.[156] Early favoured as a prime Growth Centre candidate by the Whitlamites, the conservative Bjelke-Peterson state government ensured that Townsville never made it off the map of possibilities.

One other area of likely contention for all our decentralisation dreams is the coordination of state and federal governments regarding cities. As has been made clear, state planning for cities would need to be readjusted to restrict the capital cities' growth to enable the required population decentralisation.[157] Without such (frankly unlikely) restrictions, a boosted city in the regions would falter due to the intense competition for jobs and people posed by the capital cities.

A NEW HOPE?

A complex array of impediments exists to delivering decentralisation dreams in Australia, a long-standing historical truism.[158] Nonetheless, the COVID-19 era has seen unprecedented outward migration from the capital cities occurring organically, suggesting that Australia may have reached a real tipping point towards regional population decentralisation. The pandemic prompted many Australians to rethink their urban living options, especially regarding the cost of living in the big cities.[159] It will be instructive to see whether the COVID-19 era migration of city residents to the regions will endure over the longer term. If it does, the barriers, perceived or otherwise, to a renaissance of decentralisation policy could be chipped away. However, what if we consider genuinely remote regions of Australia for urbanisation outside the strangling effect of the burgeoning state capital cities? In the next chapter, frontier fever considers this intriguing opportunity.

153 Bolleter
154 Llewellyn-Smith; Bolleter
155 Robert
156 Potts
157 Birrell
158 Colman
159 Guaralda et al.; Bolleter et al.,
   'Implications of the Covid-19 Pandemic'

PHOTO BY DR SALLY APPLETON.

5

FRONTIER
FEVER

And her five cities, like five teeming sores,

Each drains her: a vast parasite robber state

Where second-hand Europeans pullulate

Timidly on the edge of alien shores.[1]

BACKGROUND

This chapter reviews a final tranche of three alternative urban futures: the Inland, Northern and Western Cities scenarios. These seek to direct population growth towards sparsely inhabited 'frontier' regions in Australia's inland, western and northern regions, evoking the historic frontiers of America's West, China's Sinkiang and Manchuria, and Southern Africa's veldt.[2] Our 'frontier fever' scenarios emerge from a considerable history of national and regional boosterism, tapping into the roots of the decentralist ideology captured in Chapter 4.

On the auspicious 1888 centenary of the arrival of the First Fleet in Sydney Cove, the *Spectator* newspaper thundered that: 'There is every reasonable probability that in 1988 Australia will be a Federal Republic, peopled by 50 million English speaking men.'[3] Just after World War I, author and patriot Edwin Brady ambitiously pitched Australia's carrying capacity as 200 or even 500 million[4] – a projection based on a naive perception that Australia's prospective agriculture areas were 'highly fertile and unlimited in area'.[5] Following World War I, Australia's keenness for large-scale migration from Britain provoked a contentious debate on the country's capacity to support a surging population, with estimates ranging up to a more 'modest' 480 million.[6] The national Labor Government

1 A.D. Hope, 'Australia' (1939). In Gilbert, 82
2 Cohen
3 In Southphommasane, 132
4 Frost; Cathcart
5 Frost, 288
6 Harding

of the 1940s heavily promoted post-war immigration, and sceptics who highlighted environmental constraints to settlement were marginalised. Aspirational projections continued apace. As part of the National Population Enquiry in 1975, the maximum sustainable population based on assessing water resources was estimated to be 280 million.[7] In 1990, economist Phil Ruthven suggested a likely population of 150 million in 2088, settled mainly in the north.[8] Moreover, in 2010, Sydney developer Harry Triguboff speculated, with perhaps an ounce of self-interest:

> *I'd like to see 100 million because I believe we will have many things to do here besides drilling holes and selling coal .... Our agriculture has to be huge. Our desalination must be fantastic. Our rivers must flow the right way. It will all have to be developed.*[9]

As Australia's population growth became substantially tagged to waves of net overseas immigration from the 1950s, the feeling emerged again that Australia's capital cities were becoming worryingly bloated at the cost of emaciated regions.[10] Diverse justifications for spreading and intensifying settlement into regional and rural Australia and beyond (resource development, a 'balanced' population and big city angst, as we saw in Chapter 4) have lain behind calls for more intensive and sustained non-metropolitan urban development.

RESOURCE DEVELOPMENT IN FRONTIER REGIONS

So how did the boosters think Australia could sustain such vast future populations? The answer was generally by transforming thinly inhabited frontier regions, such as the interior or 'the north', into 'productive' landscapes.[11]

Edwin Brady, one of the leading advocates for the taming and development of Australia's interior, projected that, through technology and science, Australia could support a vast population by transforming Australia's 'dead heart' into the 'red heart'.[12] From his travels, he wrote of Australia's interior:

7   Rutherfurd and Finlayson
8   Harding
9   Australian Associated Press
10 Neutze
11 Hugo, 'Population Distribution, Migration and Climate Change'
12 Mirams, 272

I found wonder, beauty, unequalled resource. Under the arid seeming of the plains, I saw the possibilities of a marvellous tilth. Barren hills poured out a golden recompense in minerals. The whole continent has proved to be a vast storehouse of mainly undeveloped wealth.[13]

After successfully waging war against the Kaiser, Brady urged Australians to turn their focus to 'the last walls of nature' and to trample the 'sullen barricades' with an 'army' of White settlers rather than kowtowing and timidly accepting the interior's apparent aridity.[14] He argued that Australia's landscapes had been greatly underestimated and were 'highly fertile'; however, developing railways, water storage, irrigation, irrigation projects, better artesian supply and smaller, more intensive farms would be necessary to unlock this potential.[15] As Sarah Mirams explains:

All would be transformed when railways and roads brought civilisation to the empty lands. Nature could be moulded and coaxed to work for white settlers.[16]

New towns, and in time even cities, would be demanded to service vastly expanded agricultural districts for processing and exporting extracted resources.[17] Brady fantasised that such regions could boost Australia's anglo population to half a million within just a few generations.[18] Above all, he proclaimed: 'The empty spaces must be filled.'[19]

Promoters of a rural civilisation penned a tide of boosterish pamphlets, articles and books that likewise argued that the agricultural capacity of Australia's frontier regions had been woefully underestimated.[20] Despite the challenges reality posed, such thinking persisted into the mid-twentieth century. In 1944, author Ion Idriess (1889-1979) foresaw a surge in continental urban development (Figure 5.1):

13 Brady, 14
14 Cathcart, 220
15 Frost, 288
16 Mirams, 278
17 Bolleter
18 Cathcart
19 Mirams, 273
20 Bolleter, The Ghost Cities of Australia

FIGURE 5.1: ION IDRIESS DREAMT OF A GARDEN CITY ON THE FERTILE PLAINS AROUND LAKE EYRE TO PROMOTE THE ECONOMIC AND SOCIAL DEVELOPMENT OF THE CONTINENT. IMAGE BASED ON A PHOTO BY JOSH TAGI COURTESY OF SHUTTERSTOCK (STOCK PHOTO ID: 1906529254).

Australia's cities of the future will not be found in five or six spots on our 12,000-mile coastline – they will stretch continuously along the rivers of the plains, from Roma to the Murray mouth and from Hughenden to Lake Eyre. On the fertile plains around Lake Eyre ... will grow up a garden city.[21]

Idriess championed the scheme by Toowoomba businessman Alfred Griffiths to open up the continental interior via a vast inland railway loop linking regional centres in every mainland state and connecting to coastal ports (Figure 5.3).

Anglo-Australians have a long history of attempting to exploit Australia's mighty rivers to flood the continent's apparently 'dead' heart (Figure 5.2).[22] The grand scheme of engineer and town planning advocate John Bradfield developed in the late 1930s for 'turning back the rivers' and watering the interior through a massive system of dams, tunnels and pipelines lent authority to more populist dreamings for decades. A recent forensic analysis of Bradfield's scheme concluded it to be technically feasible but commercially unviable.[23] Michael Cathcart has called many of these schemes the imaginings of a nation of 'water dreamers'.[24]

21 Idriess, 181
22 Morgan
23 CSIRO, An Assessment of the Historic Bradfield Scheme
24 Morgan

FIGURE 5.2: THE GRAND SCHEME OF J.J.C. BRADFIELD DEVELOPED IN THE LATE 1930S FOR 'TURNING BACK THE RIVERS' AND WATERING THE INTERIOR FOR MORE INTENSIVE AGRICULTURAL PRODUCTION AND URBAN SETTLEMENT. MAP TRACED BY SHUBHAM GAUTAM. MAP BY REDRAWN BY THE AUTHORS (HTTPS://WWW.ABC. NET.AU/NEWS/2022-12-09/ QUEENSLAND-GOVERNMENT-ABANDONS-BRADFIELD-SCHEME-AFTER-REPORT/101751678).

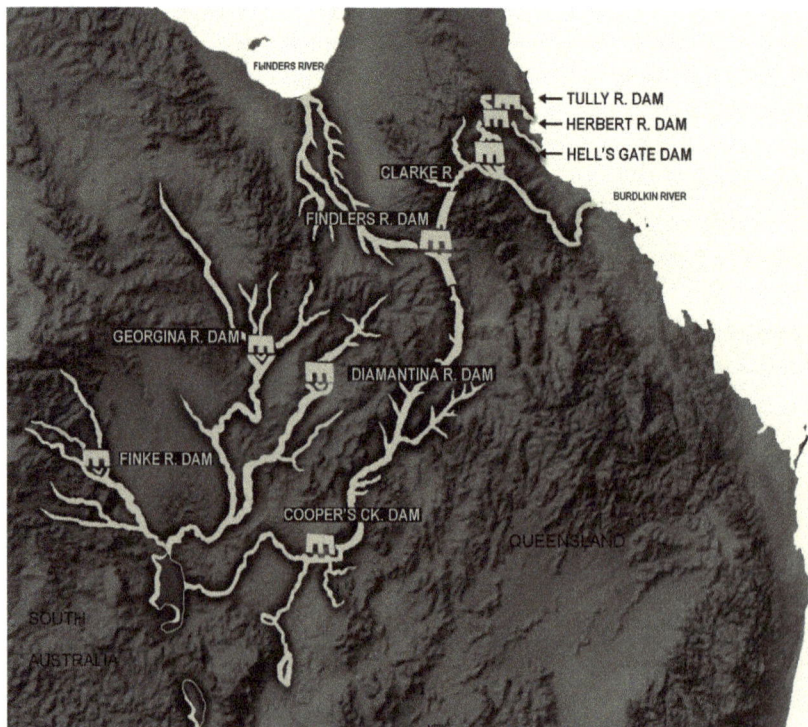

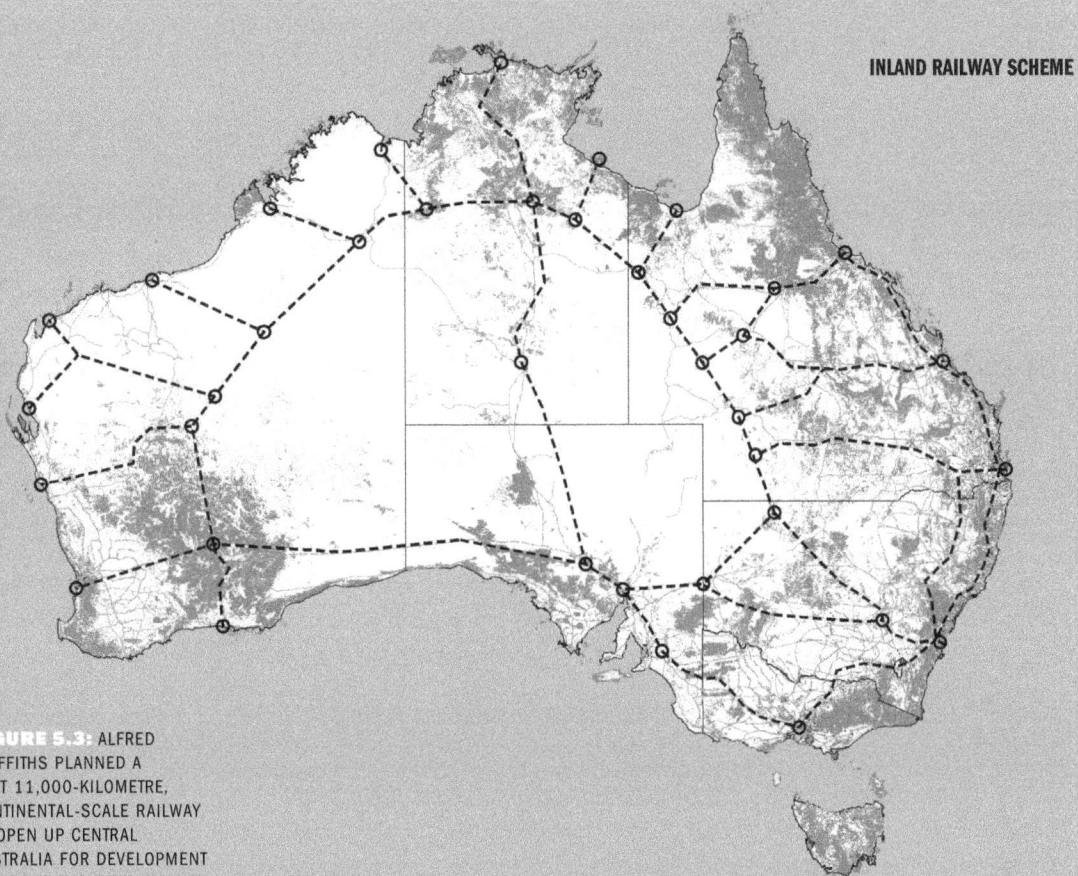

INLAND RAILWAY SCHEME

FIGURE 5.3: ALFRED GRIFFITHS PLANNED A VAST 11,000-KILOMETRE, CONTINENTAL-SCALE RAILWAY TO OPEN UP CENTRAL AUSTRALIA FOR DEVELOPMENT AND DEFEND AUSTRALIA FROM INVASION. MAP BY ION IDRIESS. REDRAWN BY THE AUTHORS.

More recent suggestions and investigations offer less-than-convincing propositions. In the 1970s, mining magnate Lang Hancock mooted bombing the Great Australian Bight so the ocean could thrust deep into the nation's parched interior, enabling evaporation to condense into rain and, once and for all, green the desert (Figure 5.4).[25] In the early 1980s, the scientist Ernest Hallsworth turned his mind to the question of prospective new communities on the major arid coastlines of southern and northwestern Australia to obviate the continual loss of productive land through 'business as usual' land development in the more temperate and favoured environments. He envisaged the desert coastlines of the northwest and the Great Australian Bight, each supporting 5 million people in new cities of 500,000 spaced 50 miles (80 kilometres) apart. The technological demands were considerable – air conditioning, treatment of sewage and, especially, water supply would be best resolved through constructing nuclear-power desalination plants.[26] Again, there was no strong business case for this venture beyond preventing the reduction of opportunity costs of further loss of prime agricultural land.

POPULATE OR PERISH

Due to Australia's sparse interior and northern inhabitation, politicians whacked the development-for-defence drum between the wars.[27] They emphasised the need to populate northern Australia to ward off other nations (mainly Asian) – a situation encapsulated by the phrase 'populate or perish'.[28] This was admittedly more a xenophobic slogan than a spatial strategy for nation-building. Maps often represented Australia's vulnerability, contrasting her vast size and minuscule population with other nations. These depictions gave the feeling of a starving, coloured, teeming world coveting Australia's wide-open landscapes.[29] As such, Imperial commentators ticked off Australia for its wanton inability to fill its emptiness with 'sturdy white defenders of the race'.[30] With no reference to Aboriginal homelands, other commentators regarded Australia's seemingly uninhabited interior as a dereliction of national duty.[31]

The approach of World War II ignited more alarm about developing and securing the north. Politician Ted Theodore even appealed for excising a separate northern state for Australia's 'defence and safety'.[32] In 1948, Queensland Premier Hanlon again emphasised to Prime Minister Ben Chifley that 'Australia's security depends on a population of two million north of the Tropic of Capricorn'.[33] He added, 'North Queensland must be developed to hold this country for European civilisation'.[34] Post-war Labor politician Nelson Lemmon, who had served in Chifley's cabinet as Minister for Works and Housing, scolded the Menzies government for failing to comprehend 'that one of the greatest defence needs of this country is the peopling of our empty north' towards which he declared '1,200,000,000

25 Bolleter and Weller, 45
26 Hallsworth
27 Bolleter, 'The Ghost Cities of Australia'
28 Babb, 10
29 Mirams
30 Murphy, 'The Modern Idea', 120
31 McGregor, 'Developing the North'
32 Dale et al.
33 In McGregor, 'Developing the North', 45
34 In McGregor, 'Developing the North', 45

Asian eyes are looking in envy' (Figure 5.6).[35] He foretold that future generations would pay the price for today's neglect. Others had long raised suspicions about any who resisted the need for populating the frontier zones with a racist zeal:

The man who thinks we do not want more community settlement in Australia is a good man to get out of Australia. He is the sort of man that will talk White Australia until he is black in the face and until Australia is itself yellow. If we do not get more people in Australia ... we will have a yellow Australia, and if we do, it will be simply because we had a yellow streak in ourselves.[36]

Post-war, many Australians looked nervously at Australia's Asian neighbours, particularly Indonesia, whose mammoth 200 million people was many times bigger than Australia's population.[37] Australian perceptions had been heavily influenced by their experience of being attacked during World War II by Japan. As such, many concluded that Australia's wide-open spaces in the north and interior would become a tempting target for invasion unless claimed and tamed by Australians.[38] As a result, the 1950s and 1960s saw a vast program to draw immigrants as a matter of public policy.[39]

Concerns about an unpopulated north persisted till at least the 1970s, with Labor Prime Minister Gough Whitlam expressing sympathy with the many Australians who had 'an uneasy feeling about an empty and defenceless north'.[40] Partly in response, expatriate architect Bill Twitchett's resuscitation of a continental settlement program in the late 1970s involved a massive immigration program for new citizens. Stage one would target immigrants from Bangladesh, Mexico and Egypt, and they would substantially populate six 'priority settlement centres': three new inland cities (near Lake Eyre, Bourke and Mildura) and three coastal cities (near Onslow, Darwin and the Gulf of Carpentaria). Here was a scheme to enable the country 'as a whole [to] grow rapidly, not only demographically and economically but also intellectually and morally'.[41]

So, what is the legacy of all this 'pre-history'? While frontier development is decidedly 'on the nose' in many quarters, in order to explore all possible options for decentralisation, this chapter distils these enduring dreams into three scenarios for frontier development: Inland Cities, Northern Cities and Western Cities.

35 McGregor, 'Environment, Race , and Nationhood', 185
36 Sir Joseph Carruthers in Lewis, 65-66
37 Diamond
38 Diamond
39 Diamond
40 In McGregor, 'Environment, Race, and Nationhood', 186
41 Twitchett, 137

FIGURE 5.4: LANG HANCOCK MOOTED BOMBING THE GREAT AUSTRALIAN BIGHT SO THE OCEAN COULD BE THRUST DEEP INTO THE NATION'S PARCHED INTERIOR. IMAGE BASED ON A PHOTO BY SAHARA PRINCE COURTESY OF SHUTTERSTOCK (STOCK PHOTO ID: 1786546988).

FRONTIER FEVER

INLAND
CITIES

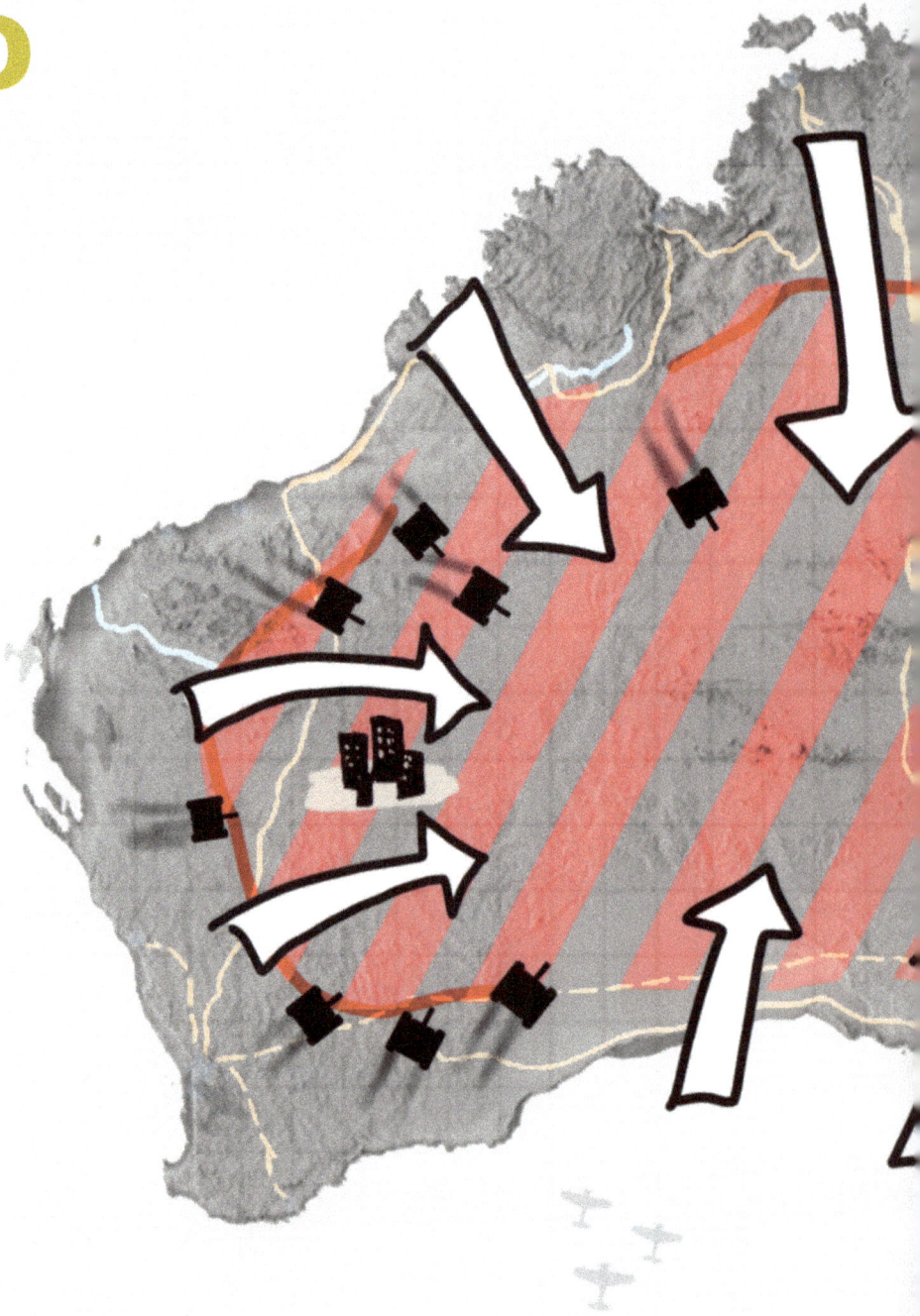

FIGURE 5.5 IMAGE BY NUR MOHD ROZLAN.

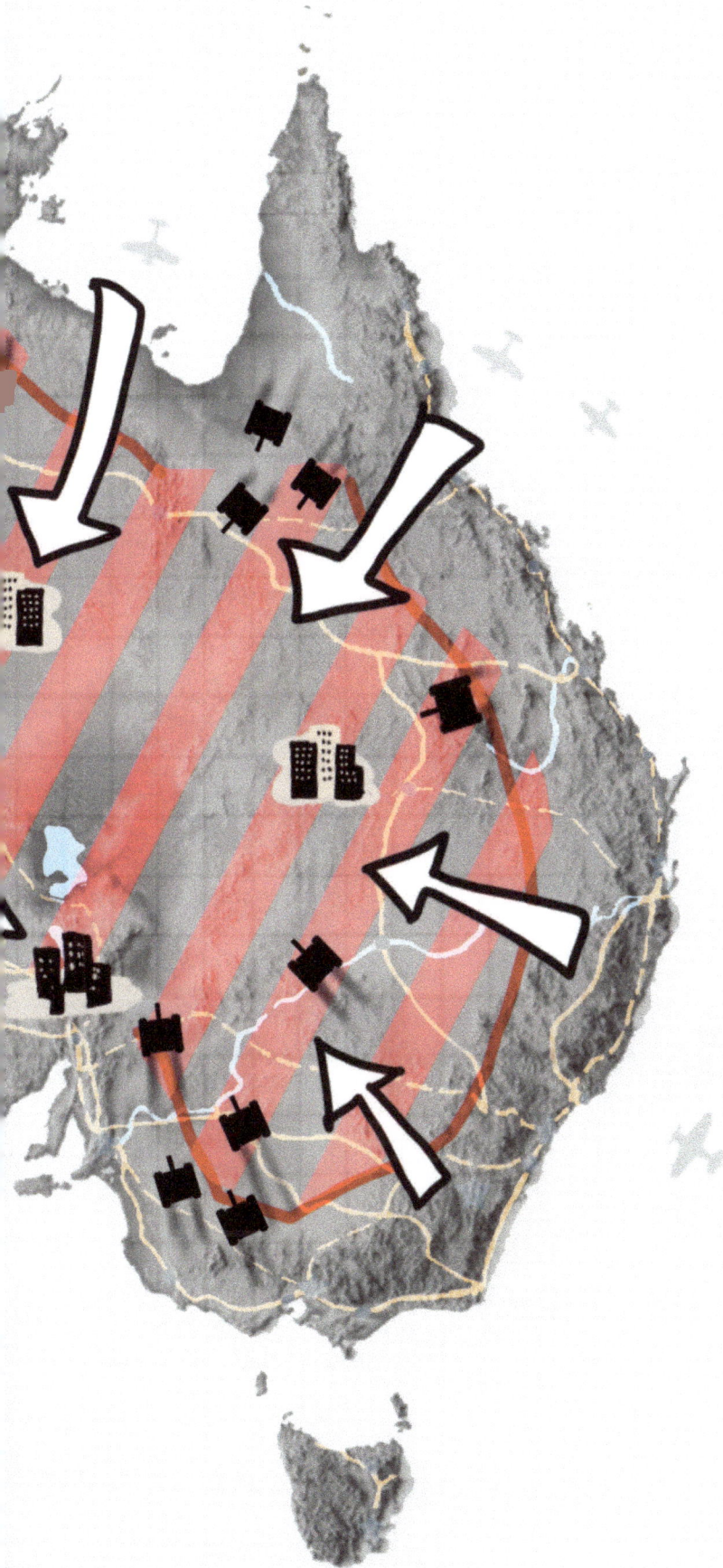

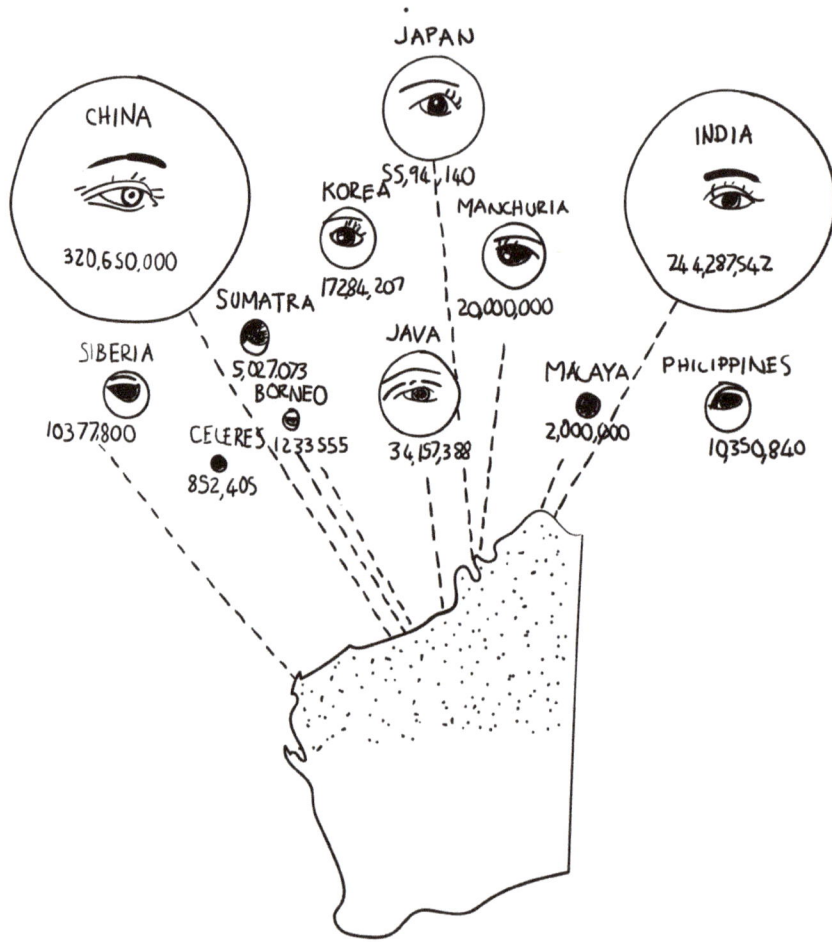

AN URGENT NEED OF WHITE POPULATION

JAPAN

CHINA
320,650,000

KOREA
17,284,207

55,94,140

MANCHURIA
20,000,000

INDIA
244,287,542

SUMATRA
5,027,073
BORNEO

JAVA
34,157,388

MALAYA
2,000,000

PHILIPPINES
19,350,840

SIBERIA
10,377,800

CELERES
852,405

1,233,555

FIGURE 5.6: COMMENTATORS IN THE INTER-WAR YEARS WARNED THAT 'STURDY WHITE DEFENDERS' NEEDED TO FILL AUSTRALIA'S 'EMPTY SPACES' LEST OTHERS 'DO THE JOB FOR US'. MAP TRACED BY THE AUTHORS FROM E. J STUART'S LAND OF OPPORTUNITIES 1923.

The White Inhabitants of our
— Northern Areas —
number less than 7,000!

INLAND CITIES SCENARIO

The Inland Cities scenario was inspired by the late nineteenth to mid-twentieth century period in which Australians endeavoured to create a 'rural civilisation' despite the harsh realities of the interior's environment.[42] It also reflects on Australia's array of inland towns and cities with at least a theoretical growth capacity that offers capital city residents reduced housing prices, traffic stress and the pull of simple country life.[43]

SCENARIO DESCRIPTION

As a reminder of the maths, the national population forecast for 2101 employed to underpin the scenarios was the Australian Bureau of Statistics' mid-range projection of 53 million. This projection represents a 28 million person increase in the current national population. We presumed, for starters, that half of this increase would naturally disperse across existing towns and cities, leaving 14 million people to allocate in each scenario. The Inland Cities scenario distributes population growth to 29 nominated inland centres boosted by over 500,000 people each by 2101 (Figures 5.7, 5.8, 5.9, 5.10).

SCENARIO SENTIMENT

Despite the harsh realities, laypeople ranked the Inland Cities scenario the third highest (evidently old dreams die hard).[44] The dominant theme in the slew of positive commentary was that inland towns 'have the capacity for growth'. This theme was reinforced in various ways, for example: 'This would be my choice for redistributing population. Life isn't all about cities and the beach.' Further, people felt that 'population growth could be the catalyst for development and infrastructure investment in inland towns and cities'. Other themes were that this scenario could 'save regional communities' and 'lead to social, cultural and economic revitalisation'. As another warned, 'regional towns need growth and jobs; otherwise, they will stagnate and be ravaged by unemployment, poverty, drugs and then crime'. A positive and now-familiar theme was that inland cities could take pressure off capital cities and rebalance Australia's lopsided settlement:

We have huge areas of uninhabited land, and populating some of these areas would solve the problem of having the coastal areas overpopulated. Australia's regional towns are sorely neglected and crying out for residents, while the cities are jam-packed.[45]

42 Murphy, 'The Modern Idea', 119
43 Department of Regional Development, *Western Australia's Supertowns*; Newman
44 This scenario was not included in the earlier expert survey.
45 Bolleter et al., 'Long-Term Settlement Scenarios for Australia'

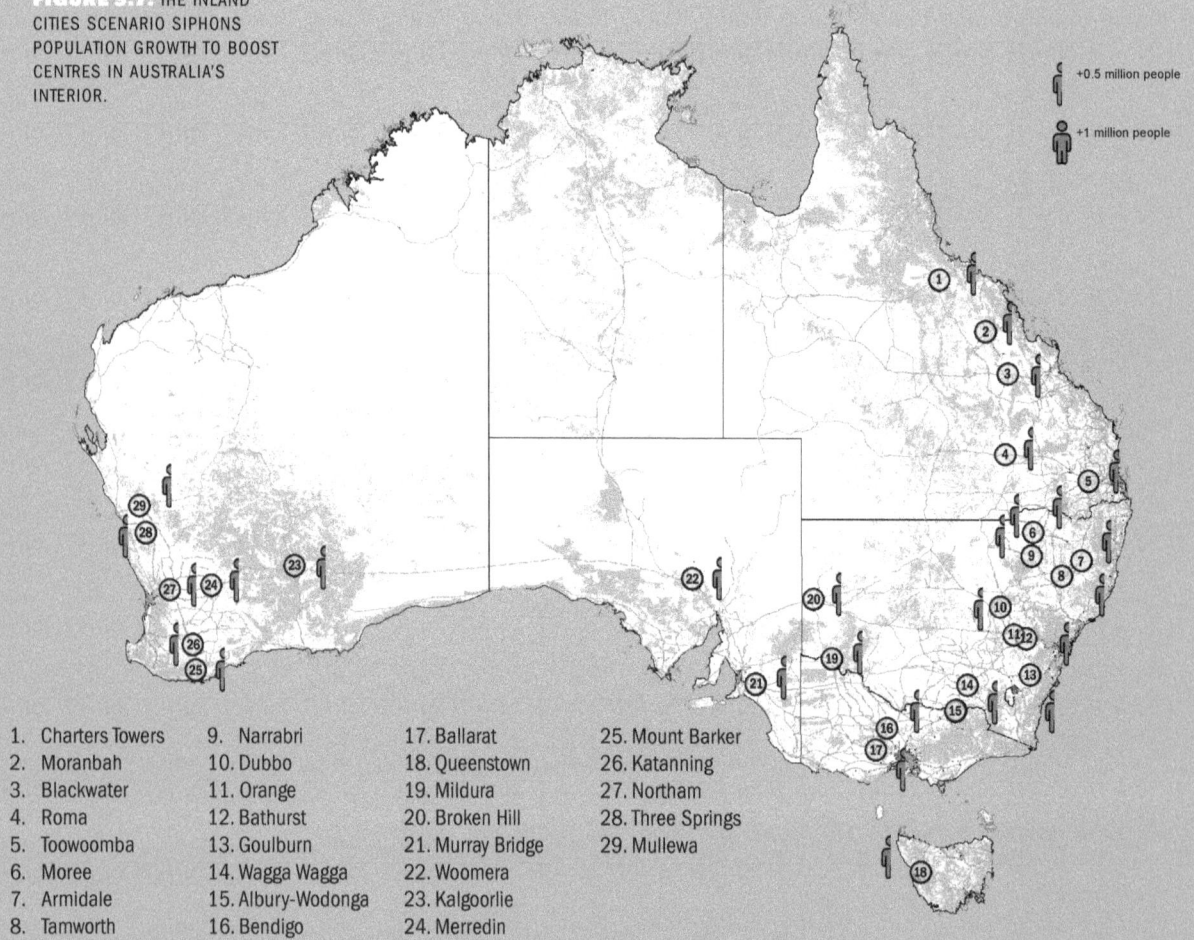

FIGURE 5.7: THE INLAND CITIES SCENARIO SIPHONS POPULATION GROWTH TO BOOST CENTRES IN AUSTRALIA'S INTERIOR.

+0.5 million people

+1 million people

1. Charters Towers	9. Narrabri	17. Ballarat	25. Mount Barker
2. Moranbah	10. Dubbo	18. Queenstown	26. Katanning
3. Blackwater	11. Orange	19. Mildura	27. Northam
4. Roma	12. Bathurst	20. Broken Hill	28. Three Springs
5. Toowoomba	13. Goulburn	21. Murray Bridge	29. Mullewa
6. Moree	14. Wagga Wagga	22. Woomera	
7. Armidale	15. Albury-Wodonga	23. Kalgoorlie	
8. Tamworth	16. Bendigo	24. Merredin	

INLAND CITIES

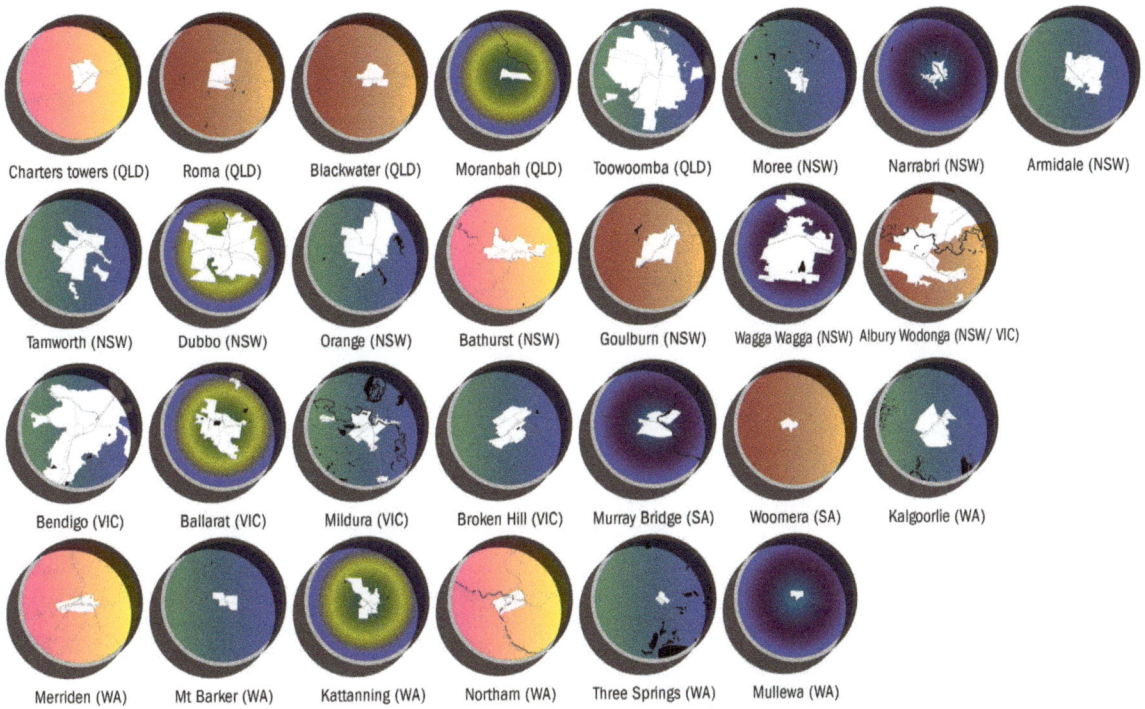

Charters towers (QLD)   Roma (QLD)   Blackwater (QLD)   Moranbah (QLD)   Toowoomba (QLD)   Moree (NSW)   Narrabri (NSW)   Armidale (NSW)

Tamworth (NSW)   Dubbo (NSW)   Orange (NSW)   Bathurst (NSW)   Goulburn (NSW)   Wagga Wagga (NSW)   Albury Wodonga (NSW/ VIC)

Bendigo (VIC)   Ballarat (VIC)   Mildura (VIC)   Broken Hill (VIC)   Murray Bridge (SA)   Woomera (SA)   Kalgoorlie (WA)

Merriden (WA)   Mt Barker (WA)   Kattanning (WA)   Northam (WA)   Three Springs (WA)   Mullewa (WA)

FIGURE 5.8: INLAND CITIES.

FIGURE 5.9: THE INLAND CITY OF BROKEN HILL IN OUTBACK NEW SOUTH WALES. PHOTO BY TARAS VYSHNYA COURTESY OF SHUTTERSTOCK (STOCK PHOTO ID: 2213234127).

FIGURE 5.10: INLAND CITY ALBURY IN 2101. IMAGE BASED ON A PHOTO BY THENNICKE COURTESY OF WIKIPEDIA COMMONS (HTTPS://COMMONS.WIKIMEDIA.ORG/WIKI/FILE:ALBURY_FROM_MONUMENT_HILL_3.JPG). SELECT BUILDINGS PHOTOGRAPHED BY JOHN GOLLINGS PHOTOGRAPHY COURTESY OF IVAN RIJAVEC.

LOCATION: ALBURY WODONGA, NSW / VIC
INDIGENOUS REGION: WAVEROO
YEAR: 2101
COORDINATES: 36.0751°S, 146.9095°E
POPULATION: 588,164

FRONTIER FEVER

Reflective of some perceived issues around cultural integration in the big cities, several people proposed that migrants be directed to 'inland towns and regional cities where they are needed most'. Furthermore, as a respondent to our expert's survey explained:...

there is plenty of anecdotal evidence to suggest that migrants and refugees survive and adapt very well in smaller regional communities, with less risk of developing ghettoes.[46]

Unsurprisingly, apparent water scarcity was dominant in the negative comments; people perceived it would limit the supportable population.[47] Moreover, they felt this issue would compound over time with the cascading effects of out-of-control climate change. Finally, climate change impacts in the interior, such as 'rising temperatures and drought', were also seen as a threat, making 'inland cities uninhabitable'.

There were other expressions of concern. A recurring worry was a 'lack of incentives for people to move inland' and a mighty misalignment with 'consumer preferences which makes the scenario unfeasible'. Others cited the cost of providing vast desalination and water pipeline infrastructure to render the scenario realistic. Another prevalent theme was the prohibitive requirement for significant infrastructure investment (transport, community services, facilities and telecommunications) to overcome 'isolation issues' and sustain the long-term growth of inland cities. In particular, people noted the importance of broadband internet connectivity:

...so that jobs that are not dependent on a specific location (e.g. creative jobs) can be free to move to these inland cities while still being connected to colleagues and clients elsewhere.[48]

46 Bolleter et al., 'Evaluating Scenarios'
47 Bolleter et al, 'Long-Term Settlement Scenarios for Australia'
48 Bolleter et al., 'Long-Term Settlement Scenarios for Australia'

A related and rational commentary thread was that inland Australia lacked job opportunities and 'inland cities and regional areas cannot compete with the pull of capital cities and coastal locations'. As one person explained:

If these towns were capable of growth, their young people would not leave them for 'better opportunities,' and they would not be struggling.

Predictably, there was also concern that substantial population growth would threaten the liveability of regional centres. In particular, there was a 'need to preserve the heritage and unique qualities of regional centres', which would be 'impossible to manage' given such a 'huge quantum of change'.[49]

In summary, while the Inland Cities scenario rated highly amongst people, it was highly contentious and raised many questions around liveability and viability, which elude easy answers.

SCENARIO SUITABILITY

The Inland Cities scenario sites present an array of barriers to growth, including blistering summers, aridity and prolonged droughts (such as the almost decade long 2001 to 2009 drought), long and tedious drives to the capitals, a scarcity of jobs, rail connectivity and port access. Nonetheless, vast swathes of cleared land for development and basic infrastructure boost suitability scores (Figures 5.11, 5.12, 5.13).

49 Bolleter et al., 'Long-Term Settlement
    Scenarios for Australia'
50 Bolleter, The Ghost Cities of Australia

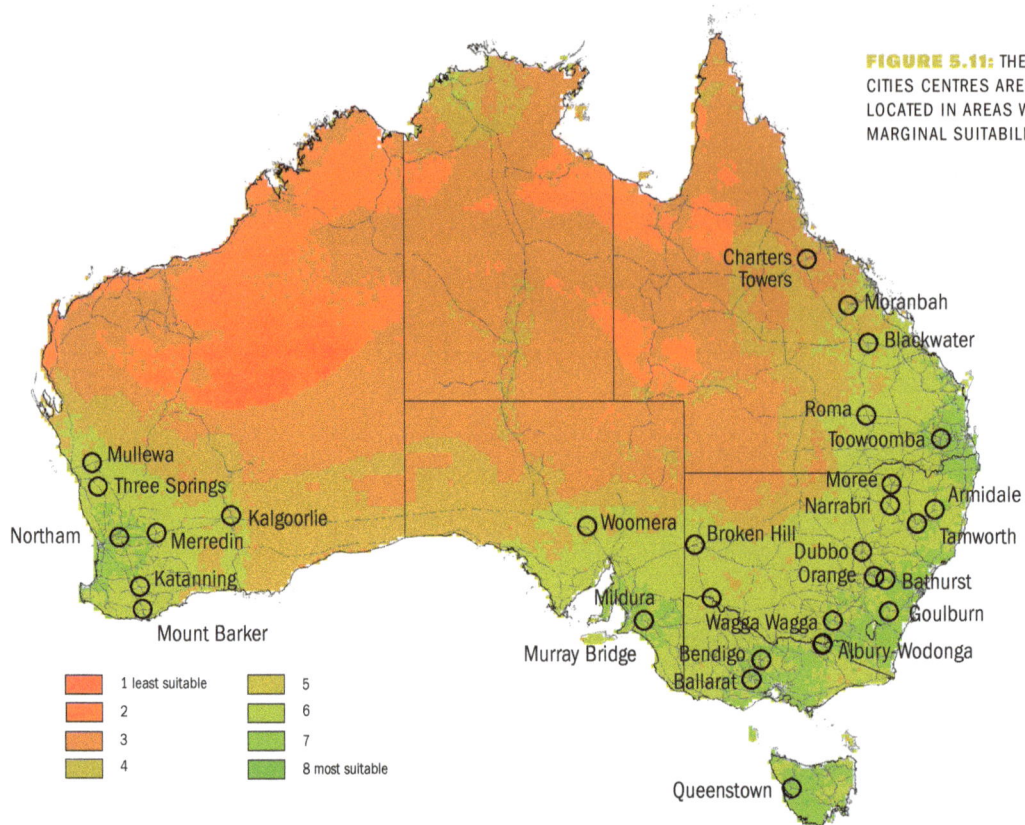

FIGURE 5.11: THE INLAND CITIES CENTRES ARE GENERALLY LOCATED IN AREAS WITH LOW TO MARGINAL SUITABILITY.

Charters Towers
Moranbah
Blackwater
Roma
Toowoomba
Moree
Narrabri
Armidale
Woomera
Broken Hill
Tamworth
Dubbo
Orange
Bathurst
Mildura
Wagga Wagga
Goulburn
Murray Bridge
Bendigo
Albury-Wodonga
Ballarat
Mullewa
Three Springs
Kalgoorlie
Northam
Merredin
Katanning
Mount Barker
Queenstown

1 least suitable	5	
2	6	
3	7	
4	8 most suitable	

Narrabri
Armidale
Tamworth
Dubbo
Orange
Bathurst
Goulburn

FIGURE 5.12: INLAND CITIES IN NEW SOUTH WALES.

FIGURE 5.13: INLAND CITIES IN WESTERN AUSTRALIA'S WHEATBELT.

Map labels: Merredin, Northam, Katanning, Mount Barker

Scale: 0 30 60 KM

NORTHERN CITIES

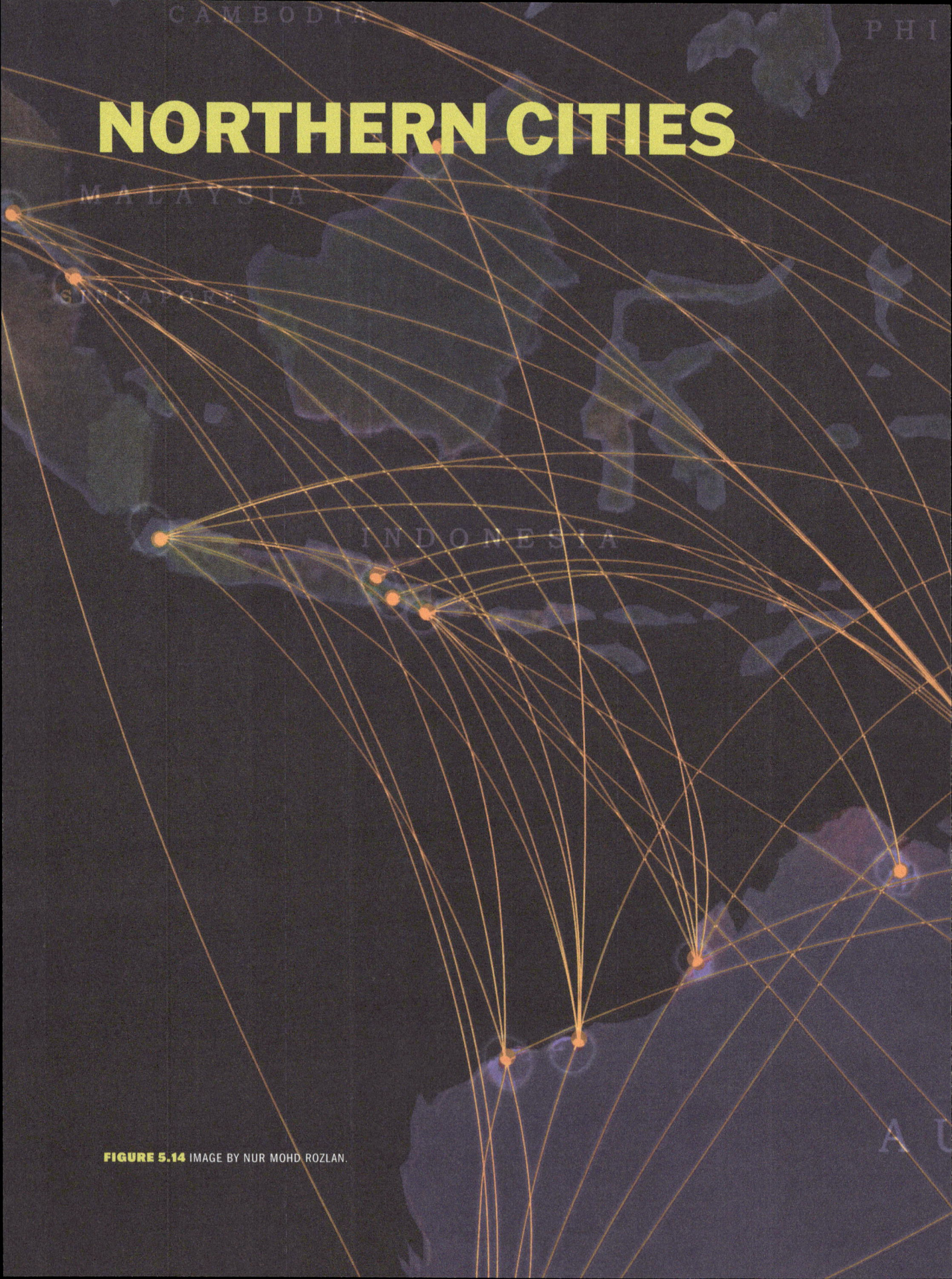

FIGURE 5.14 IMAGE BY NUR MOHD ROZLAN.

FRONTIER FEVER

PAPUA NEW
GUINEA

STRALIA

NORTHERN CITIES SCENARIO

Spruikers of northern development predict often-extreme population growth in the north, partly because of its growing geopolitical significance. [50] Indeed, they stress that northern Australia sits at the fulcrum of the 'two most important global axes of the twenty-first century: Asia and the tropics'.[51] These two regions are projected to surge in economic power and population, and proponents demand that northern Australia should surf this wave of potential prosperity.[52] As Gerald Glaskin implores:

> *The North is a country in itself, a third of the size of the United States - three times the size of Texas. It is a land that has slept through the centuries but can sleep no more. It is stirring now - stirring and waiting for man to be sufficiently civilised, sufficiently knowledgeable, to make it his own.*[53]

However, while northern Australia encompasses a vast 3.5 million square kilometres, almost half of the continental landmass, it supports only a meagre 1,300,000 people.[54] Of course, such reductive formulas overlook its cultural significance. Indeed, Indigenous cultural life in northern Australia underpins its vitality, intimately bound to the landscapes these traditional owners have lived in co-existence with for millennia.[55] Despite the north's deep cultural and ecological complexity, the federal white paper issued by the Abbott Coalition government 'Our North, Our Future' appraises northern Australia's potential through a reductive economic lens.[56] The report depicts the north as a place of endless economic bounty to be mined, proudly proclaiming:

> *Development will require many more people living in the north. Transformation won't happen if its population inches up by a few hundred thousand over the next 20 years. It would remain a high-*

51 Roux et al., xi
52 Bolleter, The Ghost Cities of Australia
53 Glaskin in Robb, 174.
54 Australian Government, Our North, Our Future
55 Raupach et al.
56 Bolleter, 'The Consequences of Three Urbanisation Scenarios'

*cost, small-scale economy, more of a pilot project
than a powerhouse. We need to lay the foundations
for rapid population growth and put the north on
a trajectory to reach a population of four to five
million by 2060.[57]*

This aspirational figure represents an almost 400% increase (an additional 3,700,000 people) in the existing population and, as the report explains, would entail the development of substantial cities of more than a million people.[58] The subsequent urban expansion required to accommodate this population surge is equivalent to building over 20 new Townsvilles in the next 35 years (keeping in mind that the existing Townsville has taken over one-and-a-half centuries to build; Figure 5.15). It is proposed that visa concessions and conditions for migrants could substantially boost the population in the north, support economic development and alleviate skills shortages.[59] The Albanese Labor government (elected 2022) did undertake to prepare a 'refreshed' 'Developing Northern Australia' white paper while committing in advance to accelerated population growth, albeit sustainably.[60]

Recent years have seen a smattering of speculative schemes for new cities in northern Australia that seek to surf the wave of northern Australia's growing significance.[61] These have often been special jurisdiction 'charter cities' incorporating designated economic or 'enterprise' zones.[62] The latter are geographic regions where bespoke taxation and regulatory arrangements apply – neo-liberal honey-pots to lure investors through minimising tax or regulatory hurdles.[63] By deploying such strategies, charter cities seek to emulate the economic success seen in Hong Kong or Singapore.[64]

Former World Bank vice president Paul Romer is a charter cities backer who describes the process as simple as:

*....picking an essentially uninhabited piece of land
of this size, creating a new set of rules, and allowing
willing participants to opt in.[65]*

57 Australian Government, Our North, Our Future, 4
58 Australian Government, Our North, Our Future, 4
59 Australian Government, Our North, Our Future, 10
60 King, 'Speech to CEDA'
61 Bolleter
62 Dovey
63 Hall
64 Bolleter, The Ghost Cities of Australia
65 Chakrabortty, 9

FIGURE 5.15: TOWNVILLE IN FAR NORTH QUEENSLAND. PHOTO BY CAM LAIRD COURTESY OF SHUTTERSTOCK (STOCK PHOTO ID: 1677592561).

In a 2014 keynote address to a Northern Development Summit, Romer referred to Manhattan's gridded street pattern as a possible spatial template for such a new charter city[66] located on one of northern Australia's 'many cattle stations' (Figure 5.16).[67] As he explained:

> *You could literally take that cattle station and lay out a grid of basically public space that would be the utility corridors, the transport corridors. But save the public space so that you can lease it back to the ranchers if the best use is as a ranch. However, if it turns out to be the best use as a city of millions of people, you have created the public space for mobility and utility corridors, then you will be able to do it in an efficient and cost-effective way.*[68]

Darwin-based academic Ken Parish has ventured another intriguing new charter city approach that could accommodate waves of refugees (particularly climate change refugees).[69] He proposes that, rather than resettling refugees in regional towns, they could live and work in a purpose-specific new charter city on Australia's second biggest island, Melville Island, north of Darwin (Figure 5.17).[70] Parish argued that separating the charter city from the other capitals would relieve the 'community tensions and divisions' often coupled with refugee resettlement.[71] Such a plan builds upon historical precedents. Indeed, in the 1970s, Darwin was a major destination for refugees fleeing violence and political turmoil in Asia, including from East Timor.[72] Parish's proposition is timely because it is estimated that there are already 25 million environmental migrants[73] and by 2050, this number could soar to between 100 million and 1 billion.[74] While these figures are subject to a contentious debate, they raise searching questions about Australia's role in responding to (or resisting?) this projected human tide.

The north continues to invite considerable speculation about alternative urban futures. So, what might a framework of future northern cities look like?

66 Bolleter, The Ghost Cities of Australia
67 In Dale al., 9
68 Romer, 182
69 Bolleter, 'The Ghost Cities of Australia'
70 Parish
71 Parish
72 Megarrity, Northern Dreams
73 Wennersten and Robbins
74 Bettini

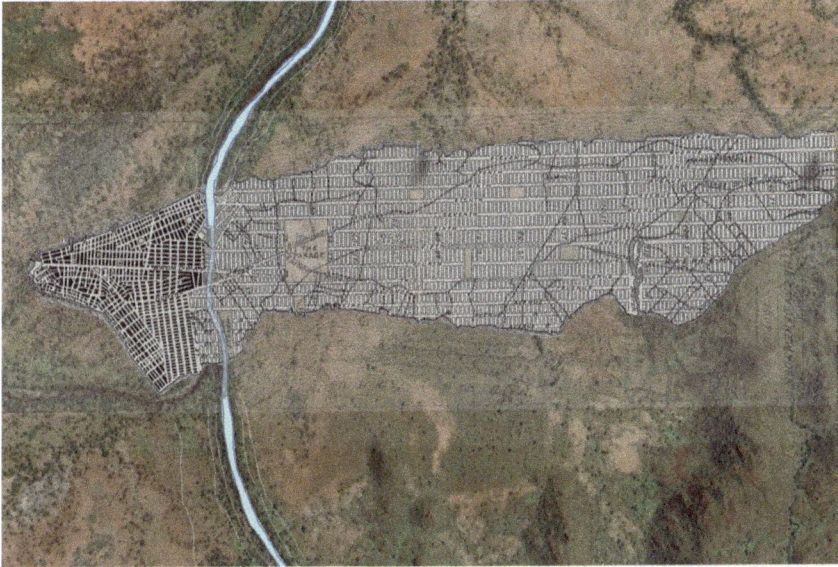

FIGURE 5.16: PAUL ROMER'S ENDORSEMENT OF MANHATTAN'S GRID LAYOUT AS A POSSIBLE SPATIAL TEMPLATE FOR A NEW OUTBACK CHARTER CITY. IMAGE BY SHUBHAM GAUTAM

FIGURE 5.17: A PROPOSED NEW CHARTER CITY FOR REFUGEES OFF THE AUSTRALIAN COAST IN THE TIMOR SEA. IMAGE BASED ON A PHOTO BY ANGATA COURTESY OF SHUTTERSTOCK (STOCK PHOTO ID: 1294357873) SELECT BUILDINGS PHOTOGRAPHED BY JOHN GOLLINGS. PHOTOGRAPHY COURTESY OF IVAN RIJAVEC.

SCENARIO DESCRIPTION

This Northern Cities scenario boosts nine northern cities by over 1.5 million people in line with the enduring vision for substantial population growth in northern Australia (Figures 5.18, 5.19, 5.20, 5.21).

SCENARIO SENTIMENT

The prospective development of northern Australia remains deeply contested, with strong opinions both for and against. So, in amongst this contentious contest, how did our Northern Cities scenario rate? Unfortunately for northern development protagonists, laypeople and experts condemned the Northern Cities scenario to a lowly fifth of the eight scenarios,[75] another comparatively rare confluence of expert and community opinion.

Nonetheless, a significant theme in the thread of positive commentary was that northern Australia provides abundant space to grow, natural resources and arable land, and, as such, presented a feasible and sustainable growth option.[76] As development enthusiasts proclaimed, 'there is lots of water and resources here to be exploited' and 'Yes, we like this - bold new growth corridors with their own identities.' Others felt that population growth 'would lead to the social, cultural and economic revitalisation of northern Australian cities'. Finally, some optimists felt that substantial population growth in the north of Australia would encourage sustainable, resilient, environmentally responsive city-building and design:

> *We would need to consider a new approach to tropical design that would create different cities from those based on European settlement. It would be an opportunity to create a new resilient 'Australian' type of city that works in our challenging environments.*

75 Bolleter et al., 'Evaluating Scenarios'
76 The respondent quotations below come from Bolleter et al., 'Long-Term Settlement Scenarios.'

The dominant theme in the avalanche of negative commentary was that potential climate change effects could see northern cities uninhabitable by 2100 and highly exposed to extreme weather events. Furthermore, one pragmatist explained, 'There are sensible reasons why northern Australia has been left comparatively undeveloped. It is a hostile country with heat, drought, humidity, monsoon, cyclones and 10-metre tides.' Crocodiles could also be added to that list.

Other cautious respondents identified adverse impacts of substantial population growth on northern Indigenous communities and heritage sites. Related commentary worried that this scenario would 'lead to degradation of pristine, biodiversity-rich and largely untouched areas', and such 'areas of greatest cultural heritage and biodiversity' should be 'left alone'.

Several nervous respondents also worried about the lack of employment opportunities, dependency on unsustainable industries and finite resources. In addition, others identified northern cities' isolation from southern state capitals and existing infrastructure, as well as the related need for significant infrastructure investment, particularly transport.

Some people also identified that population growth, on the scale proposed, would place the 'liveability of existing northern cities under threat'. However, others reasoned that this growth trajectory is unlikely anyway, given the absence of 'incentives to move to northern cities'. Moreover, 'after a century and a half of trying, we think we are better off stopping fantasies of northern colonisation and letting it remain essentially wild'.

SCENARIO SUITABILITY

As the negative survey commentary evokes, the Northern Cities scenario locations rated terribly for suitability due to an intense climate, replete with heat stress, highly seasonal rainfall and cyclone risks (Figure 5.22).[77] Moreover, the north is a complex mosaic of ecologies and cultural heritage that finds expression in a patchwork of Native Title claims and determinations, which could complicate, if not curtail, urban ambitions (Figure 5.23).[78] Finally, there is a lack of jobs and infrastructure in many regions outside the north's major centres of Darwin, Townsville and Cairns – notwithstanding substantial port operations in Port Hedland and Darwin. This overwhelmingly negative assessment doesn't necessarily mean urbanisation can't occur in the north, just that the Australian Government should proceed cautiously, in incremental steps and in a mode mindful of the challenges that are too easily overlooked from an air-conditioned office in Canberra.

77 Bolleter et al., 'Informing Future Australian Settlement Planning'.
78 Bolleter, 'The Ghost Cities of Australia'

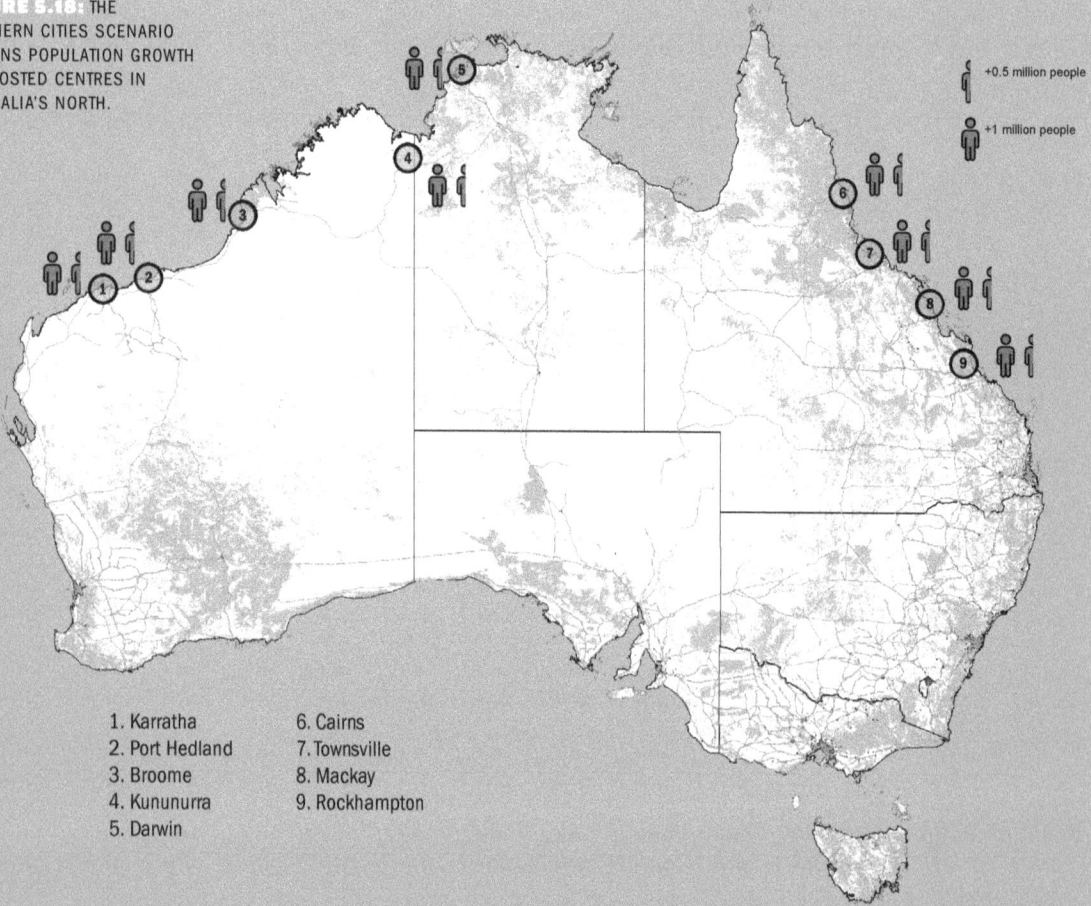

FIGURE 5.18: THE NORTHERN CITIES SCENARIO SIPHONS POPULATION GROWTH TO BOOSTED CENTRES IN AUSTRALIA'S NORTH.

+0.5 million people

+1 million people

1. Karratha
2. Port Hedland
3. Broome
4. Kununurra
5. Darwin
6. Cairns
7. Townsville
8. Mackay
9. Rockhampton

NORTHERN CITIES

Karratha (WA)

Port Hedland (WA)

Broome (WA)

Kununurra (WA)

Darwin (NT)

Cairns (Qld)

Townsville (Qld)

Mackay (Qld)

Rockhampton (Qld)

FIGURE 5.20: THE NORTHERN CITY OF TOWNSVILLE IN 2101 WOULD BE A BUSTLING CITY OF ALMOST 2 MILLION PEOPLE. IMAGE BASED ON A PHOTO BY STEPHEN GIBSON COURTESY OF SHUTTERSTOCK (STOCK PHOTO ID: 507630949). SELECT BUILDINGS PHOTOGRAPHED BY JOHN GOLLINGS. PHOTOGRAPHY COURTESY OF IVAN RIJAVEC.

LOCATION: TOWNSVILLE, QLD
INDIGENOUS REGION: BINDAL
YEAR: 2101
COORDINATES: 19.2590°S, 146.8169°E
POPULATION: 1,967,327

FRONTIER FEVER

LOCATION: DARWIN, NT
INDIGENOUS REGION: LARRAKIA
YEAR: 2101
COORDINATES:
12.4637°S, 130.8444°E
POPULATION: 1,908,652

FRONTIER FEVER

FIGURE 5.22: THE NORTHERN CITIES ARE GENERALLY LOCATED IN AREAS WITH LOW SUITABILITY.

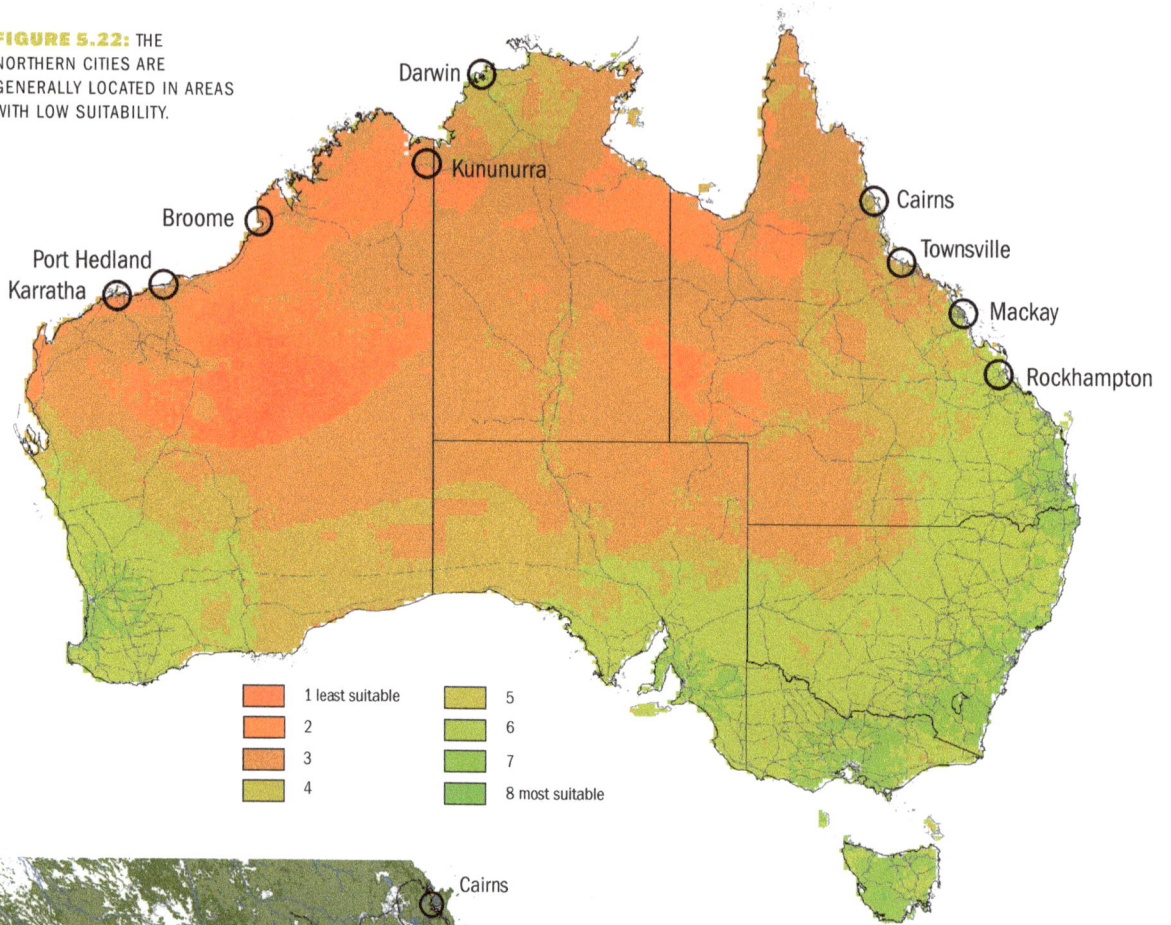

Darwin

Kununurra

Broome

Port Hedland
Karratha

Cairns

Townsville

Mackay

Rockhampton

1 least suitable		5	
2		6	
3		7	
4		8 most suitable	

Cairns

Townsville

Mackay

FIGURE 5.23: NORTHERN CITIES ON THE QUEENSLAND COAST.

Rockhampton

WESTERN CITIES SCENARIO

Australia contains a relative imbalance of lopsided populations on its east and west coasts. Indeed, Western Australia comprises a whopping one-third of Australia's landmass but houses only one-tenth of its population (figure 5.24).[79] Moreover, population distribution within WA is extremely bottom-heavy. The southwest corner was favoured in the colonial era as the most attractive, and settlements occurred wherever ports could be developed. Once established, these ports (Perth, Bunbury, Geraldton, Busselton and Albany) served regions that promised and delivered rich rewards from rural activities (Figure 5.25).[80]

From these port centres, Perth/Fremantle has emerged as the giant, the others remaining relative 'pygmies'.[81] In the 1970s, this perceived imbalance led to concerns that population overconcentration in Perth was degrading the city's liveability, in line with similar sentiments nationally.[82] The Western Australian government was convinced that effective decentralisation was desirable and necessary 'if we are to preserve the way of life for which we are envied by other people in other countries throughout the world'.[83] As the Minister for Decentralisation and Town Planning, Herbert Graham, noted:

Perth must be protected from unchecked and undesirable growth. It must not be allowed to become another London, New York, or Tokyo, choked with crowds, cars and the wastes and excesses of a population that has outgrown the city in which it chooses to live. We cannot erect a barb-wired fence or a concrete wall to keep people out, definitely not, there has got to be a constructive and positive move to attract people elsewhere than the metropolis.[84]

79 Bolleter et al., 'Long-Term Settlement scenarios'
80 Brodie-Hall
81 Brodie-Hall
82 Change to: Bolleter, 'The Ghost Cities of Australia'
83 Graham, 15
84 Graham, 3

Attempts to take the pressure off Perth focused on a scattering of candidate centres. Initially, in the 1950s, the satellite town of Kwinana, south of Perth, was developed as

WESTERN CITIES

FIGURE 5.24
IMAGE BY NUR
MOHD ROZLAN.

FRONTIER FEVER

FIGURE 5.25: GERALDTON ON AUSTRALIA'S WEST COAST. PHOTO BY TRABANTOS. COURTESY OF SHUTTERSTOCK (STOCK PHOTO ID: 1900843567).

a necessary adjunct to major industrial expansion. Under the Whitlam government's decentralisation program, the provincial cities of Geraldton, Bunbury and Albany, a dispersed group between 180 and 400 kilometres from Perth, were all identified as potential growth centres. For Perth itself, a growth corridor along the coast to the northwest, anchored by a prospective centre known as Salvado, was also tentatively proposed to take pressure off central areas.

While Salvado was considered seriously by the Western Australian Government at the time, it was ultimately scrapped following a change of government.[85] Nonetheless, the ambition for a substantial centre defining the northwest corridor eventually found expression in Joondalup, now surrounded by a sea of suburban sprawl. Moreover, while Whitlam government Growth Centres planning never eventuated for Geraldton, Bunbury and Albany – this crop of second-tier cities (alongside others) in Western Australia has remained the focus of state-based policymakers and advocacy groups as candidates for serious growth.[86] Nonetheless, in the fevered imaginations of decentralisation proponents, the Pilbara region in the northwest of the state has remained an area of particular fascination.

In the 1960s and 1970s, mining companies received generous government concessions through lower rates and taxes for building communities in the remote Pilbara region.[87] Consequently, by the 1960s, a meagre population in the Pilbara lived in far-flung mining company towns such as Dampier and Tom Price, and later Karratha, Port Hedland, Newman and Onslow in the 1970s and 1980s.[88] While some of these settlements were designed on innovative lines, including relatively dense and compact inward-looking communities, and suburban 'Radburn' schemes organised around networks of walkable open space, sociological studies undertaken by the CSIRO revealed gaps between designer intentions and resident satisfaction. The suggestion was made for a more centralised regional pattern of larger settlements to reduce social isolation, increase resident choice, and leaven aggregate infrastructure costs.[89]

In parallel, and with broader aspirations to reduce pressure on Perth, in 1972, the state government considered comprehensively developing the Pilbara region and forging a network of shiny new towns with a projected population of a quarter of a million people (Figure 5.26).[90] These ambitions were captured in the Pilbara Study in 1974.[91] This 'entirely new urban system' was to find an economic base in the development of resource-based industries (e.g. pastoralism, forestry and tourism), interlinked with resource extraction, the forging of steel from vast iron-ore reserves, and even the enrichment of uranium (ambitions that have proven elusive).[92] As Herbert Graham noted in strangely biological terms:

85 Lloyd and Anderton
86 Department of Regional Development, 'Royalties for Regions'
87 Storey
88 Bolleter
89 Newton and Brealey
90 Brodie-Hall
91 Technic 10, and Crooks Michael Peacock Stewart
92 Rushman

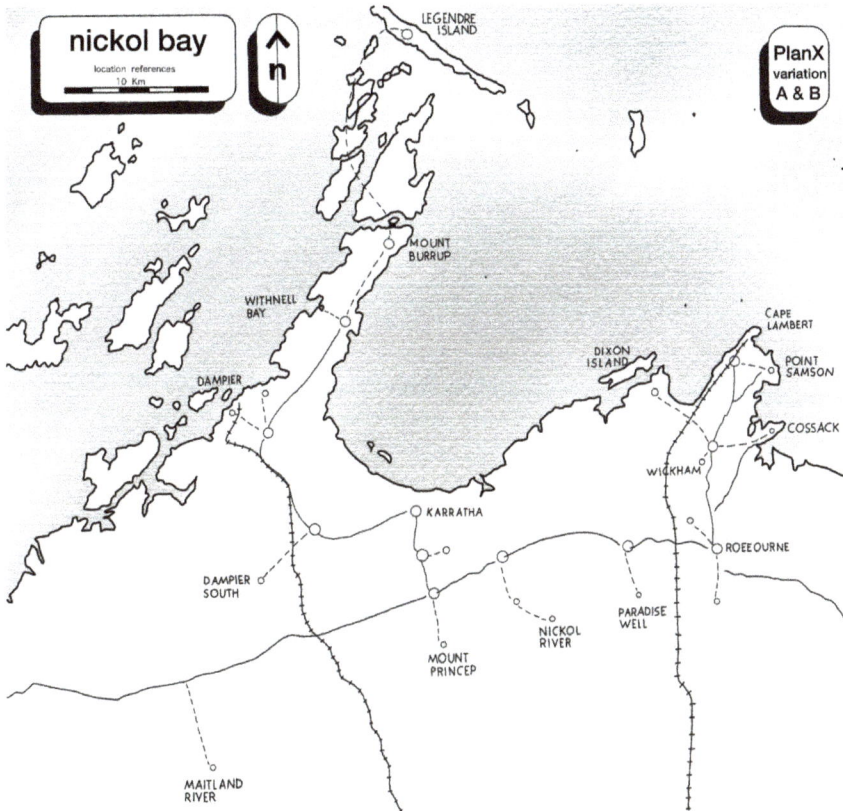

FIGURE 5.26: A NETWORK OF NEW TOWNS PROPOSED FOR THE NICKOL BAY SUBREGION OF WESTERN AUSTRALIA IN THE EARLY 1970S. MAP BY TECHNIC 10, AND CROOKS MICHAEL PEACOCK STEWART. TRACED BY SHUBHAM GAUTAM.

Our major mineral development projects have given us a skeleton of non-metropolitan growth. We are now encouraging flesh to grow round the bones so that the animal can ultimately begin feeding itself.[93]

93 Graham, 9

FRONTIER FEVER

Ultimately, such aspirational planning foundered and, in recent decades, there has been a move away from the new town model. Instead, mining companies now depend on a fly-in fly-out (FIFO) system, which allows them to employ miners who live thousands of kilometres away without being responsible for the urban system in which they reside.[94] The prevalence of the FIFO system in the Pilbara has understandably raised fears that it could ultimately lead to:

> *...fast growth mining towns with limited infrastructure and services and no sense of community; dormitory slums where life is endured away from family left behind in centres like Perth, Darwin, Mackay and Townsville.[95]*

Despite the very real problems of FIFO living, the Pilbara region had become the economic engine-room of Australia because of its massive mineral deposits, producing 18.4% of Western Australia's gross state product and 3.2% of Australia's GDP.[96] Nevertheless, only 60,000 Australians live there (roughly equivalent to the provincial town of Wagga Wagga in NSW), a curious inversion of economic power and population.[97]

In response, in 2009, the Western Australia Government, led by Colin Barnett, upscaled the Pilbara Study model into the Pilbara Cities policy to deliver boosted cities with, ambitiously, all the amenities, infrastructure and services of Australia's capital cities. The policy framework to transform lightweight, drab mining towns like Port Hedland or Karratha into activated and amendable cities was bankrolled by the Royalties for Regions program. The Royalties for Regions program which sought to counterbalance the concentration of capital collected by resource companies in Perth through redistribution to the regions.[98]

The Kimberley region (north of the Pilbara) has presented other planning and development opportunities. Queensland's Gold Coast has been seen as a model for boosted city development in the Kimberley. In 2010, Bernard Salt proposed that Broome, a largely tourism town of 15,000 people, could be developed into a bustling, bold city by the middle of the twenty-first century (inevitably 'like a Gold Coast of the west'), accommodating surges in population and consolidating Australia's 'claim to the riches of the northwest'.[99]

94 Megarrity, "Necessary and Urgent'?
95 Dale, 138
96 Remplan
97 Bolleter, 'The Ghost Cities of Australia'
98 Chapman et al.; Pilbara Development Commission
99 Salt, 236

Other recent proposals for the Kimberley include law lecturer Ben Gussen's 2017 proposal for a charter city, 'Dilga' (named for the local Indigenous Karadjeri goddess of fertility), to cultivate synergies between Singapore and northern Australia. As Gussen reasons, Singapore is a tiny island city-state 'starved of land', which seriously inhibits growth. Meanwhile, vast landscapes (apparently) 'lie empty' in the north of Western Australia.[100] The proposal envisages that Dilga be developed by a company as a joint venture between the governments of WA and Singapore (Figure 5.27).[101] As part of the bargain, WA obtains equity by providing the land, and Singapore by bankrolling the infrastructure.[102] By harnessing such arrangements, Gussen's charter city would be hacked out of the Kimberley wilderness on a massive site, roughly equivalent to the size of Hong Kong.[103]

Clearly, the northwest invites considerable speculation about alternative urban futures, while the southwest provides an array of amenable urban centres. So, what could a framework of future western cities look like?

SCENARIO DESCRIPTION

Given its size and scarcity of population, the Western Cities scenario boosts cities and towns along the west coast, in the northwest (e.g. Broome and Karratha), and also closer to Perth (in Geraldton and Albany, amongst others) by over 1.5 million people (Figures 5.28, 5.29, 5.30).

SCENARIO SENTIMENT

The Western Cities scenario received a credible fourth rating by laypeople,[104] but was slapped down by the experts, who voted it into seventh. The dominant positive commentary was that WA (particularly in the southwest) still has untapped potential (e.g. underutilised resources and underdeveloped land). Moreover, WA could support a much-increased population: 'WA is the economic powerhouse of Australia; it makes sense to increase its population.'

Some people felt that population growth would lead to diversification of the state's economy, away from mining and 'increase its output and economic growth'. Other boosters felt that the support of manufacturing and processing facilities could generate jobs growth.

100 Gussen
101 Bolleter, The Ghost Cities of Australia, 68-69
102 Gussen
103 Gussen
104 The respondent quotations below come from Bolleter et al., 'Long-Term Settlement Scenarios.'

FIGURE 5.27: BEN GUSSEN'S DILGA. IMAGE BASED ON A PHOTO BY SARA WINTER. COURTESY OF SHUTTERSTOCK (STOCK PHOTO ID: 307587383).

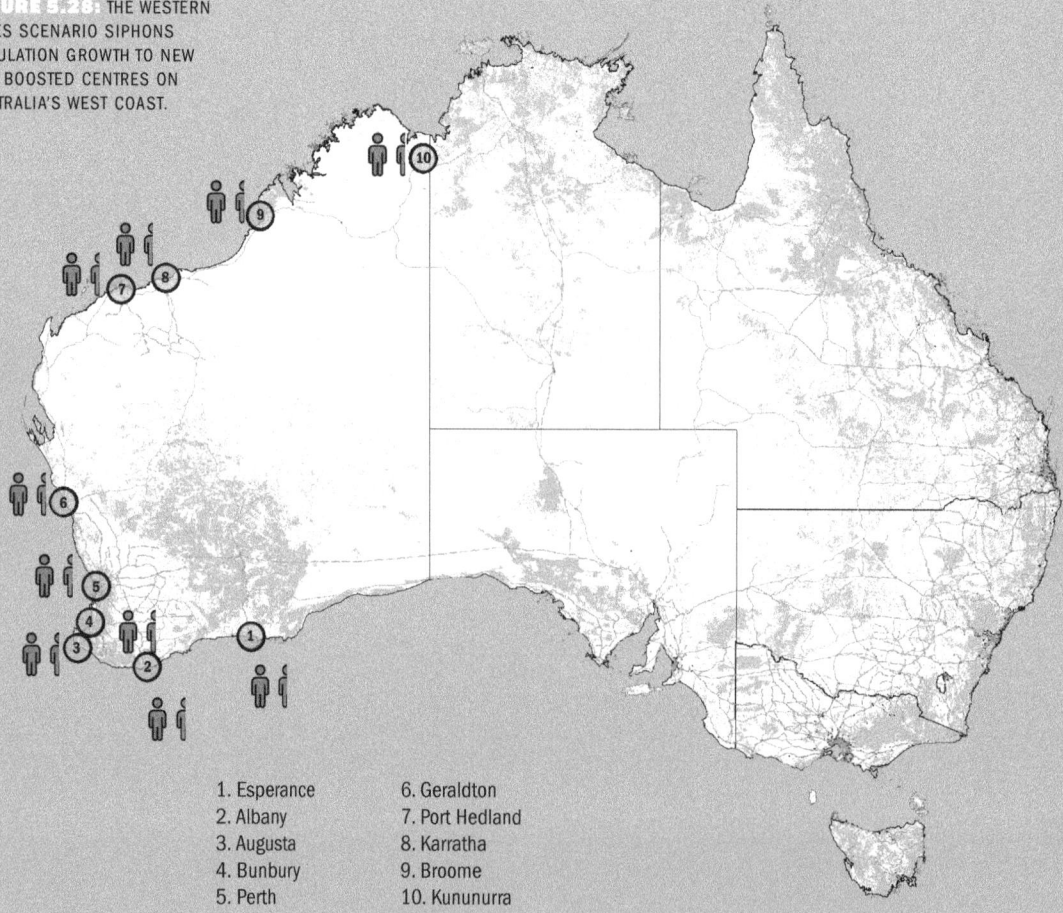

FIGURE 5.28: THE WESTERN CITIES SCENARIO SIPHONS POPULATION GROWTH TO NEW AND BOOSTED CENTRES ON AUSTRALIA'S WEST COAST.

1. Esperance
2. Albany
3. Augusta
4. Bunbury
5. Perth

6. Geraldton
7. Port Hedland
8. Karratha
9. Broome
10. Kununurra

WESTERN CITIES

Kununurra (WA)

Broome (WA)

Port Hedland (WA)

Karratha (WA)

Geraldton (WA)

Perth (WA)

Bunbury (WA)

Albany (WA)

Esperance (WA)

FIGURE 5.30: THE WESTERN CITY OF KARRATHA AS A GROWTH POLE FOR WESTERN AUSTRALIA'S PILBARA REGION IN 2101. IMAGE BY SHUBHAM GAUTAM BASED ON A PHOTO BY AN UNKNOWN PHOTOGRAPHER COURTESY OF DEVELOPMENTWA (HTTPS://DEVELOPMENTWA.COM.AU/PROJECTS/RESIDENTIAL/TAMBREY-NEIGHBOURHOOD-CENTRE/FOR-SALE). SELECT BUILDINGS PHOTOGRAPHED BY JOHN GOLLINGS. PHOTOGRAPHY COURTESY OF IVAN RIJAVEC.

LOCATION: KARRATHA, WA
INDIGENOUS REGION: JABURRARA
YEAR: 2101

COORDINATES: 20.7337°S,116.8447°E
POPULATION: 965,532

FEVER

Finally, in a now familiar refrain, some people felt the 'shift of population to the west would take pressure off the east coast' and Melbourne and Sydney in particular.

One of the dominant themes in the negative commentary was that substantial population growth in WA would need significant infrastructure investment and planning to address water security issues. As one doubter articulated:

> *There is a reason why the population is low in Western Australia! Lack of infrastructure, harsh environment, distance from other capital cities both in Australia and overseas, lack of water, all make it difficult to think this is viable.*

Other cautious types worried that significant population growth 'would see the liveability of Australia's Western cities and towns under threat', resulting in the 'loss of unique character'. Other 'sand gropers' echoed these sentiments, 'Nope, nope, nope. We like being remote and forgotten about - leave us alone' and 'I moved back to Western Australia from the east coast after seeing how the population over there has ruined the quality of life'.

Many people were also rightly concerned about climate change impacts (extreme weather events, rising temperatures) in the state's north. One warned:

> *I do not mind the southern half, but the northern half is a tough sell, particularly the Pilbara cities; cyclones, heat, huge tides, deadly animals on land and sea, drought, floods.*

Other people surveyed fretted that population growth would damage the west's fragile coastal environment and biodiversity:

There are many concerns around vegetation clearing and coastal impacts on native species. The Western Australian government has a terrible habit of clearing high-quality bushland and leaving areas that are degraded or already cleared.

A substantial number of people cited a 'lack of incentives to move or live in Western Cities' and 'this growth trajectory is unlikely'. Others reinforced this sentiment, proclaiming, 'How do you attract people to move so far from home to the end of the earth?' and 'WA is the forgotten state and should stay that way'. Finally, in telling fashion, one person noted that the scenario reflected 'frontier mentality thinking, not good urban planning'.

SCENARIO SUITABILITY

Our suitability analysis of the Western Cities scenario focused on climatic factors, such as heat stress, annual rainfall and cyclone risk; natural and cultural heritage in the form of significant native vegetation; hydrological features; slope; conservation reserves and native title determinations; and infrastructure in the form of major ports, airports, regional railway lines, water pipelines, major power lines, telecommunications and principal roads – to name a few.[105] Measured against these factors, the suitability of the Western Cities scenario varies considerably from the northwest to southwest, reflecting the state's vast scale stretching between opposing climate zones and economic regimes (Figure 5.31). Starting at the bottom, the southwest benefits from reasonable proximity to Perth and its economic opportunities and the existing thick infrastructure networks, as well as reasonable climate comfort and cleared land with minimal constraints. Moving north, the urban centre locations rated poorly for all the opposite reasons (Figure 5.32).

105 Bolleter et al., 'Informing Future
Australian Settlement Planning'

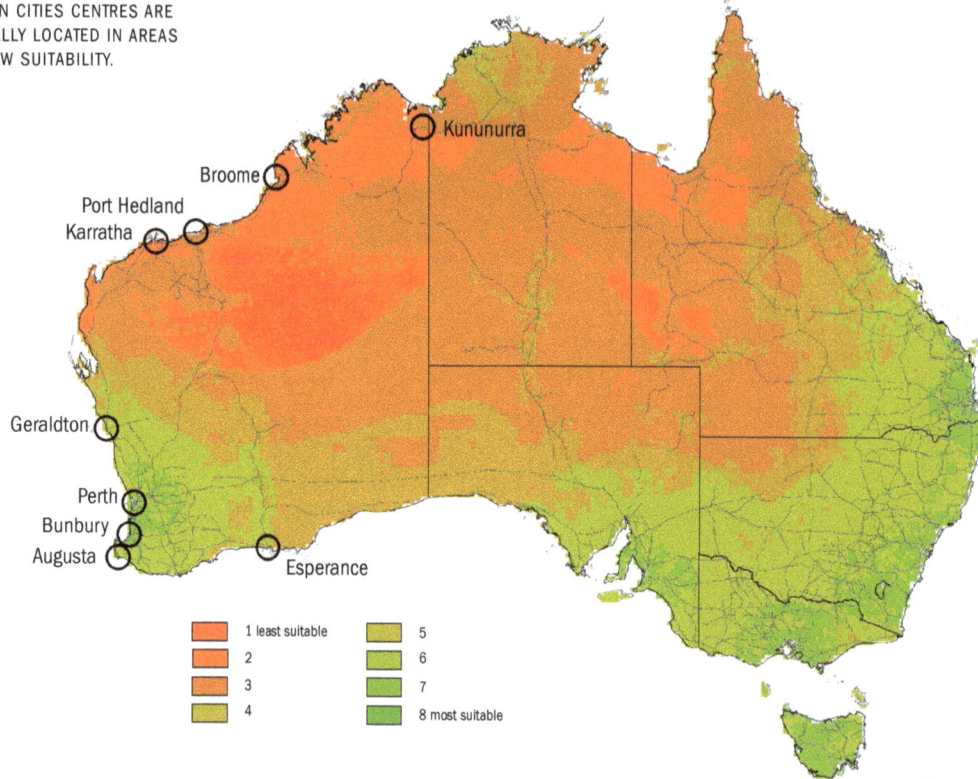

FIGURE 5.31: OUTSIDE OF THE SOUTHWEST CORNER, THE WESTERN CITIES CENTRES ARE GENERALLY LOCATED IN AREAS WITH LOW SUITABILITY.

Kununurra

Broome

Port Hedland
Karratha

Geraldton

Perth
Bunbury
Augusta

Esperance

1 least suitable	5
2	6
3	7
4	8 most suitable

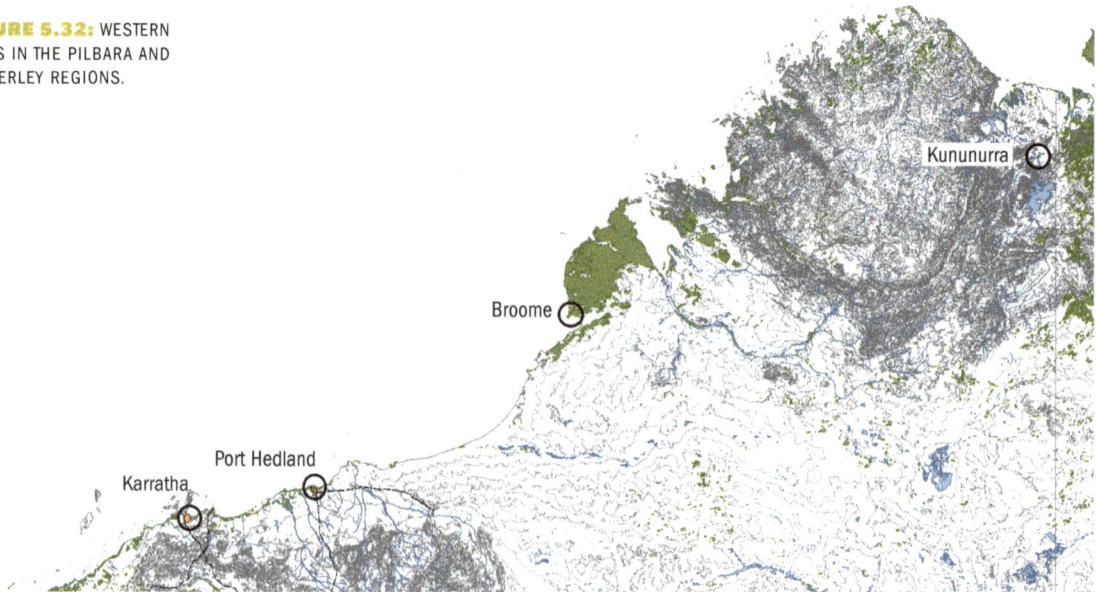

FIGURE 5.32: WESTERN CITIES IN THE PILBARA AND KIMBERLEY REGIONS.

Kununurra

Broome

Port Hedland
Karratha

DISCUSSION

New and expanded settlement at a substantial scale in relatively remote locations in Australia's north and interior spaces is technically feasible. But at what cost? Endeavouring to forge development in frontier environments confronts what may be insurmountable barriers, such as ensuring liveability for prospective residents; adapting to an uncomfortable climate; overcoming carrying capacity constraints; costly infrastructure provision; doubts regarding the job creation and worker migration potential, especially in an era of increasing mechanisation and automation; loss of biodiversity accompanying urban development; and assurance of Indigenous rights, values and interests. We look at each of these in turn below.

LIVEABILITY

As discussed in Chapter 4, coastal access is a crucial component of liveability for many Australians. In this regard, the Inland Cities scenario will be a hard sell (Figure 5.33). Moreover, while mining entrepreneur Gina Rinehart claims that 'there are thousands of miles of coastline in our north that could be populated', readers should remember that the north's coastline is not the generally amiable south coast.[106] In the wet season of the tropical monsoonal climate, wild cyclones lash the north, and floods inundate large areas (indeed, the Kimberley region was struggling to get back on its feet more than 12 months after widespread flooding in 2022-2023).[107] Moreover, as Allan Dale explains, 'the heat and humidity sap your strength', and you can 'forget going to the beach, as marine stingers could be wafting past'.[108] These lifestyle factors would be challenging to overcome in populating our Northern Cities scenario and, to some degree, the Western Cities scenarios.

CLIMATE CHANGE

Climate comfort, in the form of mild winters and summers, is a major driver of population distribution.[109] As such, blisteringly hot temperatures will likely constrain the development of northern, northwest and central Australia. Moreover, the climate of northern Australia could, in time, become unliveable and even dangerous. This alarming situation could

106 Rinehart, 152
107 Woinarski et al.
108 Dale, 85
109 Duranton and Puga

FIGURE 5.33: THE INLAND TOWN OF NORTHAM IN WESTERN AUSTRALIA'S WHEATBELT IS JUST UNDER 100 KILOMETRES FROM PERTH BUT HAS A MODEST POPULATION OF ONLY 12,000, REFLECTING THE BARRIERS TO EVEN MODEST INLAND DECENTRALISATION. PHOTO BY ROSE BOLLETER.

arise because of the interaction between high heat and humidity, measured in terms of 'wet-bulb' temperature. When heat and humidity reach a wet-bulb temperature of around 35°C, the human body battles to cool down through sweating, and it has been estimated that even generally fit people in the shade, even undertaking no physical activity, can die as a result.[110] In the Northern Territory, the wet-bulb temperature already tops 30°C for almost all year and already drives down liveability and economic productivity.[111] Humidity in the north remains high, even with climate change.[112] Therefore, it is possible that, in time, intermittently, the compounding confluence of high humidity and extremely high temperatures could be lethal.[113] Whether or not such events consistently occur before 2101 isn't the point, as climate change impacts will now cascade over centuries to come.

Moreover, most climate modelling for the northern project show that there will be more cataclysmic cyclones, even with a possible drop in the number of cyclones.[114] The number of category 3 to 5 cyclones is forecast to rise, and by 2070, there could be a 140% increase in the intensity of the most severe cyclones.[115] These projections are to be taken seriously because other modelling also correlates to a disproportionate rise in death and damage with an increase in the extremity of cyclones.[116]

These considerations raise questions about the wisdom of further populating the north or northwest, such as in the Northern Cities and Western Cities scenarios, in our age of climate change.[117] Given that climate comfort proves to be a fundamental driver of population patterns, the most heavily affected cities and towns will likely bleed population to the more amenable southern capital cities. Moreover, mundane issues, such as obtaining insurance, could spur on this migration. Indeed, Dale predicted in 2014:

Climatic risks could mean a red-line from Rockhampton to Port Hedland, above which, the insurance industry would prefer not to provide cover... suddenly, the north becomes too much trouble for the rest of Australia.[118]

This prediction is eerily prescient, given the catastrophic flooding in the Kimberley region in the summer of 2022–23.

110 Sherwood and Huber
111 Hyndman
112 CSIRO, Climate Change in Australia
113 Bolleter et al., Projected Extreme Heat Stress
114 Hugo, Population Distribution, Migration and Climate Change
115 DCCEE in Hugo, Population Distribution, Migration and Climate Change, 48
116 McMichael in Hugo, Population Distribution, Migration and Climate Change, 580
117 Bolleter, The Ghost Cities of Australia
118 Dale, 138-139

Climate modelling also suggests rainfall will continue to decrease in most interior regions.[119] As such, rainfall will likely be a particularly constraining factor for the Inland Cities scenario. Many thriving cities worldwide experience only very intermittent rainfall (Dubai is one example), but in Australia, urban settlement has tended to coalesce in areas that receive moderate rainfall. This common-sense trend is unlikely to change.

OVERESTIMATED CARRYING CAPACITY

Current thinking about the development of northern Australia hubristically presumes 'the future of northern Australia is whatever we are prepared to make it'.[120] However, research by Murray Lane shows northern and central Australia's meagre human carrying capacity (which extreme climate will further diminish) will curtail schemes for settlement on the scale described by the white paper for Northern Australia or, indeed, our Northern Cities or Inland Cities scenarios.[121] This analysis calculates the land area required per person and estimates the maximum population able to be supported based on productive land availability within the chosen region.[122] The results show that all Australian states, except Western Australia, are over-capacity in the long term (Figure 5.34). This outstripping of carrying capacity is most severe in the Northern Territory.[123] As such, it is worth being circumspect about the potential of frontier regions (such as the north, the northwest or the interior) to sustain massively boosted populations as long-term settlement scenarios. There are 'compelling environmental reasons why, even after more than two centuries of European settlement, Australia has not filled itself up' through frontier development.[124] Indeed, as former secretary to the Department of Treasury Ken Henry explains:

> *With a population of 22 million people, we haven't managed to find accommodation with our environment. Our record has been poor and ... we are not well placed to deal effectively with the environmental challenges posed by a population of 35 million.*[125]

119 CSIRO
120 Sheriden Morris in Office of Northern Australia and Australian Government Department of Industry, 22
121 Lane, 318
122 Lane
123 Lane
124 Diamond, 397
125 Walker, 39

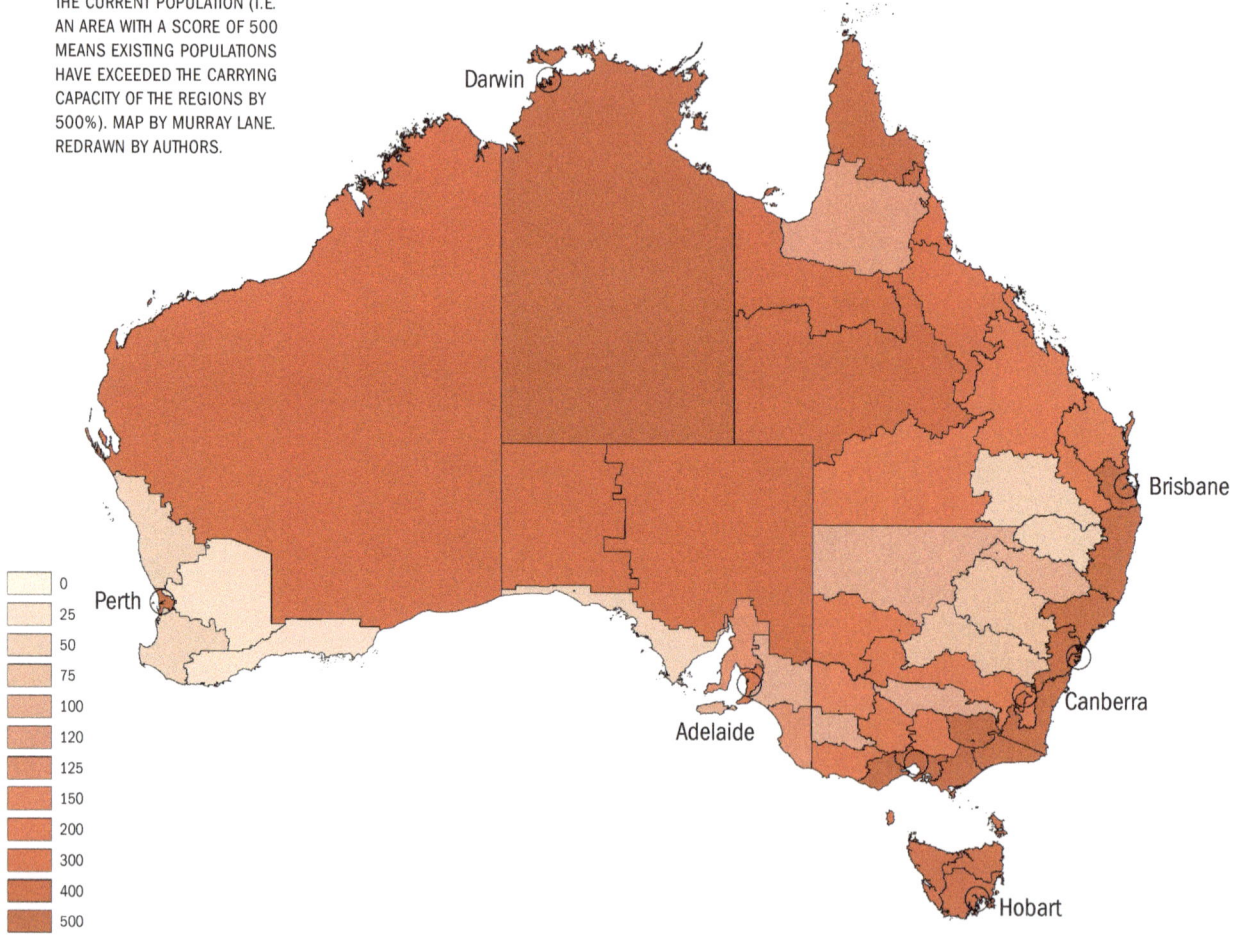

FIGURE 5.34: THIS MAP SHOWS CARRYING CAPACITY BY REGION AS A PERCENTAGE OF THE CURRENT POPULATION (I.E. AN AREA WITH A SCORE OF 500 MEANS EXISTING POPULATIONS HAVE EXCEEDED THE CARRYING CAPACITY OF THE REGIONS BY 500%). MAP BY MURRAY LANE. REDRAWN BY AUTHORS.

INFRASTRUCTURE COSTS

Beyond carrying capacity issues, cities in the north, northwest and interior of Australia would be dogged by economic barriers, such as the cost of constructing the enabling infrastructure necessary to support population growth on the scale of our scenarios.[126] Indeed, the current picture of infrastructure in northern Australia is patchy at best and, in many cases, simply not up to the task of supporting major population growth. For instance, only Darwin and Port Hedland have deep-water ports (needed to deliver the materials required to construct cities and generate revenue through trade).[127] In particular, the investment required to extend enabling port, rail and airport infrastructure for massively boosted northern cities would be vast.[128] Australian federal or state governments could seek investment from other nations; however, cautionary tales abound. For instance, leasing Darwin's main port to a Chinese corporation has elicited a storm of controversy. The inland cities centres would also likely struggle. Why? Long distances to major ports by road and rail inevitably mean the costs of goods and services spiral upwards, putting remote inland cities and towns at a comparative disadvantage to the larger coastal cities with deep-water ports.[129]

ABSENT ECONOMIC DRIVERS

Inland centres are also hounded by a relative lack of economic drivers for stimulating population growth.[130] This lack of drivers is crucial because, despite what regional planners may draw on a map, the population essentially 'ends up where the jobs are'.[131] Traditionally, inland centres functioned as service centres for the surrounding agricultural area; however, the increasing mechanisation of farming, global competition, market liberalisation and sociotechnical transformations have decimated employment in agriculture.[132] These days, farm dinner conversations gravitate 'around driverless tractors and small-scale swarm robotic technology to solve paddock problems'.[133] Reflecting this mechanisation, the proportion of workers employed in agriculture in Australia has free-fallen from 30% in 1911 to a minuscule 2.2% in 2016.[134] In human terms, an average of 294 farmers (and, in many cases, their families) left their properties each month between 1980 and 2011.[135] Moreover, given the rise of robots 'that can plant, fertilise, spray, weed, monitor and ultimately harvest, pack and transport crops', this situation will only get bleaker.[136]

Automation of mining also has worrying implications for employment prospects in the mining centres in our Northern Cities scenario. While the construction of new mines

126 Bolleter, The Ghost Cities of Australia
127 Barrie et al.
128 Bolleter, The Ghost Cities of Australia
129 Regional Australia Institute
130 Bolleter, The Ghost Cities of Australia
131 Barrie et al., 60
132 Plummer et al.
133 Chan 258
134 Binks et al.
135 Daley
136 Daley, 271

and liquid natural gas projects in the Pilbara require a considerable workforce and drives development in adjacent towns, once constructed projects are operational, the workforce needed is substantially smaller.[137] Furthermore, as robotics expert Hugh Durrant-Whyte concludes: 'In the next decade, most mines will operate with less than a third of current workforces, with a significant number of these engaging remotely.'[138] This situation will undoubtedly call into question the need for boosted cities to house populations to service mining operations.[139]

In general terms, mining remains an uncertain driver for centres in our Northern Cities scenario and the northern half of the Western Cities scenario. The fortunes of towns whose economies are driven by mining will always fluctuate with commodity prices. Transitions in the resources industry are usually drastic, and their timing is wildly unpredictable.[140] Indeed, nineteenth-century mining booms spawned towns that have since vanished into the dust (Figure 5.35).[141] Of course, it's unlikely that today's boom towns, like Port Hedland or Karratha, will fade back into the Pilbara's red earth anytime soon. At the same time, it is doubtful that mining will provide the stable foundation required to grow populations on the scale our related scenarios propose.

RURAL MIGRATION SCHEME CHALLENGES

In response to the difficulty of populating frontiers with 'locals', advocates of population growth in frontier regions see a role for 'dispersal' migration policies to build populations and workforces rapidly. Indeed, since the mid-1980s, many Western countries have adopted dispersal policies to siphon the flow of asylum seeker arrivals and humanitarian migrants away from major cities towards regional towns on the grounds of 'burden sharing' and regional development.[142] Indeed, in the mid-1990s in Australia, a set of regional migration schemes was introduced explicitly to facilitate growth in stagnating areas and meet regional skilled labour shortages.[143] The federal government has also established Designated Area Migration Agreements (such as in the Northern Territory), which allow regional employers to sponsor specific skilled workers to meet local needs under the temporary skill shortage visa for occupations unavailable under the standard visa arrangements.[144] Proponents from big business have proposed turbo-charging such schemes. Gina Rinehart (the daughter of Lang Hancock who wanted to A-bomb the Great Australian Bight) has proposed the creation of special, low-tax economic zones in the north that would be powered by a colossal labour force of foreign 'guest' workers, in time perhaps resulting in the emergence of a Dubai-like city out of the north's mangroves.[145]

While 70% of Australians support conventional dispersal programs (i.e., not Gina's dream) requiring some new migrants to live in regional towns or cities for a stipulated period, such programs are not always popular with those in receiving communities.[146] Indeed, there is a consistent pattern of lower support outside capital cities for immigration and cultural diversity (although we note the high variability between areas).[147] Also, for some migrants relegated to regional areas, 'we are condemning them to a pretty ordinary outcome'[148] because they can struggle to find work or are trapped in underpaid and insecure employment that doesn't require their often high-level skills.[149] As such, while nearly a third of skill-stream visas stipulate that skilled temporary migrants live regionally for a maximum of two years, the problem is finding jobs that enable them to stay once the mandatory period has elapsed.[150] Indeed, contemporary data affirms a longer-term trend of skilled migrants (63%) settling in our capital cities. Understandably, they are attracted by the demand for their skills and the cities' economic and lifestyle opportunities.[151] In this respect, settling frontier regions, like those proposed in the Northern or Inland Cities scenarios, with targeted migration programs, is not the silver-bullet proponents might be looking for.

137 Bolleter, 'The Ghost Cities of Australia'
138 Daley, 275
139 Bolleter
140 Regional Australia Institute
141 Watson
142 Schech
143 Hugo, 'Change and Continuity in Australian International Migration Policy'
144 Australian Government, Planning for Australia's Future Population
145 Southphommasane, 161
146 Biddle
147 Chan
148 Chan
149 Schech
150 Button and Rizvi
151 Tuli

LOSS OF BIODIVERSITY

If mass urbanisation did occur in the frontiers of the north, it would threaten the largest intact savanna 'remaining on Earth, an extraordinarily vast, natural landscape with a rich biodiversity of international significance'.[152] If not worth protecting for its own right, there will be an economic cost of trashing such an important wilderness. Indeed, in an age when global biodiversity is rapidly diminishing, areas with wilderness qualities will surge in global attractiveness for tourism and tradeable offsets.[153] In these respects, northern Australia's preservation predominately as a wilderness may make ecological and economic sense over the medium to long term.

NATIVE TITLE

Last but by no means least, Aboriginal cultural links to this northern landscape are equally essential to protect as part of the world's cultural heritage.[154] Indigenous people have finally had their property rights protected in law through native title, producing an Indigenous estate encompassing more than 30% of the Australian landmass[155] and 50% of the Northern Territory.[156] Development, such as proposed in the Northern Cities scenario, would be posited within this complex cultural-institutional landscape, raising moral and legal issues.[157] As such, northern development policymakers are now compelled to consider the Indigenous presence.[158] While large-scale urbanisation deals are theoretically possible, support for such development by Indigenous custodians of the land (and others) remains uncertain. Moreover, unresolved claims for native title and disputes about balancing economic development, conservation and traditional uses linger.[159]

Support for development on the scale of the Northern Cities scenario (amongst others) will centre on how it can benefit Indigenous people who still confront chronic disadvantage.[160] It is worth noting that traditional Indigenous culture has tended to thrive in far-flung regions, such as central Australia, Arnhem Land and the Kimberley, that are isolated from Australia's teeming cities.[161] Therefore, a genuine reconciliation of city building with Indigenous custodianship of the land will require a sweeping reconceptualisation of how we have forged Australian cities to date.

152 Woinarski et al., 85
153 Dale
154 Dale
155 Porter
156 Pearson and Gorman
157 Bolleter, 'The Ghost Cities of Australia'
158 Megarrity, Northern Dreams
159 Regional Australia Institute
160 Raupach et al., 29
161 Blainey

AN UNREALISTIC DREAM?

In the long term, the result of the wholesale implementation of the Inland, Northern and Western Cities scenarios (presuming this is even possible) would be to compound population growth in areas to which it is ill-suited on a large scale. The upshot would likely be a massive drain on resources and limited progress on the ground. While the continental settlement distribution would look more spatially 'balanced', significant urban development on these frontiers must overcome many barriers, such as a lack of existing infrastructure, an inhospitable climate, a relative lack of economic opportunity and the ever-present pull of the established large cities.[162]

For two centuries, our colonial imagination was 'dominated by dreams of conquering a land we always perceived as somehow alien. We wanted to tame, cultivate and exploit it. We wanted to mould it to the purposes we had brought with us.'[163] The comparative popularity of scenarios, such as Inland Cities, suggests that, to some degree, such old dreams die hard. Historian Geoffrey Bolton observed that urban Australians 'like to feel that they have not lost the capacity to pioneer new frontiers', and have typically projected their pioneering fantasies northward[164] and to the interior. If our analysis is to be trusted, these fantasies should be recognised for what they are – fantasies.

In chapters 3 to 5 of this book, we have proposed and assessed continental-scale settlement patterns. However, there has been little exploration of how these may 'hit the ground' in urban design terms. To address this lacuna, in the following penultimate chapter, we look to the next generation of city planners to speculate on their ideal future cities for Australia as part of an ideas competition.

162 Bolleter, 'The Ghost Cities of Australia'
163 Gleeson, 'Lifeboat Cities'
164 McGregor, 'Environment, Race, and Nationhood ', 197

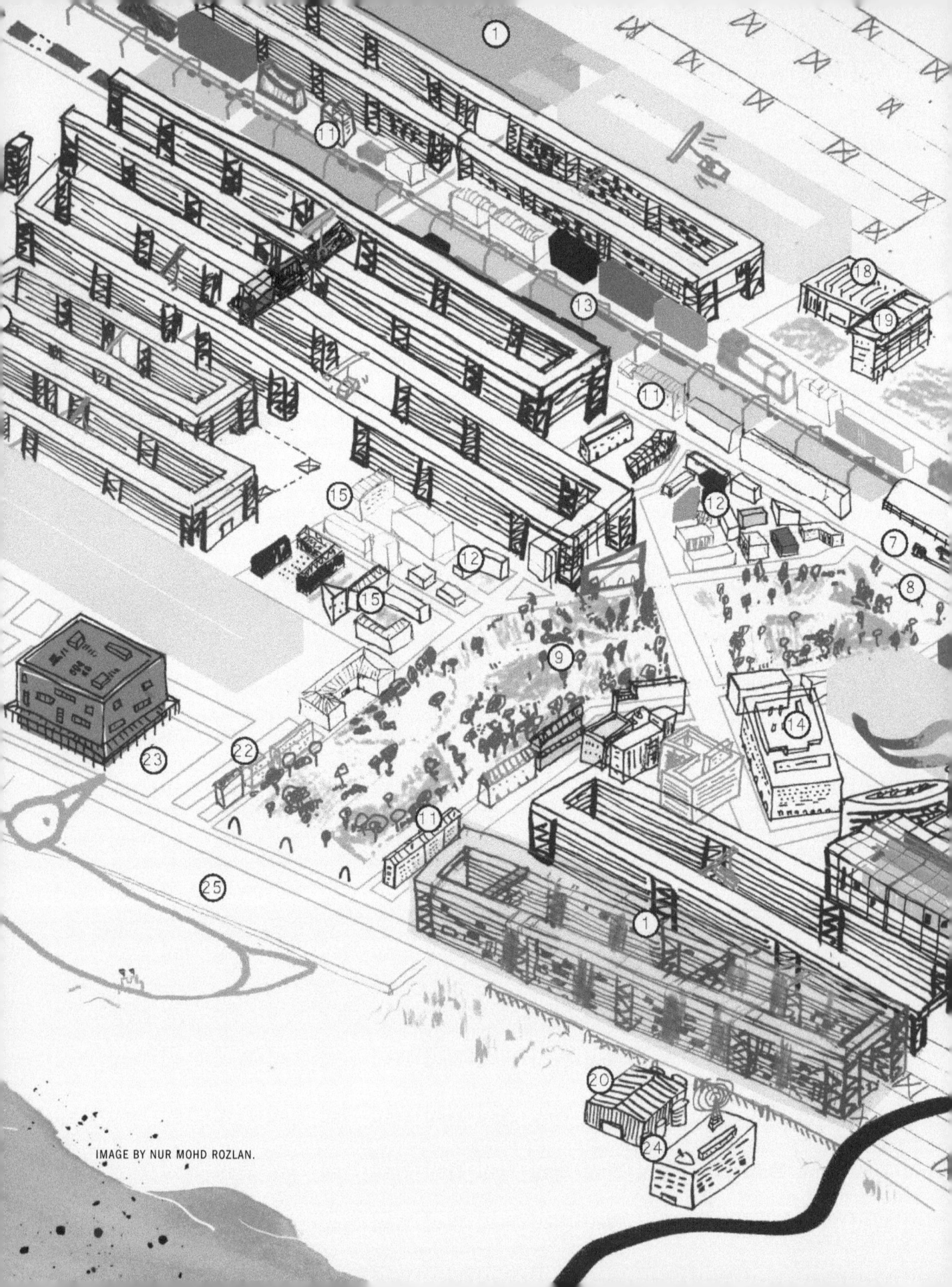

IMAGE BY NUR MOHD ROZLAN.

6

IMAGINING FUTURE URBAN SETTLEMENT

INSERT DREAM HERE

1km²

BUSINESS AS
Unusual

FIGURE 6.1: BUSINESS AS (UN)USUAL UNIVERSITY (BAU) COMPETITION PROMOTIONAL IMAGERY. IMAGE BY ROBERT CAMERON.

BACKGROUND

O ur depiction and evaluation of settlement scenarios have been high-level scans grounded in a broad-brush survey and suitability analyses. Even at that indicative regional scale, more detailed research is required, but an important question is: What might new urban settlement look like in different geographic settings? This attempt is integral to ensuring that new urban spaces go in the right place and are fit for purpose, location and long-run sustainability.

Historically, there has been no shortage of suggestions for ideal town designs. These schemes capture the evolving aspirations of Australian city planning from the eighteenth century. Moreover, they mirror the broader design ideologies au courant across the decades: gridded town forms of the colonial era; set-piece geometries in the City Beautiful idiom; the low-density city of garden suburbs; the modernist efficiency of the city scientific; the greenbelt metropolis; the stellate morphology of the corridor city; and the turn to more compact, smart and sustainable typologies around the turn of the millennium.[1] Only the more recent formulations pay due heed to Indigenous values, knowledge and presence.

A previous work, *Made in Australia,* has speculated on the structure and look of the new and expanded cities required to accommodate the surging urban populace projected by the ABS a century hence. That work was mindful of similar development opportunities

1   Freestone et al., 'Pragmatic Utopianism'

and constraints acknowledged in the present analysis. Seeking to avoid the megacity's extensive sprawl and hyper verticality, the future depicted therein looked like mega-regional planning for decentralised urbanisation facilitated by high-speed rail.[2]

Here, the approach is different. In an inclusive enterprise complementing our research, we looked to the next generation of city planners to speculate on their ideal future cities for Australia, given the likelihood that we might need some moving forward. Their aspirational brief was to conceptualise, design and visualise a future city for Australia responsive to one or more of the urban challenges that we confront: not only future population and migration, but climate change, affordable housing, social equity, pandemics, future technology, Indigeneity and distinctive place-making. The vehicle for this was a national student competition. We describe this below and then showcase the four winning designs.

BUSINESS AS UNUSUAL: IMAGINING A FUTURE AUSTRALIAN CITY

The Business as (Un)usual University (BAU) Competition in 2021–22 invited both tertiary and secondary school students to imagine a future Australian city that embodied a new Australian Dream for the twenty-first century. We report only on the tertiary here. The brief invited students to weave a new dream for Australian cities and express it in a proposal for a future Australian city of 50,000 people or more. Entrants were briefed on the predominant challenges bedevilling Australian cities, as tabled in Chapter 2 of this book. They were also asked to consider their proposals accounting for the projected doubling of Australia's population by 2101. The students' proposals needed an overall vision and the design of a 1 square kilometre precinct (both of which had to be set in the year 2101). Entrants could choose any site within Australia except for the currently urbanised areas of existing state, territory and federal capital cities. The proposals could adapt or expand an existing centre or strike out into unurbanised territory (Figures 6.1, 6.2).

BAU's interdisciplinary jury comprised Abel Feleke (Norman Foster Foundation scholar and advisor to the Aga Khan Agency for Habitat), Beth George (University of Western Australia), Robin Goodman (RMIT), Perry Lethlean (Taylor Cullity Lethlean), Rebecca Moore (Government Architect, WA), Richard Weller (professor and chair of Landscape Architecture and executive director of the McHarg Center at The University of Pennsylvania) and the two authors of this book. Of the initial 494 registrations, there were 72 entries. Entrants were primarily from Australia, but also China, Thailand, Poland and India. BAU's interdisciplinary jury agreed on four winners (each receiving $2500) and five honourable mentions. The winning designs were announced at the Planning Institute of Australia (WA) state awards event in November 2022 and featured on the Australian Urban Design Research Centre's website.[3]

Despite the pessimism of our times (brought on by war, plagues and climate change, among other things), the entries reveal a strain of utopian optimism uniting the next generation of planners and designers. Some recurring themes across entries were transit- and pedestrian-oriented development, eco-cities, flood resilience, landscape rehabilitation, Indigenous values, solar power and energy efficiency, recycling and regenerative, mixed-use, agrihoods (neighbourhoods that integrate agriculture into residential functions), waste management, public health and climate change adaptation and mitigation.

THE WINNING ENTRIES

Below, we include (lightly edited) text from the four winning entries structured around five questions:

1. Where is your city located?
2. What is the ideal population of your city?
3. What is the impetus behind your city?
4. Describe the design of the city.
5. How does your city embody an alternative Australian Dream?

3   Australian Urban Design Research
    Centre

BUSINESS AS
Unusual

imagining an Australian City for the 21st Century

Competition

INSERT DREAM HERE

PLACEMAKING FUTURE URBAN SETTLEMENT

1km²

1. THE GREEN RAIL

Entrants: Natalie Keynton and Bridget Foley

WHERE IS YOUR CITY LOCATED?

South Morang, Melbourne, Victoria

Our city is both highly specific and general in nature. We propose a model for creating green precincts around rail stations throughout Australia, leveraging and extending existing active transport infrastructure. In the next 20 to 30 years, we imagine these cities will emerge around existing stations. We also imagine these train lines extending into new territory and connecting to regional hubs. This model of strategic expansion outside of the city boundary combines the convenience of the city – with high-speed connections – and the quiet of the country town.

We chose Middle Gorge railway station, over 20 kilometres north of Melbourne's CBD, as a test case. It is a 25-kilometre drive, taking between 45 minutes and two hours, or a train ride of over an hour (Figure 6.3). Already designated as a growth zone, this northern corridor is developing with very low-density housing estates. We propose an alternative vision for future growth at the fringes of our cities – and a new Australian Dream.

WHAT IS THE IDEAL POPULATION OF YOUR CITY?

106,000

WHAT IS THE IMPETUS BEHIND YOUR CITY?

The traditional 'Australian Dream' is today riddled with problems. Our fantasy – borrowed from overseas – of the single-dwelling on a quarter-acre block has replicated itself in sprawling cookie-cutter suburbs at the city fringe. 'Affordable' home ownership, delivered through house-and-land packages, creates hot, isolated, unsustainable neighbourhoods.

Poorly designed and constructed houses lead to increased heating and cooling requirements, lack of urban greening and the urban heat island effect. In addition, they result in longer commuting and travel times as critical services and infrastructure are not delivered along with new housing.

The Australian Dream of 2022 – barely achievable even now – will lead us to an unsustainable and unliveable 2100. It is time for a new Australian Dream. How can we reinvigorate the Australian Dream to create a better, more environmentally friendly future? Many Australians are calling for more climate action: We have designed a road map for strategically revitalising fringe urban areas into environmentally friendly, lush precincts. Continually expanding our cities by taking over valuable farming land is not viable; instead, we can create delightful density within existing and emerging fringe centres and create attractive neighbourhoods residents will want to live in (Figures 6.4, 6.5, 6.6).

In this small way, we challenge the brief to create new rural centres. We recognise that Australia has one of the highest rates of urbanisation globally (86%), and urbanisation is likely to continue between now and 2100. While COVID-19 saw many people relocate to rural areas, we believe this was a response to prolonged lockdowns and a desire to escape them. However, it is our challenge to create attractive, green neighbourhoods surrounded by natural landscapes and small-scale farming to allow us to appropriately densify our existing urbanised areas to manage the effects of climate change and population growth.

DESCRIBE THE DESIGN OF THE CITY

Step 1: Invest in a high-frequency, elevated rail network and install a high-speed bike network underneath the railway line.

Step 2: Create a masterplan for each precinct to create a delightfully dense, highly walkable, 20-minute neighbourhood and leverage existing infrastructure at the city fringe, such as roads, schools and large-format retail.

Step 3: Consolidate existing railway parking in one demountable multi-deck car park.

Step 4: Create several medium-density buildings on former car parking sites to bring activity into the centre.

Step 5: As car usage declines and more citizens begin to travel by active transport, shift all car usage to a high-speed road parallel to the railway to free the precinct centre from cars. Simultaneously, create a network of pedestrian- and bike-friendly connections using existing roads, accessible only by service and slow-speed vehicles.

Step 6: As existing low-density homes deteriorate, transform blocks into medium-density apartment living suitable for all.

The Green Rail

Getting us where we need to be

FIGURE 6.3: THE GREEN RAIL.

(Development Stage 6. Year: 2052)

Step 7: In newly dense precincts, ensure that the service and infrastructure needs of the community are met by ensuring that each precinct is an actual 20-minute neighbourhood.

Step 8: Because the increased density will accommodate residents from the old Australian Dream houses and a growing population, regenerate former housing estates into local-scale farming or natural environments to create a source of local food production and recreational activities, such as bushwalking.

HOW DOES YOUR CITY EMBODY AN ALTERNATIVE AUSTRALIAN DREAM?

We believe COVID-19 has strengthened our need for connection to community and country. With this in mind, we have designed our city with four different scales of community.

In the Green Rail, no building will have more than 30 apartments. Each floor should have eight or fewer apartments, meaning that you will know the people you see in the stairwell and be able to make collective decisions with your neighbours about shared communal spaces and their uses.

Using the existing road infrastructure, 'super lots' will be created by amalgamating individual housing lots. Each super lot should be developed at a rate of no less than 120 dwellings per hectare, meaning there could be between four and 10 building communities per super lot.

Each railway station will be the hub of a 20-minute neighbourhood, each with approximately 21,000 residents (based on density rates). These 20-minute neighbourhoods are each the same size as regional towns, such as Echuca or Griffith. However, all are within a 20-minute walk from high-speed rail, which connects several towns into a linear city, an expansive network of communities, limiting environmental impact while connecting people to their friends, communities and city. Five linear cities working together will house over 106,000 people.

1km2 Precinct Design

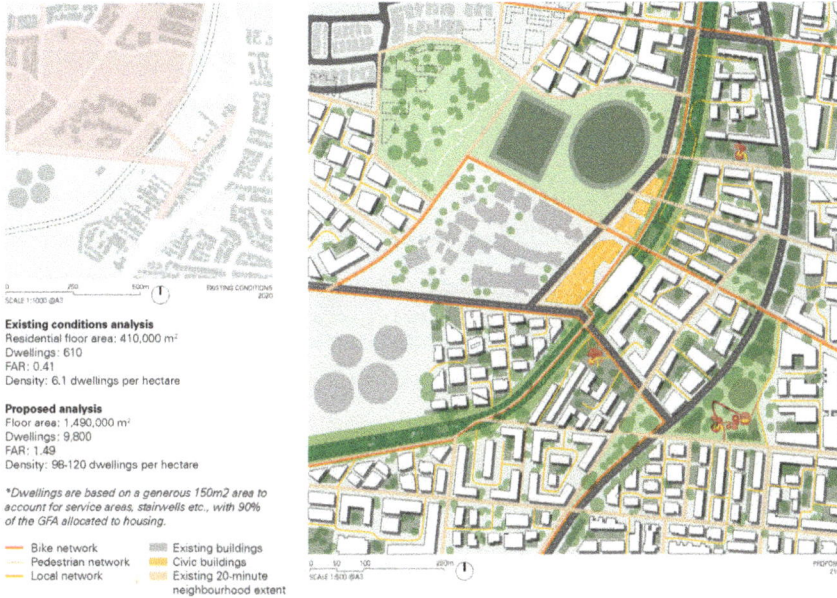

SCALE 1:1000 @A7

EXISTING CONDITIONS
2020

Existing conditions analysis
Residential floor area: 410,000 m²
Dwellings: 610
FAR: 0.41
Density: 6.1 dwellings per hectare

Proposed analysis
Floor area: 1,490,000 m²
Dwellings: 9,800
FAR: 1.49
Density: 96-120 dwellings per hectare

*Dwellings are based on a generous 150m2 area to
account for service areas, stairwells etc., with 90%
of the GFA allocated to housing.

— Bike network   ▓ Existing buildings
— Pedestrian network   ▓ Civic buildings
— Local network   ▓ Existing 20-minute
                              neighbourhood extent

SCALE 1:500 @A3

PROPOSED
2100

A Century of Cities in Review, 1 July 2100:

Around 2010, residents began to be aware of how ill-equipped their houses and communities
were to cope with climate change in Australia. As a result, whole neighbourhoods
overheated in the summer, causing loss of life; people's health deteriorated as residents
drove everywhere; and 'affordable' houses became expensive to heat, cool and maintain.

However, it took another decade or so for real action to begin. It started slowly – a few
trial neighbourhoods here and there – but we found what worked. The Green Rails were
created thanks to the strong political will in the 2020s, which saw large-scale investment
in our eco-rail network. It must have seemed like a dream back then to create cities that
worked with nature rather than in isolation from it, as was so often the practice with the
24/7 use of air conditioners.

External Life

STAGING: Maintain existing road structure and develop incrementally over time

STAGING: Provide a multi-deck carpark to supply parking needs in the interim and begin transformation on existing at-grade carparks

BUILT FORM: A maximum of 5 storeys aiming for a density of 120 dwellings per hectare

BUILT FORM: Ensure design diversity with each building delivered by a different architect

INFRASTRUCTURE: Create a parallel, arterial road for high-speed vehicular traffic to service industry

CONNECTIONS: Every street is to support a pedestrian-priority movement network

CONNECTIONS: Elevate the railway line and provide high-quality recreation spaces underneath to encourage permeability

CONNECTIONS: Create a high-speed bicycle network underneath the elevated rail to support active transport

CONNECTIONS: Every building must have active transport connections and end-of-trip facilities

SUSTAINABILITY: All streets to support WSUD initiatives, with city-wide water harvesting practices

SUSTAINABILITY: Built form to explore mass-timber construction

SUSTAINABILITY: Once the population is more condensed, land outside the 20-minute neighbourhood could be used for small-scale, community farming or other productive land uses

SUSTAINABILITY: A precinct-wide approach to sustainability must encourage neighbourhood waste disposal, neighbourhood rainwater harvesting, renewable energy generation and micro-grids

Internal Life

How Nat met Bridget ...

Bridget lives in Yerra building and loves to grow her popular rich, red tomatoes from her neighbourhood green roof and cook using ingredients fresh from the market a 10 minute walk away. She works remotely from her favourite café below whose delivious aromas she can smell every morning.

Nat mostly works in Melbourne CBD but enjoys living away from the hustle and bustle. She loves her quick 5 minute walk to the station.

She works from her favourite café in The Commons where she met Sally and is looking forward to Saturday where she'll be enjoying a quiet dinner of spaghetti marinara made with tomatoes fresh from Sally's garden.

Both wanted to find a balance between the convenience of a city but the quiet of a country town, they finally found solace here, a city and neighbourhood combined to create a an all-inclusive community.

Bridget's home grown tomatoes in the community graden next door

Bridget's apartment

Favourite remote work station

Nat's apartment

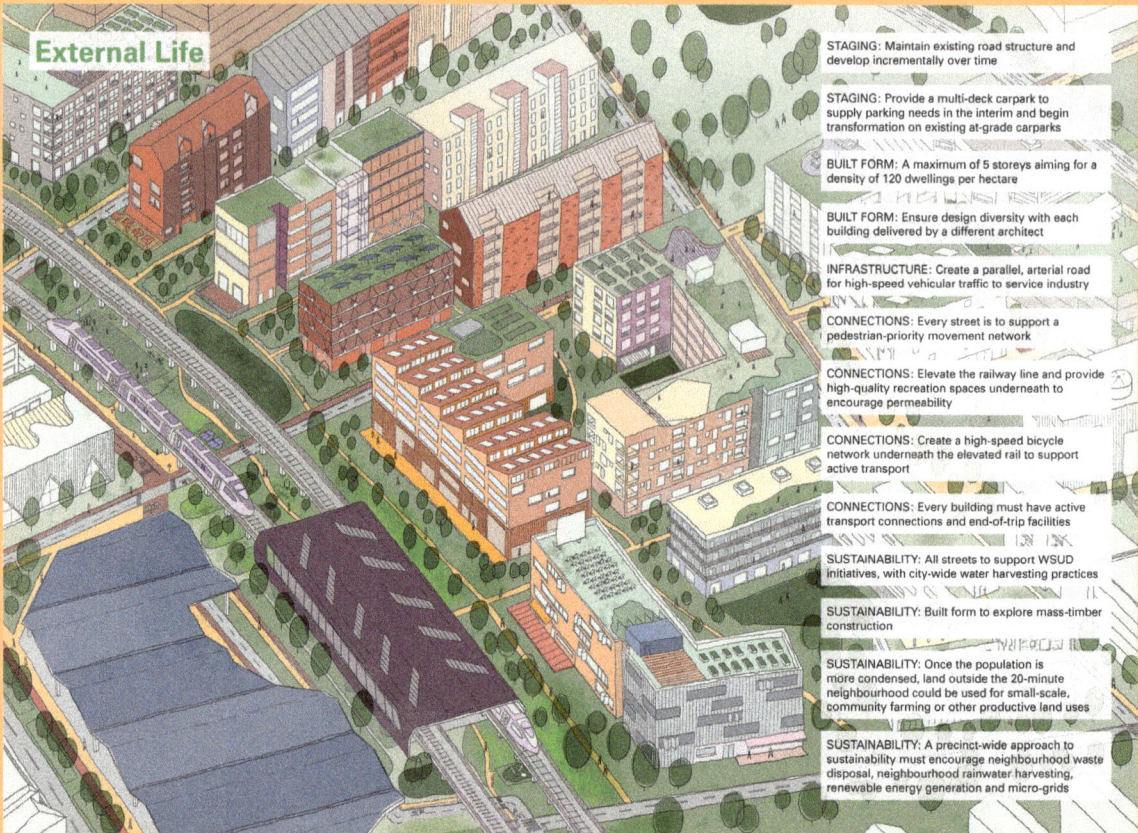

FIGURE 6.5, 6.6: GREEN RAIL: EXTERNAL AND INTERNAL LIFE.

However, thanks to those early pioneers, 98% of cars have now been removed from our roads, our emissions have been reduced by 89%, and countless businesses have been created in a whole new industry around closing our waste loops and creating circular economy neighbourhoods. In addition, by elevating infrastructure and residents' collective effort to plant trees and regenerate landscapes, our native flora and fauna are no longer threatened by extinction, but thriving in a breathable environment.

Every time you open your windows for the breeze, eat a home-grown tomato or enjoy your community movie night or long-table lunch, remember that this is a turning point for current and future generations. This is the first stop of where we need to be, and if we continue along this road together, who knows what the future will hold.

2. TRANSIT CITY Entrant: Nur Mohd Rozlan

WHERE IS YOUR CITY LOCATED?

Port Augusta, South Australia

The future city centre, the main arrival point for those travelling by high-speed rail from other major cities, will be Port Augusta on Spencer Gulf's eastern side. However, much of the future city will grow beyond this area, parallel to the water body and on the gulf's western side (Figure 6.7).

WHAT IS THE IDEAL POPULATION OF YOUR CITY?

1,500,000

WHAT IS THE IMPETUS BEHIND YOUR CITY?

The modern nation of Australia is primarily founded on a migrant population. Going into the future, we will continue to rely upon this pattern to sustain our economy. So far, Australia has been largely selective in whom it welcomes; its intake is mostly skilled migrants. On the other hand, its refugee and humanitarian intakes are much lower. This cannot remain the

PANEL 1: FUTURE CITY LOCATION

Service 1
home-moving freight line

E-W

local train line

local point of arrival

education

"old city"

PORT
AUGUSTA

home-production
industry & workyards

local & international
point of arrival

solar energy farm

port

case. Moreover, the number of cross-border migrants is increasing worldwide, mainly due to political conflicts and the onset of climate change. Australia must step up and provide refuge for more people and expand its migration policy to become more inclusive.

Transit City, a charter city, will support migrants' initial settling-in journey (i.e., a temporary stay of various time spans, depending on the individual's support and needs) before moving on to a new town/city they will call home. The city also has the potential to provide a more humane solution to lifeless detention and offshore processing centres. With its governing system, the city will be able to respond more promptly to the diverse needs of new migrants and represent their voices in decision-making. The city invests in migrants' well-being and recognises each individual's ability to make Australia a better place.

Port Augusta is an ideal location for the following reasons. Firstly, its strategic location and existing train infrastructure connecting eastern and western Australia allow for easier distribution of new immigrant populations across the country, especially in regional towns that require a population boost. Secondly, as a major service hub in the region, there is potential to develop more industries and increase career pathways for new migrants (e.g., education, renewable energy, tourism, hospitality, manufacturing and marine studies). Thirdly, port access will assist in the distribution of goods; and fourthly, the location's temperature will be ideal for living in the next century.

DESCRIBE THE DESIGN OF THE CITY

The new city is structured in a grid to respond to the constantly changing and temporary population (Figure 6.8). Freight networks run on this grid to assist in sculpting the urban landscapes and insert or remove interventions onto flexible metal structures. The grid only provides a framework, however, while still encouraging the city to grow organically and allowing residents to add their personality to the city. The urban form is compact and controlled by the airport to the west, water bodies to the south, and work and train yards to the north. The grid is divided into precincts, each with its data collection and processing centred on human activities and changes that take place in the area.

Upon arrival, residents are given their own housing unit to develop and customise. They can choose where to reside in the new city (Figures 6.9, 6.10), and once their temporary stay ends, they will choose whether to take their housing unit. If they choose not to take the unit, it will be dismantled or repurposed to house new residents.

Essential services, commercial areas and other non-residential land uses are close to transit corridors for easy access beyond community green spaces. In addition, green corridors located along tram lines provide an escape from density and serve as wayfinders.

The city will be primarily car-free, with private transport limited for service functions. Instead, residents get around the city by train, trams and active transport, including electric bikes.

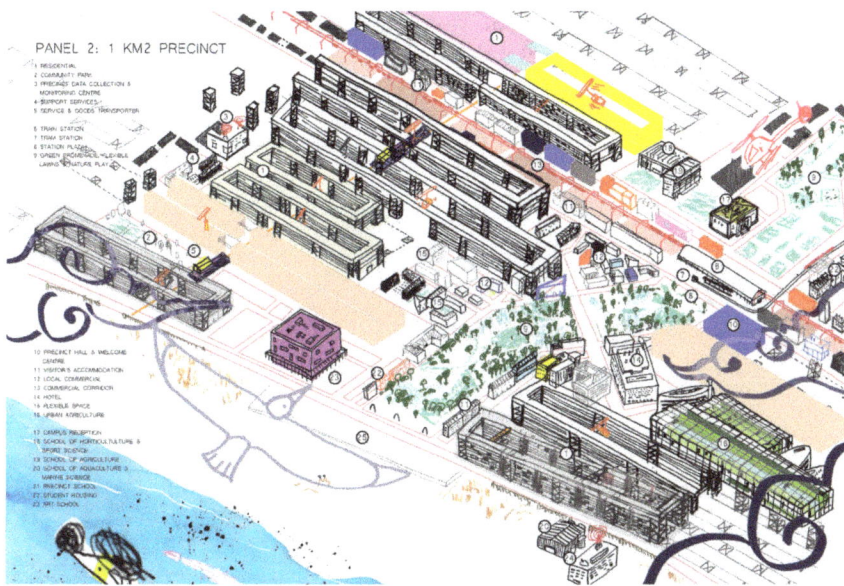

PANEL 2: 1 KM2 PRECINCT

1 RESIDENTIAL
2 COMMUNITY PARK
3 PRECINCT DATA COLLECTION & MONITORING CENTRE
4 SUPPORT SERVICES
5 SERVICE & GOODS TRANSPORTATION

6 TRAIN STATION
7 TRAM STATION
8 STATION PLAZA
9 GREEN PROMENADE, FLEXIBLE LAWNS & NATURE PLAY

10 PRECINCT HALL & WELCOME CENTRE
11 VISITOR'S ACCOMMODATION
12 LOCAL COMMERCIAL
13 COMMERCIAL CORRIDOR
14 HOTEL
15 FLEXIBLE SPACE
16 URBAN AGRICULTURE

17 CAMPUS RECEPTION
18 SCHOOL OF HORTICULTURE & SPORT SCIENCE
19 SCHOOL OF AGRICULTURE
20 SCHOOL OF AQUACULTURE & MARINE SCIENCE
21 PRECINCT SCHOOL
22 STUDENT HOUSING
23 ART SCHOOL

FIGURE 6.8 A 1 KILOMETRE SQUARE CITY PRECINCT.

PANEL 3: TRANSIT CORRIDOR

WARWICK

FIGURE 6.9: TRANSIT CORRIDOR.

IMAGINING FUTURE URBAN SETTLEMENT

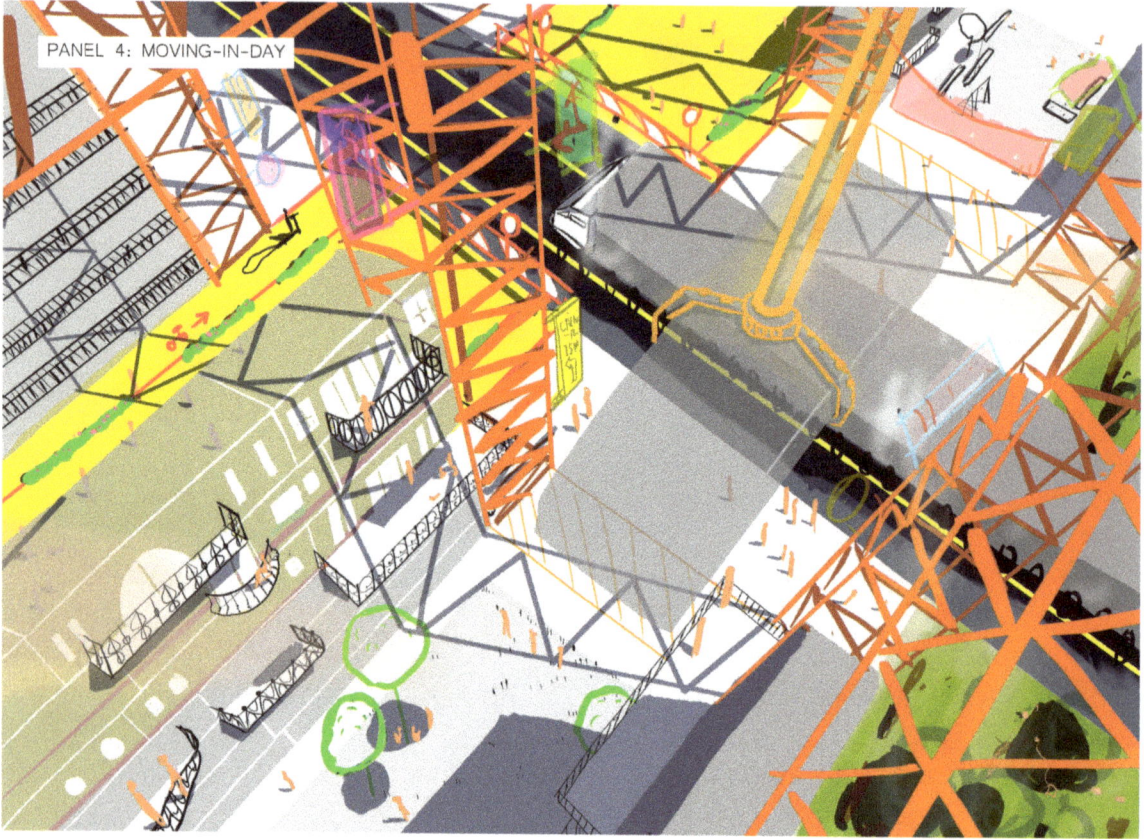

PANEL 4: MOVING-IN-DAY

FIGURE 6.10: MOVING-IN DAY.

HOW DOES YOUR CITY EMBODY AN ALTERNATIVE AUSTRALIAN DREAM?

Transit City envisions a dream where migrants are given the best opportunity to establish a new life in Australia regardless of their cultural or socioeconomic background. This is not only by providing social and economic support, but by integrating new residents into 'normal' everyday life, giving them opportunities to be part of and contribute to communities, explore various job pathways and interests, gain education and qualifications, and reconnect with previously separated relatives and friends.

The city is not solely for new migrants. Australian citizens can also come to visit, work and live here. Opening the city up to other Australians allows new migrants and Australian citizens to form social networks and learn about each other's cultures. The migrants can also leave the city and visit other towns and cities for leisure or work purposes, such as internships or training in a different city. They would require a special pass registered on a system to regulate movement, ensure safety and protect the agreement of special considerations bestowed and agreed upon between the Australian and Transit City's governments.

During their stay in the city, residents will attend workshops, schools or universities to develop language, cultural and technical skills. In collaboration with Transit City, the Australian Government may also provide incentives for migrants to pursue specific courses to address job shortages in the country. Private companies can also invest in job training for new employees.

Despite the prevalent use of technology in the city to monitor and collect data, face-to-face interaction is still valued and highly prioritised. Robots and artificial intelligence (AI) take up the more mundane tasks of keeping the city clean and functioning. However, activities involving value-based interaction between individuals are conducted in person wherever possible, such as in educational and service settings, to help foster belonging and a sense of place among new migrants.

In addition, the city provides various types of climate-suitable outdoor spaces to encourage outdoor activities and social events for residents to join and engage with other community members. Residents are also encouraged to join or form community groups and organise events or volunteer their time for the community.

3. PORT NEXUS Entrant: Jeremy de Lavaulx

WHERE IS YOUR CITY LOCATED?

Between Woodside and Woodside Beach, South Gippsland, Victoria

WHAT IS THE IDEAL POPULATION OF YOUR CITY?

65,000

WHAT IS THE IMPETUS BEHIND YOUR CITY?

The year is 2100. The government has implemented fast rail infrastructure between Melbourne, Canberra and Sydney on the coastal side of the Great Dividing Range. Gippsland continues growing as a mega-region endowed with natural resources, attracting residents and workers alike. Its main cities and satellite cities range in population from 50,000 to 1 million.

Neural interface infrastructure connects 97% of the population to the Global Digital Database. As a result, thought, sense and emotion are effortlessly encoded and decoded into the digital realm, allowing instant communication and stimulation. Most people are connected intimately to their host, decreasing the need for long-distance movement. People stay closer to where they dwell; their lives are entirely integrated into the network for convenience, interest, need and efficiency.

Automation and robotics have primarily overtaken workplaces, reducing errors and increasing efficiency. Due to this, much of the labour required has been allocated for overseeing operations, implementation and monitoring of automation maintenance.

There has been an increased focus on holistic health, nutrition, empathy, spirituality and care for non-human species. This has resulted in a shift away from high-impact agriculture, such as dairy and beef, and intensive forestry practices. Alongside this, colonial cultures of private land ownership have mainly been dissolved, with industry asking how the land can do more while growing more resilient.

Pastoral land has been gradually given back to Indigenous custodians and science ecology to achieve this decolonising impetus. Within the cool contexts of southern Gippsland, this land is starting to encode complexity through Indigenous and Western land management practices. Indigenous kinship with Country is established alongside networks of Westernised research.

DESCRIBE THE DESIGN OF THE CITY

If we break down the existing layers as the inputs, we can process these layers individually to identify the elements recombined into the prototype model (Figures 6.11).New 'interjections' are made along rural mobility links and run parallel to watersheds or existing water lines. Slower intra-city routes link city clusters, allowing a slower perception of nature. The hierarchy of these mobility routes determines velocity, density and capacity and is aided by FareShare™ interchanges.

Existing use and lack of biodiversity are questioned, divided and made more complex through patchwork ecology.

Water is aided by technological intervention to enrich, distribute, mineralise and soak the depleted soils and systems currently on site. This is aided by linking into sub-surface geological enrichments.

Industry shifts towards sustainable, nuanced, long-term practices revolving around forestry, engineered timber and vertical farming. Similarly, new technologies for supporting infrastructures make use of existing and future resources relating to the regional context.

When zooming inwardly, small-to-medium cluster cities emerge as urban centres bounded by parallel dwelling islands (Figure 6.13).These cluster cities have limited height and density, moving away from larger morphologies and taking advantage of the sky to favour all species. However, sparsity is not as it seems due to the proximity of nearby cluster cities, working industry and inter-species kinship.

HOW DOES YOUR CITY EMBODY AN ALTERNATIVE AUSTRALIAN DREAM?

Port Nexus provides an alternative Australian Dream that emerges and shifts away from the Australian Dream grown within Australian towns and cities. Historic towns have often emerged along main mobility routes with the 'strip and grid' layout, an ideal infrastructural layout to support processes of resource extraction, land title and centralism.

As centralised urban centres develop concentration and density, interstitial mobility links are formed, allowing further categorisation of land use and zoning requirements. The grid spreads, intensifies, and embeds over time, with increased densities affecting amenity and liveability. This is a shift towards undoing the complexity of the land.

Port Nexus reverses this simplification and categorisation through water infrastructures, growth and mobility phasing, programming, modes of dwelling, specific dimensioning and the deployment of local electric vehicle charging infrastructure. These aspects curate the balance between intimacy and prospect while contributing towards a unique spatial

Existing

Colonial Sparsity
Woodside TP
Woodside Beach TP

Limited use and Resilience

Watershed and River

Economy: Pastoral and Intensive Forestry

Servicing Infrastructures

Process

Probe, Make Field, Densify

Divide, Diversify, Repair

Intervene and Infrastructure Link

Shift

Sustainable Creation

Proposed

Interlinked: Mobility Hierarchy, Density per Cluster, Field Generation
Mobility Hierarchy (1)
Dimensioning (2)
FareShare™ Interchange (3)
City Programming (4)

Woodside TP
Woodside Beach TP

Resiliency: Kinship Mobility, Patchwork EVCs and Ecology
EVC Research (1)
EVC Forestry (2)
EVC Research Centre (3)
River Reparation (4)
Ecological Mobility (5)

Water Cyborg: Harvest, Distribute, Mineralise, Soak
Desalination (1)
Wastewater Treatment (2)
Calcium Enrichment Wells (3)
Water Processing Plant (4)
Distribution (5)
Soaking Complexity (6)

Multi-Species Sustainable Forestry, Engineered Timber, Vertical Farming
Forestry Industry (1)
Engineered Timber (2)
Industry Training (3)
Shipping at Port Nexus (4)
Vertical Ocean Farming (5)

Implementation and Infrastructural Link
Future Gen Nuclear (1)
HAWT Wind Turbines (2)
Wave Field Generation (3)
Geothermal Energy Generation (4)

500m
0m
-1000m
-2000m
-4000m

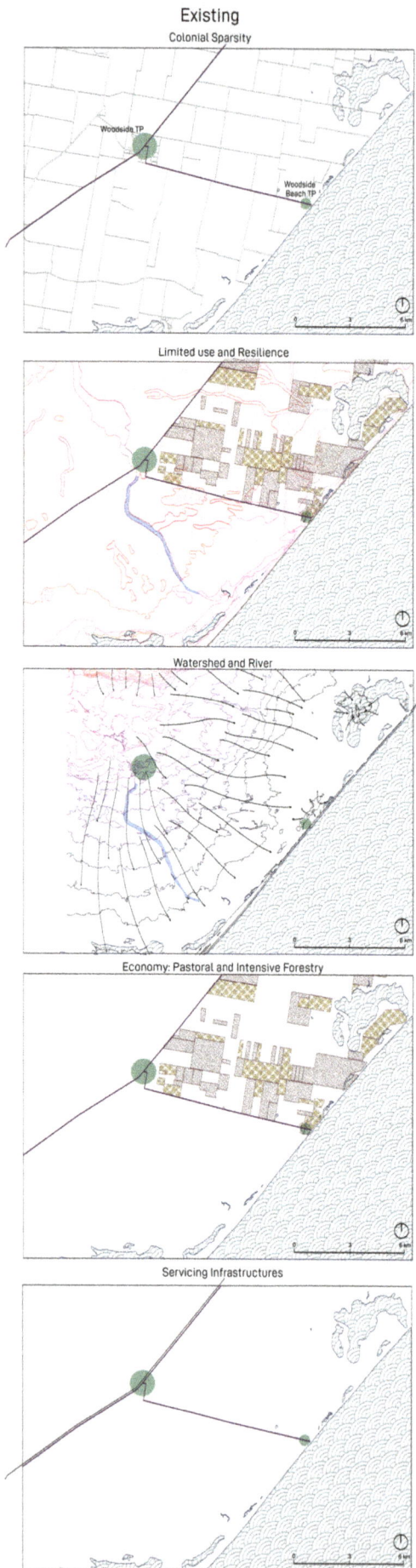

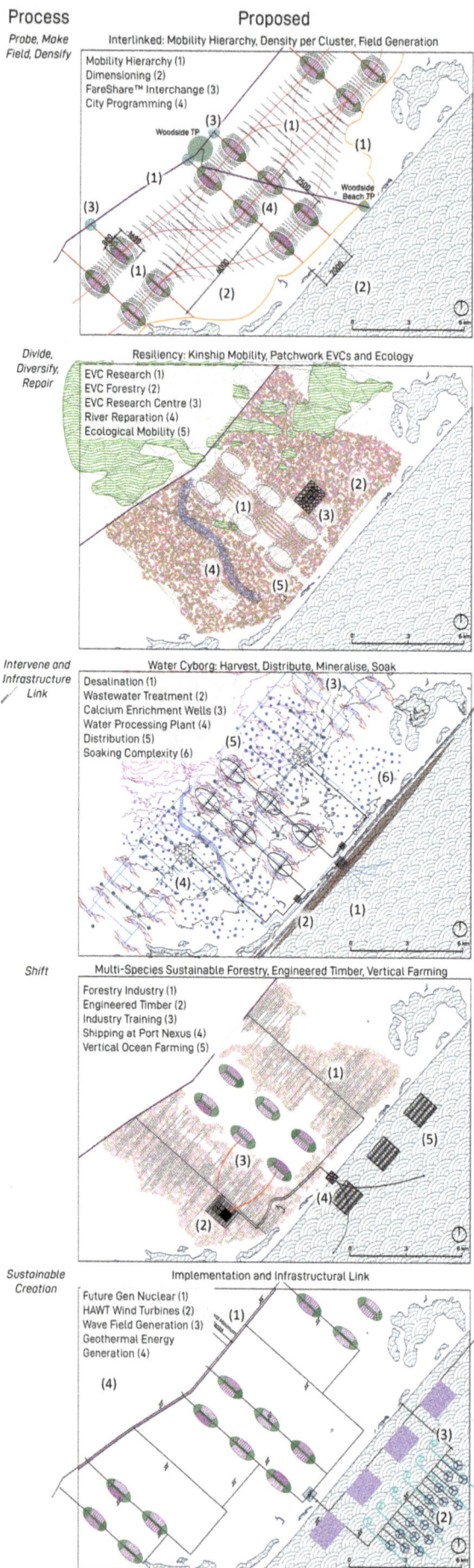

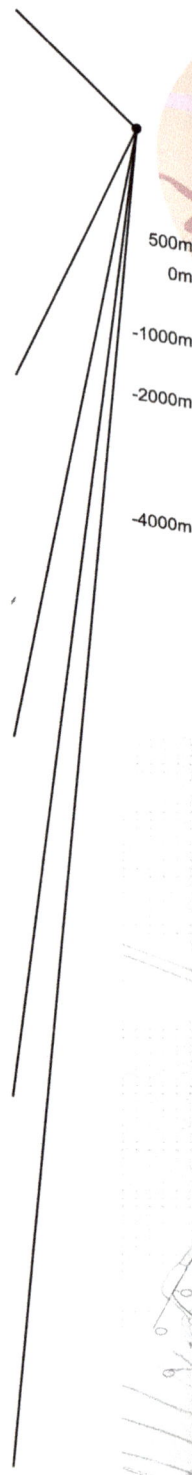

FIGURE 6.11:
VISION AT PORT NEXUS.

Spatialising Systems (Colour Coded)

Vision at *Port Nexus*

Patchwork EVC restoration, research experimentation

Seaweed harvesting for water mineralising and treatment

Coastline

Seaspray Group

Quatemary and Haunted Hill Formation

Seaspray group: calcarous (1), silty (limestone & shady (2), moderate water consolidation (3), terrigenous (4), carbonate sediments (fossils) (5)

Haunted Hills group: Cross bedded lenticular sands, gravels, clays

Latrobe group: Non-Carbon silicate rocks, quartz, clay (6), coal horizons (7)

Podosols, Tenosols, Hydrosols, Swamp (mud and sand flats)

Strzelecki Group

Latrobe Group

300:1 seabed gradient

0

5

km

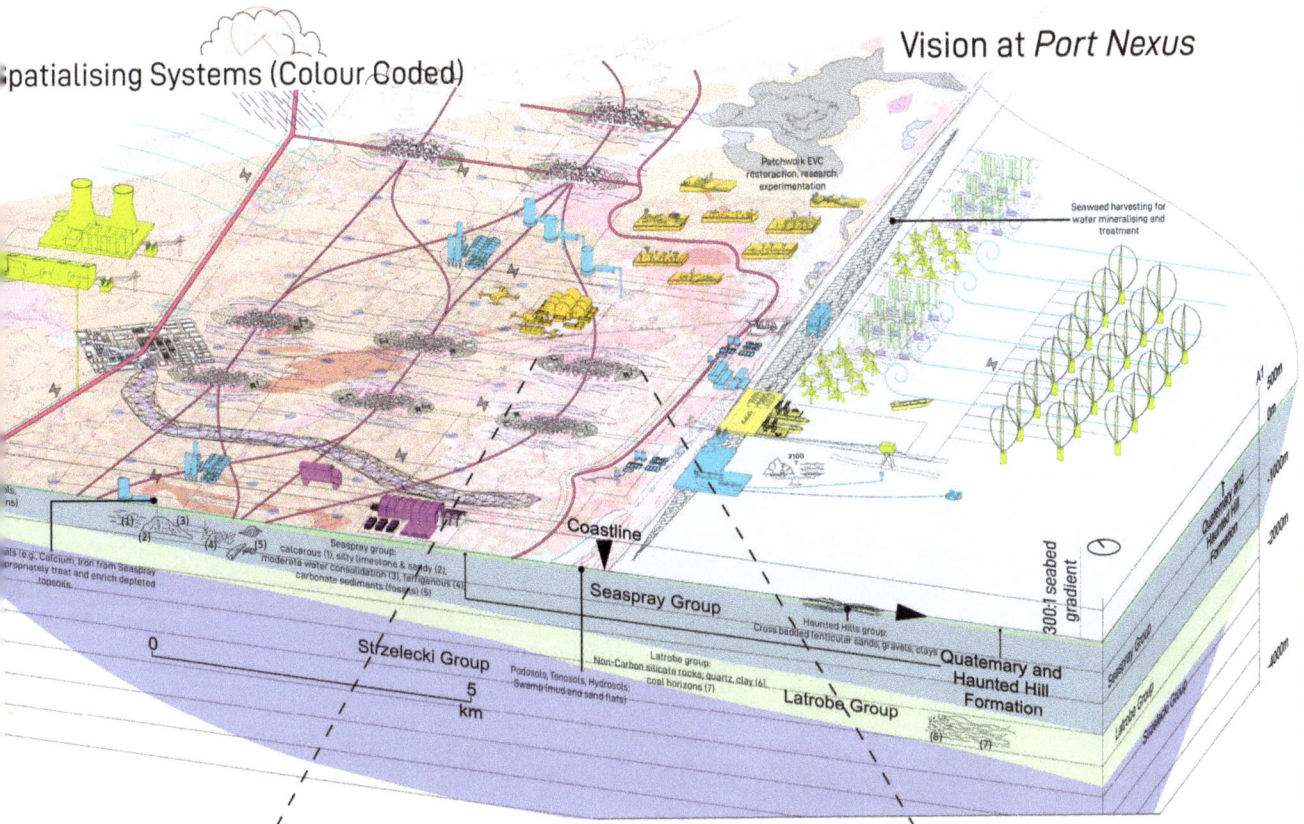

Cluster city node (In Concert)

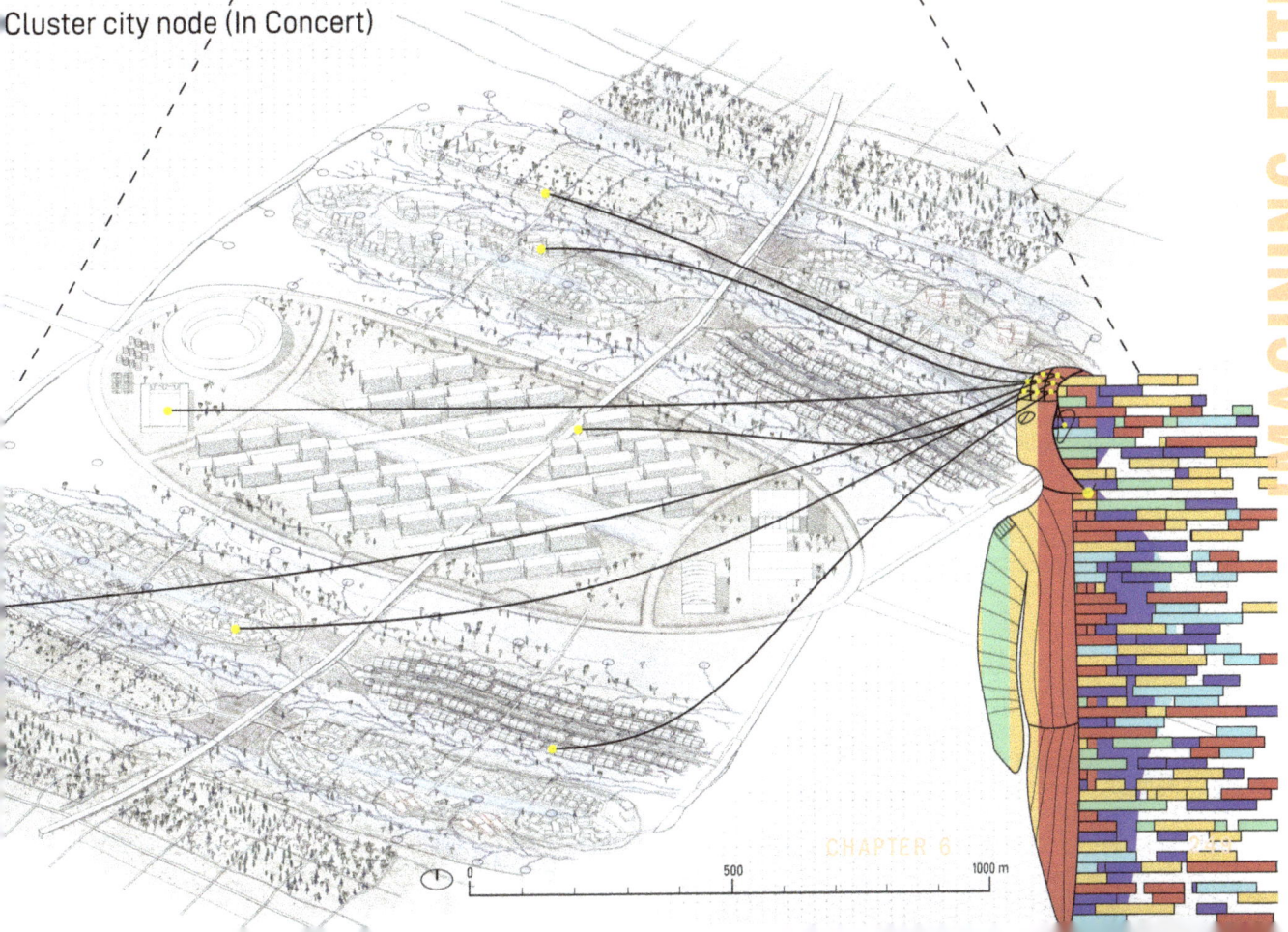

0

500

1000 m

IMAGINING FUTURE URBAN SETTLEMENT

FIGURE 6.12: NOMADISM 2.0.

identity: the experience of a new Australian horizon.

This new Australian horizon of intimacy and prospect can further privilege non-human species by questioning what it means to live above the earth with a minimal footprint. Port Nexus supports this exploration into new modes of dwelling (Figure 6.12). Systems of the 2100 context help define and enable such explorations.

Connection with kinship and the other has assisted the decentralising of self, whilst illuminating impermanency and detachment. This introspection questions patterns of habit and ownership and promotes bodily protection through the impermanent or nomadic dwelling.

To promote the land to do more, Port Nexus is a field of growth, using 'cyborg-water', research and land management to modulate humanity and non-humanity while enabling multi-species mobility and kinship.

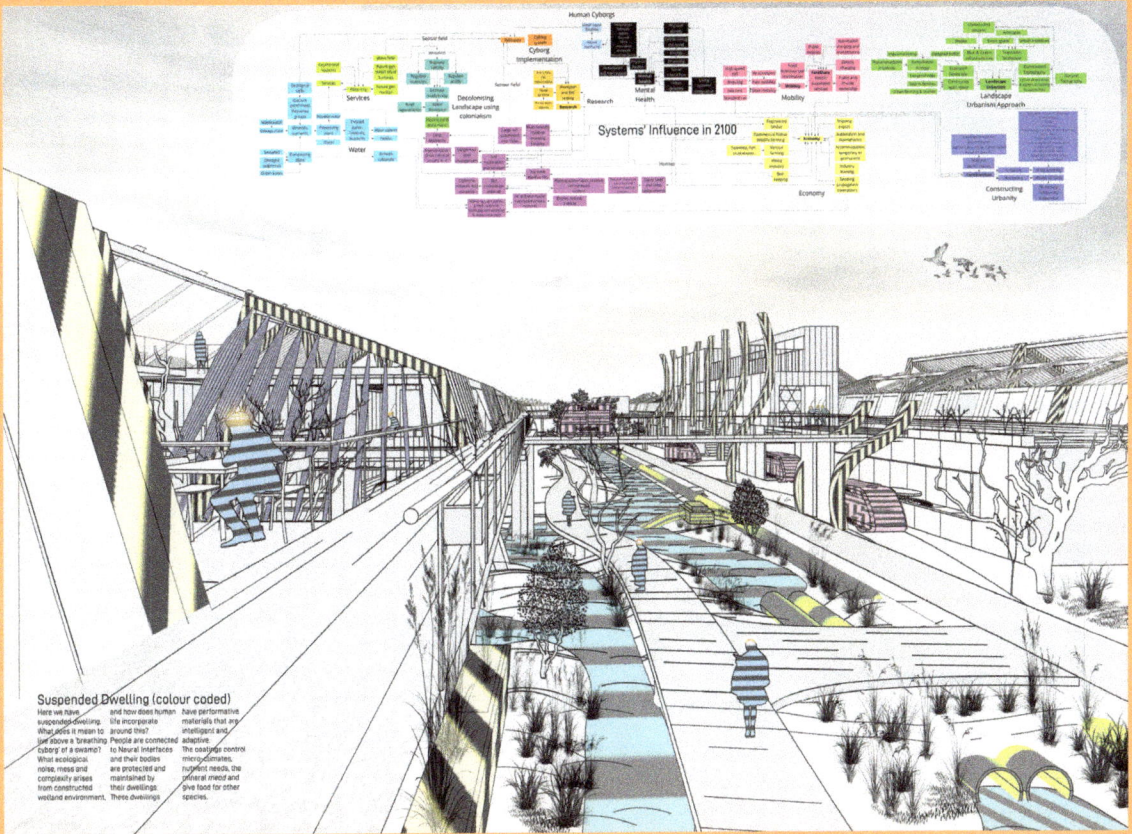

Suspended Dwelling (colour coded)

Here we have suspended dwelling. What does it mean to live above a 'breathing' cyborg of a swamp? What ecological noise, mess and complexity arises from constructed wetland environment. These dwellings and how does human life incorporate around this? People are connected to Neural Interfaces and their bodies are protected and maintained by their dwellings. have performative materials that are intelligent and adaptive. The coatings control micro-climates, nutrient needs, the mineral mend and give food for other species.

FIGURE 6.13: SUSPENDED DWELLING.

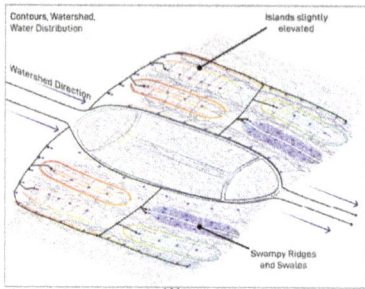

Contours, Watershed, Water Distribution

Watershed Direction

Islands slightly elevated

Swampy Ridges and Swales

Water

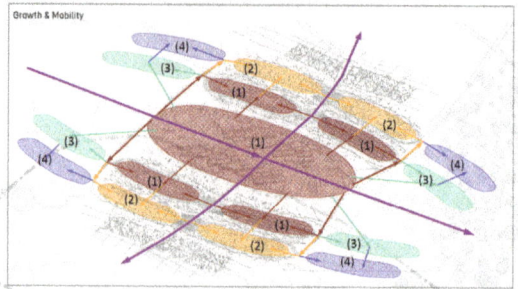

Growth & Mobility

(4) (3) (2) (1) (1) (2) (1) (3) (3) (4) (1) (1) (2) (2) (1) (3) (4) (2) (3) (4)

Phasing

Legend - Colour Coded EVCs

T - Tree
S - Shrub (Sm, Med)
H - Herb

G - Graminoid
GF - Ground Fern
R - Rush

Sc - Scrambler
Se - Sedge
Su - Succulent

100x100m estimate density - per hectare

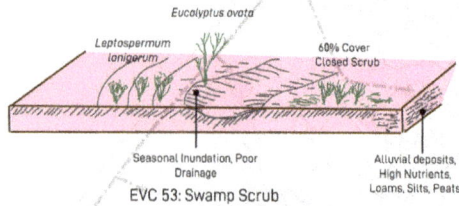

Eucalyptus ovata

Leptospermum lanigerum

60% Cover Closed Scrub

Seasonal Inundation, Poor Drainage

Alluvial deposits, High Nutrients, Loams, Silts, Peats

EVC 53: Swamp Scrub

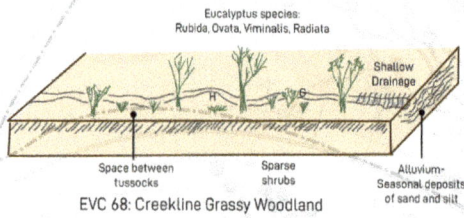

Eucalyptus species: Rubida, Ovata, Viminalis, Radiata

Shallow Drainage

Space between tussocks

Sparse shrubs

Alluvium- Seasonal deposits of sand and silt

EVC 68: Creekline Grassy Woodland

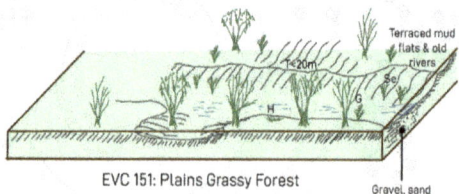

T<20m

Terraced mud flats & old rivers

Gravel, sand clay

EVC 151: Plains Grassy Forest

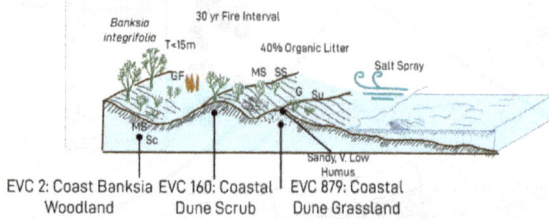

Banksia integrifolia
T<15m

30 yr Fire Interval

40% Organic Litter

MS SS

Salt Spray

Sandy, V. Low Humus

EVC 2: Coast Banksia Woodland

EVC 160: Coastal Dune Scrub

EVC 879: Coastal Dune Grassland

Island Low Point
RL 7.0

Ridge Peak
RL 7.0

More Private perspective (Page 4) Nomadism

Ridge Peak
RL 8.5

Water Retention Base
RL 7.5

Island Peak
RL 9.0

Ridge Peak
RL 8.5

Ridge Peak
RL 6.5

Highway Underpass
RL 1.0

1x1km Plan

Indicative Section

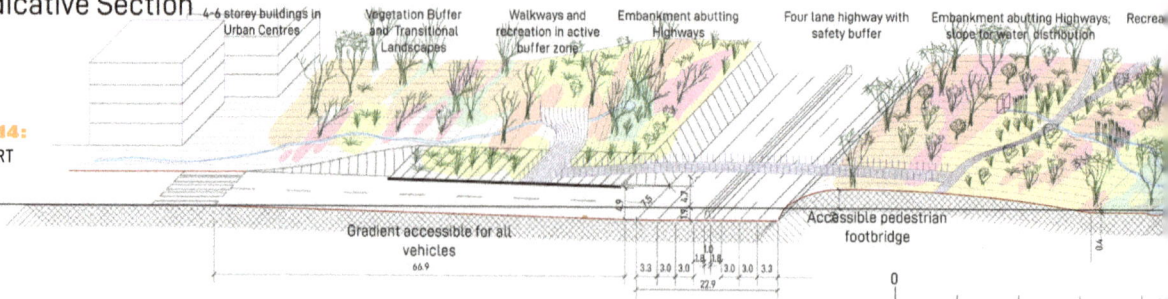

4-6 storey buildings in Urban Centres

Vegetation Buffer and Transitional Landscapes

Walkways and recreation in active buffer zone

Embankment abutting Highways

Four lane highway with safety buffer

Embankment abutting Highways; slope for water distribution

Recrea

Gradient accessible for all vehicles
66.9

Accessible pedestrian footbridge

3.3 3.0 3.0 3.0 3.3
22.9

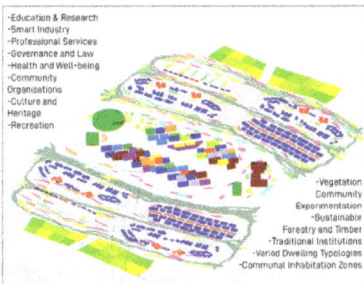

Programming

- Education & Research
- Smart Industry
- Professional Services
- Governance and Law
- Health and Well-being
- Community Organisations
- Culture and Heritage
- Recreation

- Vegetation
- Community
- Experimentation
- Sustainable
- Forestry and Timber
- Traditional Institutions
- Varied Dwelling Typologies
- Communal Inhabitation Zones

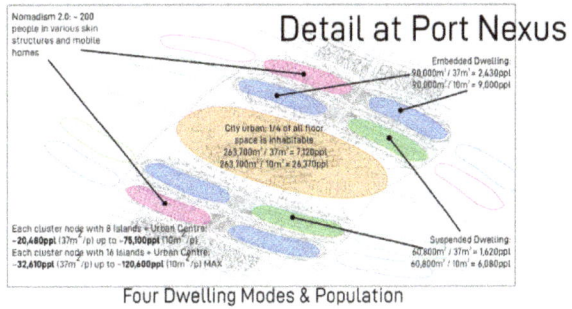

Four Dwelling Modes & Population

Detail at Port Nexus

Nomadism 2.0: ~ 200 people in various skin structures and mobile homes

Embedded Dwelling:
90,000m² / 37m² = 2,430ppl
90,000m² / 10m² = 9,000ppl

City urban: 1/4 of all floor space is inhabitable
263,700m² / 37m² = 7,128ppl
263,700m² / 10m² = 26,370ppl

Suspended Dwelling:
60,800m² / 37m² = 1,620ppl
60,800m² / 10m² = 6,080ppl

Each cluster node with 8 islands + Urban Centre:
~20,480ppl (37m²/pl) up to ~75,100ppl (10m²/pl)
Each cluster node with 16 islands + Urban Centre:
~32,610ppl (37m²/pl) up to ~120,600ppl (10m²/pl) MAX

Forestry Landscape
RL 5.0

Ridge Peak
RL 6.5

Highway Road Level
RL 11.2

Ridge Peak
RL 6.5

Water Retention Base
RL 5.5

Island Peak
RL 7.0

Landscape
RL 4.5

More Public perspective (Page 3)
Suspended dwelling.

250   500 m

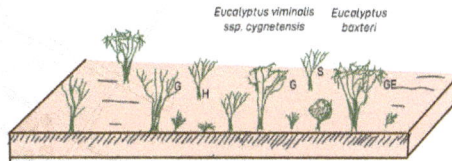

Eucalyptus viminalis ssp. cygnetensis   Eucalyptus baxteri

EVC 3: Damp Sands Herb-Rich Woodland

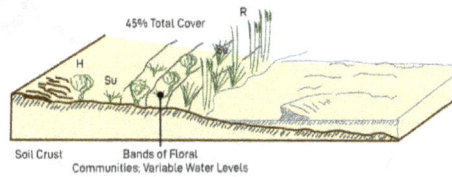

45% Total Cover

Soil Crust   Bands of Floral Communities; Variable Water Levels

EVC 9: Coastal Saltmarsh

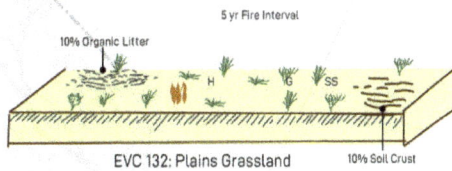

5 yr Fire Interval

10% Organic Litter

EVC 132: Plains Grassland   10% Soil Crust

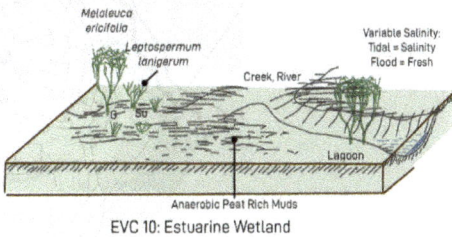

Melaleuca ericifolia
Leptospermum lanigerum

Variable Salinity:
Tidal = Salinity
Flood = Fresh

Creek, River

Lagoon

Anaerobic Peat Rich Muds

EVC 10: Estuarine Wetland

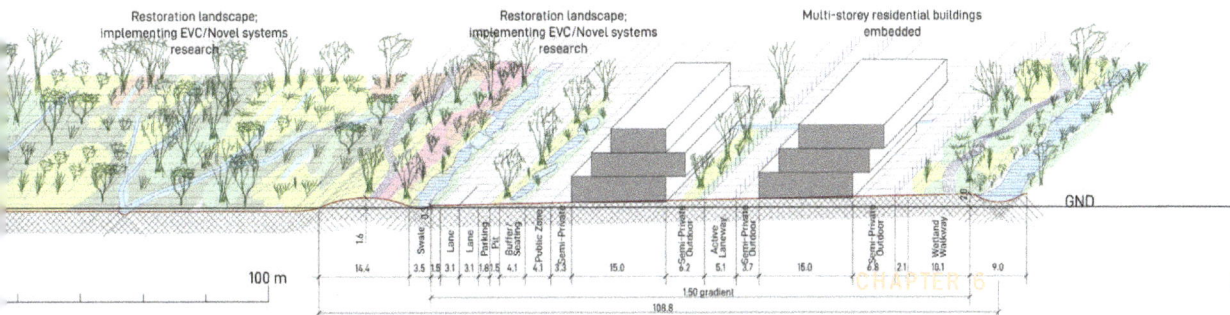

Restoration landscape; implementing EVC/Novel systems research

Restoration landscape; implementing EVC/Novel systems research

Multi-storey residential buildings embedded

GND

100 m

1:50 gradient

108.8

4. WHAT'S MINE?

Entrants: Gemma Robinson and Maisie Matthews

WHERE IS YOUR CITY LOCATED?

Lima South, Benalla, Victoria

Our proposal aims to connect abandoned quarry sites across Victoria and, potentially, nationally and repurpose them. Our first city focuses explicitly on the LS Quarry on Williams Road south of Benalla in north-central Victoria. In the surrounding area of Lima South, there are more than eight quarry sites within a 60 kilometre radius, and the linkages between these abandoned quarry sites form the crux of our 'subscription cities'.

WHAT IS THE IDEAL POPULATION OF YOUR CITY?

60,000

WHAT IS THE IMPETUS BEHIND YOUR CITY?

In 2100, structures will grow from abandoned quarry and industrial sites, revitalising, recycling and rehabilitating forgotten locations. A re-framing of landscape design and architecture to promote context and living on Country will enhance how we live and connect. Living primarily in free-standing dwellings, Australians have the capacity to individualise their homes more than other home-owning nations. We want to allow for a capacity of individualisation as people can manipulate their houses whilst they live in them. A monthly payment of varying tiers will allow people to move and relocate between municipalities. As circumstances change, so can the way one lives, yet prices remain predictable and affordable. Short-term and long-term solutions are accounted for, and a sense of community will be prioritised at all levels. 'What's mine?' is a speculative interrogation into what the future of Australian cities could look like when they address the technological, environmental and cultural shifts within our country. As our requirements and world change, so too should our cities, and so should our dreams.

DESCRIBE THE DESIGN OF THE CITY

Landscapes and rural settings will be preserved and rehabilitated while hosting city lifestyles (Figure 6.15). We have chosen to repurpose old quarry sites as we believe these sites will no longer be in use in the year 2100. The case site's abandoned rock crushers and machinery inform our architecture and form private and public space base structures. The previously excavated and scarred landscape will be utilised and rehabilitated using native species from the Ecological Vegetation Classes (pre-1750: Grassy Dry Forest). The history of this site will be honoured and will add to the character of the architecture and experience.

Types of subscriptions will vary and evolve depending on users. Subscription options include traveller subscription (renewed six monthly for those who intend to travel between the revitalised locations and stay for periods shorter than two months in each location); single subscription (renewed bi-monthly); couple subscription (renewed bi-monthly); concession subscription, which can also be applied to other subscriptions (renewed bi-monthly); short-term/trial subscription (for those who may only wish to trial or stay in a location for one month or less), and a small/big family subscription (renewed bi-monthly). These 'homes' will come fully furnished and be used like hotels. An additional benefit is that they can accommodate someone on holiday or requiring emergency housing.

HOW DOES YOUR CITY EMBODY AN ALTERNATIVE AUSTRALIAN DREAM?

The quintessential Australian dream is a traditional housing model, including a quarter-acre block, single detached dwelling, a hills-hoist clothesline and a back garden. When this dream is interrogated in our current context, it is metropolitan, capital-oriented and Western. As home and land ownership over the past 80 years has become increasingly unattainable, our cities have rapidly expanded to engulf the city fringes as people attempt to fulfil this dream. Our cities are beset with environmental problems, and the lines of inequality are only becoming more and more apparent. The traditional Australian housing model will not be feasible for the future, but what if we flipped the narrative for our future? What if homeownership does not have to be the goal?

Our proposal considers how we lived in the twentieth century and how our lives are becoming more subscription-based – our music, movies and recreational activities. What

FIGURE 6.15: WHAT'S MINE?
SITE PLAN.

2022

2080

2100

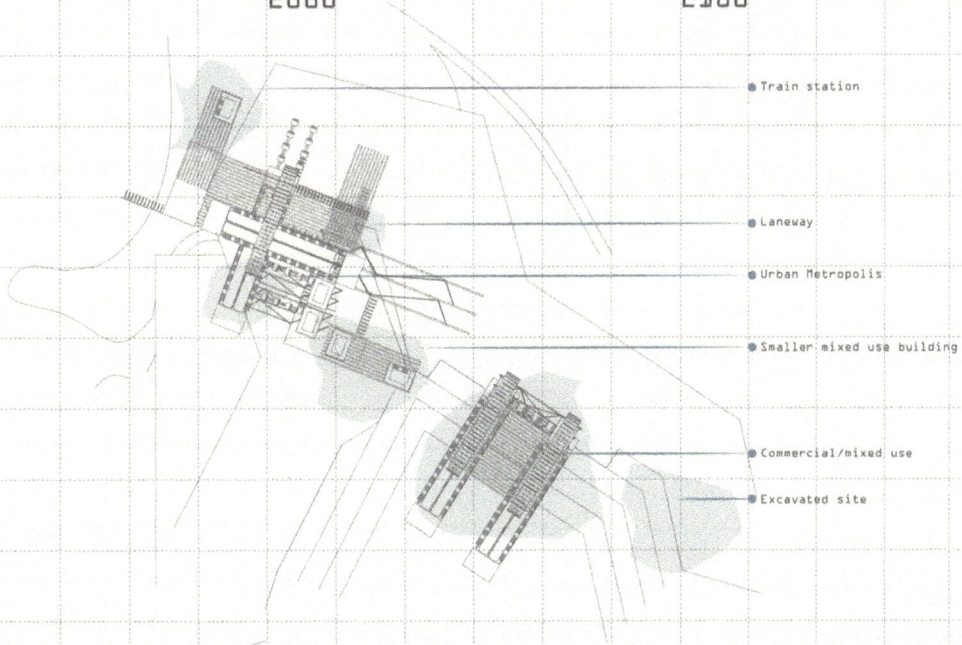

- Train station
- Laneway
- Urban Metropolis
- Smaller mixed use building
- Commercial/mixed use
- Excavated site

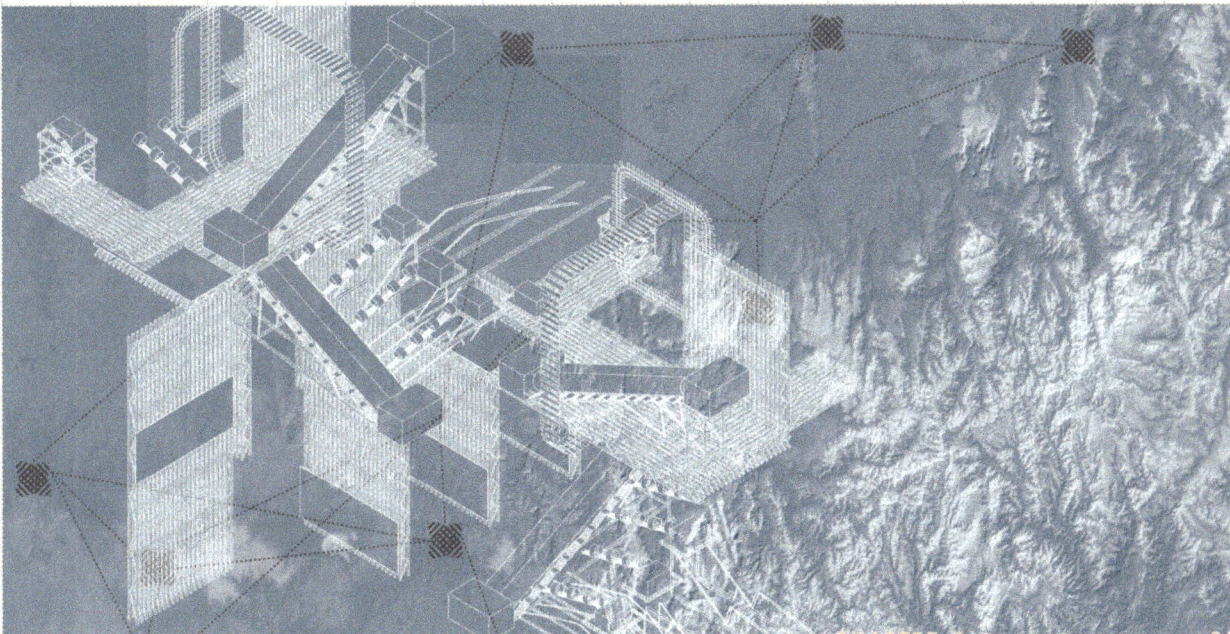

WHAT?S MINE?

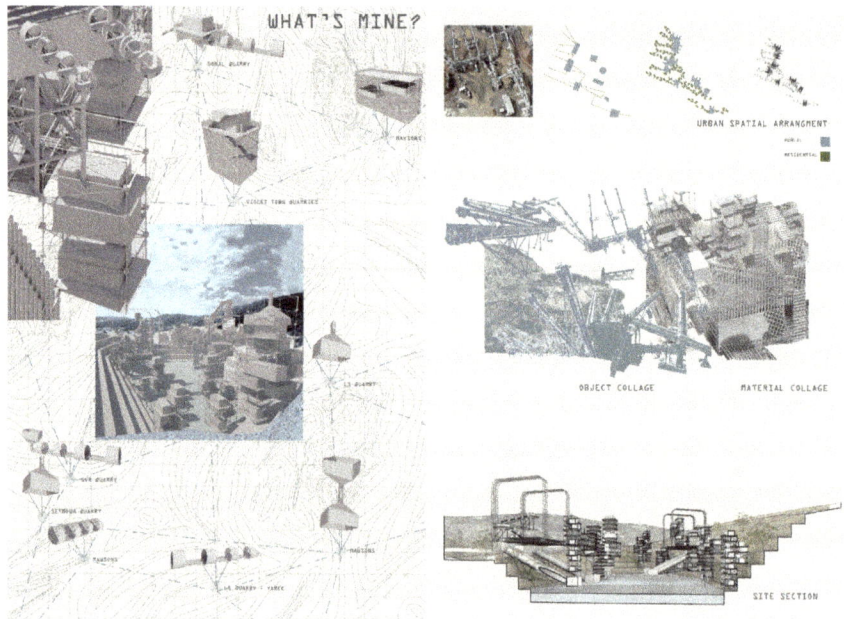

if our housing and cities followed a similar model? What if we lived in a subscription-based city, where a monthly contribution allows us to live in any participating municipality? Could a typology of housing address our changing notions of home ownership: a more flexible, accessible housing model, rather than the traditional mortgage-based purchase or deposit-based contractual rentals (Figure 6.16)?[4]

The idea of subscription living moves users away from ideas of profit, ownership, excess and permanence. It instead focuses more on shared success and living with what you need at a reasonable cost. This model would also buy you greater flexibility and quality. For example, the flexibility to come and go at short notice, to upgrade and downsize as life circumstances inevitably change, and to readily move locations and travel to different cities – countries even – with the same provider. Competition would come in the form of the quality of the communal spaces, amenities, event programs and travel opportunities.[5] In this case, 'leasing' does not result in one individual profiting at the cost of another, and no one person owns everything. The recurring payments will ultimately be ploughed back into the community and be spent on improving the lives and living conditions of all in the subscription model.

4   Merlin
5   Merlin

Our proposal speaks to an emerging philosophy concerning our relationship with ownership, possession and place. That feeling of belonging, community or sense of place no longer depends on owning bricks and mortar in a specific and fixed location.[6] Instead, we propose an Australian Dream that should become an attainable reality that embraces cohabitation, living on Country, and unsubscribing from home ownership.

DISCUSSION

These new settlement proposals speak to the scenarios canvassed in this book: Green Rail to the satellite city thinking, Port Nexus to the rail-based city, and What's Mine and Transit City to variations on new inland city propositions. A policymaker might be left scratching their head over how such new city visions could be reconciled with the reality of business-as-usual planning and development in our cities. Indeed, the visions tap into the tendency of romantic new town planning, which has 'some magic that fires the imagination, stirring some Promethean impulse to create a better place and way of life, a calm and healthy community of crystalline completeness'.[7] While challenging to reconcile with current practice, they are nonetheless representative of the kind of joined-up thinking and deeper cultural, social, economic and environmental rationales required of urban design interventions in this century of challenge, with a sense of the aesthetic being of second-order importance. In the next chapter, we weave together the divergent strands of this book to arrive at some ideas and recommendations for moving forward.

6   Merlin
7   Alonso, 4

IMAGE BY THE AUTHORS.

7

MOVING FORWARD

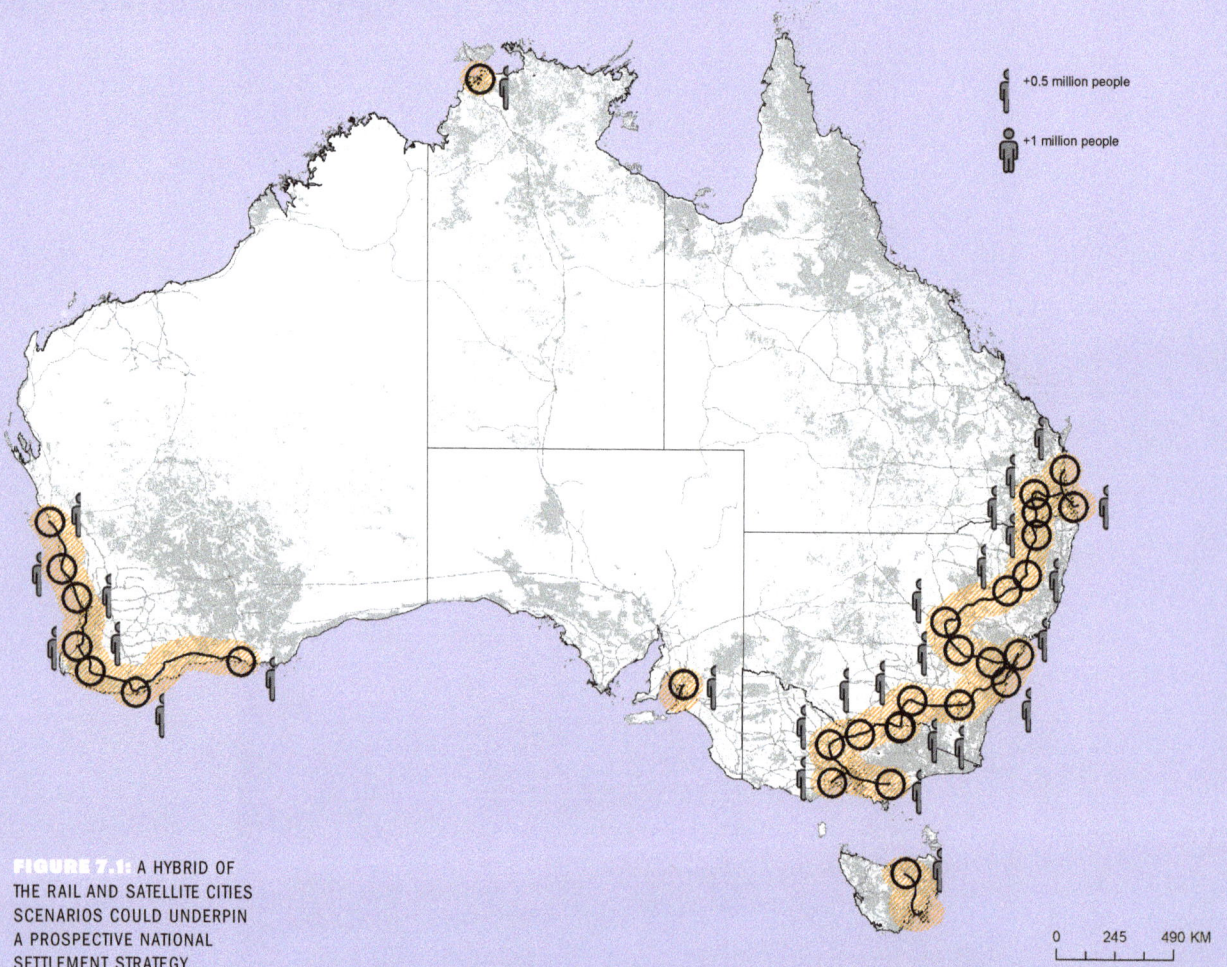

FIGURE 7.1: A HYBRID OF THE RAIL AND SATELLITE CITIES SCENARIOS COULD UNDERPIN A PROSPECTIVE NATIONAL SETTLEMENT STRATEGY.

+0.5 million people

+1 million people

0   245   490 KM

BACKGROUND

Our book has ventured into the question of Australia's long-term urban settlement. It has highlighted the many factors requiring deliberation, apparent even at the broad-brush scale considered here, and, in the process, makes a case for the national importance of our urban futures and the need to take this on board within some form of national settlement strategy (NSS). The findings reported indicate that the Australian public favours two possible settlement patterns: satellite cities orbiting the state capital cities (the Satellite Cities scenario) and regional cities on rail links connecting the capital cities (the Rail Cities scenario). There was also a relative consensus among the experts surveyed who rated these scenarios first and third, although opinion was more divided for some of the other scenarios. While the survey findings indicate a groundswell of support for population decentralisation away from the capital cities, particularly Melbourne and Sydney, the converse of compounding population growth in these major cities was loathed by laypeople. Indeed, the two scenarios that adopted this approach (Mega Cities and Secondary Capital Cities) were ranked last and second-last in the community survey, respectively. Of course, as we have suggested, there could also be national-scale NIMBYism at work. Moreover, it is intriguing that the boosted Secondary Capital Cities ranked second, not second-last, in the expert survey[1]; perhaps this is because the experts have more faith in planning systems to deliver liveable growth in these cities than laypeople.[2]

1 Bolleter et al., 'Evaluating Scenarios'
2 Bolleter et al., 'Long-Term Settlement Scenarios'

Regardless, the findings have clear implications for current state and federal government planning in Australia. The most popular scenario, Satellite Cities, resembles (to some degree) the previous Morrison government's proposed transport-driven decentralisation program for 'fast rail projects' to improve regional connectivity to the state capital cities (particularly Melbourne and Sydney). More recently, it aligns with the polycentric regionalism under investigation by the NSW Government and catalysed by its Greater Cities Commission (now subsumed within the state Department of Planning and Environment), which lifted its initial gaze as the Greater Sydney Commission beyond metropolitan Sydney to consider more seriously the interconnections with Newcastle to the north and Wollongong to the south – mega-region strategic thinking.[3] This planning generally conforms with our respondents' preference for satellite city development orbiting capital cities.

Notably, the planned satellites are not the neat greenfield 'moons' propounded by the garden cities and new town movements that produced the London new towns. While they would likely entail greenfield development, these are essentially expanded and more connected existing towns and communities within a multi-centred urban quilt. Southeast Queensland, as an urban region, stretches from the Sunshine Coast via metropolitan Brisbane to the Gold Coast - already a formidable 200 kilometre city1[4]; Sydney from the Illawarra to the Hunter; while Melbourne is interlinked with an arguably neater halo of regional centres.

The second-most-popular scenario, Rail Cities, is somewhat reminiscent of the 2010 federal (Rudd) government plan for high-speed rail along the eastern seaboard connecting Melbourne, Canberra, Sydney and Brisbane.[5] The Albanese government also moved closer to high-speed rail with its High-Speed Rail Authority. In the first instance, the authority is prioritising feasibility assessment and corridor planning for the Sydney to Newcastle section of the high-speed rail network and, subsequently, will advance plans for other sections of a potential larger network, eventually connecting Brisbane to Melbourne, with stops in Canberra, Sydney and regional centres (electoral fortunes allowing of course).[6]

In conjunction with the regional dispersion of migrants, this infrastructure planning generally conforms with our respondents' preference – and sometimes the preferences of migrants themselves – for population growth to occur in regional areas.[7] However, the initial investigation still seems metropolitan-focused. The more extensive possibilities for new and expanded regional centres on longer-distance high-speed inter-city links – advocated by the CLARA consortium[8] and Weller and Bolleter,[9] and which our Rail Cities scenario accommodated – still seems a very distant possibility.

3   Greater Cities Commission
4   Spearritt
5   AECOM
6   King, 'High Speed Rail Gathers Speed'
7   Klocker et al.
8   Consolidated Land and Rail Australia
9   Bolleter and Weller

At the other end of the scale, the lowly ranked Northern Cities scenario reflects the previous Liberal-National federal government's planning to populate northern Australia, which worryingly remains on the national settlement agenda to some degree.[10] Indeed, the Minister for Northern Australia in 2022 affirmed the Albanese government's commitment to northern Australia's development, backed by the government's $5 billion Northern Australia Infrastructure Facility (NAIF).[11] The Albanese government returned to an infrastructure-project-driven approach rather than eye-glazing new demographics.[12] However, if our respondents' judgement is correct, and factoring in the suitability analysis for urban development, any ambitions to deliver substantial population growth in northern Australia will likely stall.

The Mega Cities scenario ranked eighth in the public survey[13] and even a lowly sixth in the expert survey,[14] a concerning outcome given the scenario's close relationship to existing policy. Indeed, the Victorian and New South Wales state governments have metropolitan plans anticipating significant population surges in Melbourne and Sydney by mid-century. Our survey results indicate that this approach to accommodating long-term population growth is, to put it mildly, not wildly popular and is likely to entrench contestation around further urban densification and expansion.

Of the eight scenarios we have tabled, there is probably no one 'correct' scenario for steering Australia's twenty-first-century urbanisation. Indeed, they were simplified to begin with to form the basis for assessment in the national Plan *My* Australia survey. Instead, the answer likely lies in a hybridised approach that utilises the best aspects of scenarios 1 and 2, factoring in determinants arising from changing conditions related to climate, economic fortunes, governance, geopolitics and disruptive transport technologies, amongst a host of others. The preceding figure (Figure 7.1) lays out a sketch of this vision, but is not the vision itself, which would require the expertise of state and federal government departments, engineers, economists, planners, urban designers, ecologists, statisticians and sociologists, amongst others.

Undoubtedly, some readers will detest all the scenarios we evaluated and consider the idea of a 'Big Australia' as asking for trouble. Nonetheless, regardless of ideological stances, if projections for Australia's population to double to 53,600,000 by the early twenty-second century are borne out, we have little choice but to adopt a scenario or, more realistically, a combination of scenarios. Alternatively, if we sleepwalk into this calamity, population growth will likely compound in our capital cities. As a result, Sydney and Melbourne will slide downhill into megacity status with a population of 10,000,000 or more – with the attendant liveability issues, such as chronic congestion, lack of housing

10 Australian Government, Our North, Our Future

11 Northern Australia Infrastructure Facility, 'New Government Commits to Northern Australia Development'

12 Northern Australia Infrastructure Facility, 'Investing for Impact across the North'

13 Bolleter et al., 'Long-Term Settlement Scenarios'

14 Bolleter et al., 'Evaluating Scenarios'

affordability, pollution and declining access to nature, amongst others. Of course, we could go down this path, and plenty of countries have. However, we believe that compromising the liveability of our capital cities in this way will serve none of our interests well.[15] So, what is an alternative path?

TOWARDS NATIONAL SETTLEMENT PLANNING

While usually overshadowed by policy discourse around defence, employment, social security, health and the cost of living, the urban environment is vital and often the connective tissue between singular sectoral concerns. Many considerations come into play that can blur just how urban policy can be best targeted and effective, but to specifically deliver a hybrid of both favoured settlement patterns, a national settlement framework must help coordinate planning and development considerations across state borders.[16]

WHY AUSTRALIA NEEDS A NATIONAL SETTLEMENT STRATEGY

Urbanisation pressures globally have seen a spate of advocacy for developing national urban policies (NUP) to steer urban and regional planning strategies.[17] Indeed, the Organisation for Economic Co-operation and Development (OECD) has identified 162 countries with national-level urban policies, although in different forms, at diverse development stages and with contrasting thematic foci.[18]

Fair enough, but why are they important? NUPs are considered a vital component of policy frameworks to deliver sustainability, productivity and liveability, as well as to implement global agendas, notably the United Nations (UN) Sustainable Development Goals.[19] Such agendas are furthered by NUPs which can align different sectoral policies and ensures that all urban policies support (and don't hinder) such overarching programs.

15 Bolleter, 'The Ghost Cities of Australia'
16 Freestone et al., Australian Urban Policy
17 United Nations, 'National Urban Policy'
18 OECD, UN Habitat and Cities Alliance
19 United Nations, 'Draft Outcome Document'

In mid-2024 the Labor Government released for consultation a draft NUP aimed at establishing 'a shared vision for sustainable growth in our cities and suburbs' and to better integrate Australian Government actions into urban policy making. This document ranged widely across numerous challenges, well-intentioned objectives and principles, and a host of possible actions. The initiative was seen as 'an opportunity to consider our historical and contemporary settlement patterns'.[20] In November 2024 after consultation with key stakeholders (especially state and territory governments) and invitations for public submissions a final NUP was released. This is a high-level document endorsing sensible goals to make urban places 'liveable and equitable, productive and innovative, and sustainable and resilient' and a suite of best implementation principles to realise these aspirations in practice.[21]

While a welcome but politically low-key initiative the NUP does not venture into canvassing any kind of national plan of settlement although specific strategic directions have regional implications and funding for special initiatives is available nationally. The opportunity was not taken to advance thinking in that bigger direction undoubtedly because of Australia's multi-tier federal governance with the state and territories being the major urban governments for their jurisdictions. However, this did not inhibit a parliamentary inquiry chaired by John Alexander MP in 2018 to recommend a 'national plan of settlement, providing a national vision for our cities and regions across the next fifty years'.[22]

The case can and still clearly has to be made for the value of a national settlement strategy (NSS) to help guide macro-level decisions about desirable long term patterns of urbanisation. Some people might perceive an NSS as a federal government violation of state and local domains, all from the incestuous isolation of Canberra. However, notably, an NSS would not supplant local urban and regional policies but complement them to create the necessary coordinating conditions for sustainable urban development.[23] Nor can it be so imperially comprehensive that it is simultaneously everything and nothing. The particular dimension we are stressing here is moving towards an optimum long-range, continental-scale settlement pattern supported by state, regional and metropolitan planning policies. Australia has never had that. Only briefly in 1972, when the McMahon government established the short-lived National and Regional Development Authority, was that seriously entertained, but more as a political manoeuvre, not accorded deep and appropriate diligence, and ultimately bequeathing the rather half-hearted Growth Centres program.

20 Australian Government, National Urban Policy: Consultation Draft
21 Australian Government, National Urban Policy
22 Australian Government, Building Up & Moving Out, xxiii.
23 United Nations, 'National Urban Policy'

Given Australia's escalating growth pressures following and driven by the COVID-19 interregnum, there is increasing recognition of the benefits of national planning for cities and regions that would tackle the Australian urban system as a dynamic integrated network of settlements. This frame of reference was conspicuous in the 1970s and 1980s but has seemingly fallen out of fashion.[24] However, the result is that there is effectively no national land use and infrastructure planning in Australia, yet many issues we confront (such as climate change) demand this scale of response. While the federal government has a role in funding projects and services, implementing major planning and infrastructure happens virtually exclusively at the state level.[25] We have a series of well-intentioned ideas with no prioritisation, no strategic intent and few objectives.[26] A dangerous absence in our uncertain times.

There is a range of economic reasons why the federal government should assume part of the responsibility for safeguarding the health of our existing and future urban regions. Firstly, the Commonwealth raises the vast bulk of tax and excise revenue generated and collected in the cities. Sydney, for example, is a prodigiously crucial national asset. As a proper global city, it generates a large share of national income for the nation. As such, enduring problems, such as Sydney's sclerotic circulatory system, need ongoing surgery.[27] Sydney's problems entail a nation-building task beyond the capacity of a state government alone, and this has been recognised in the Western Parkland City initiative emerging around the second Sydney airport – a federal asset.[28] We need to manage Australia's global cities in the national interest and ensure that some of the fruit of their new productivity is redistributed to assist other regions to grow in economic potency.[29]

INADEQUACIES OF EXISTING PLANNING REGIMES

The federal government must link up its initiatives – population research, high-speed rail, housing, biodiversity, employment, migration, climate change and energy – within a strategic overall framework. Supportive of initiatives for elevating city and regional planning into nation-building enterprises at a national scale, the Planning Institute of Australia highlights that the problem in perpetuating a spatially fragmented approach is that state, territory and local governments are trying to plan for a future where they 'all have different views about our common future'. The result is a 'collective coverage of plans looking like a patchwork quilt' (Figure 7.2).[30]

Indeed, planning frameworks are not well coordinated between the various tiers of government (e.g., national-to-state and state-to-city level planning). This situation

24 Bourne and Simmons; Burnley
25 Seamer
26 Haratsis
27 Gleeson 'Rescuing Urban Regions'
28 Gleeson 'Rescuing Urban Regions'
29 Gleeson 'Rescuing Urban Regions'
30 Planning Institute of Australia

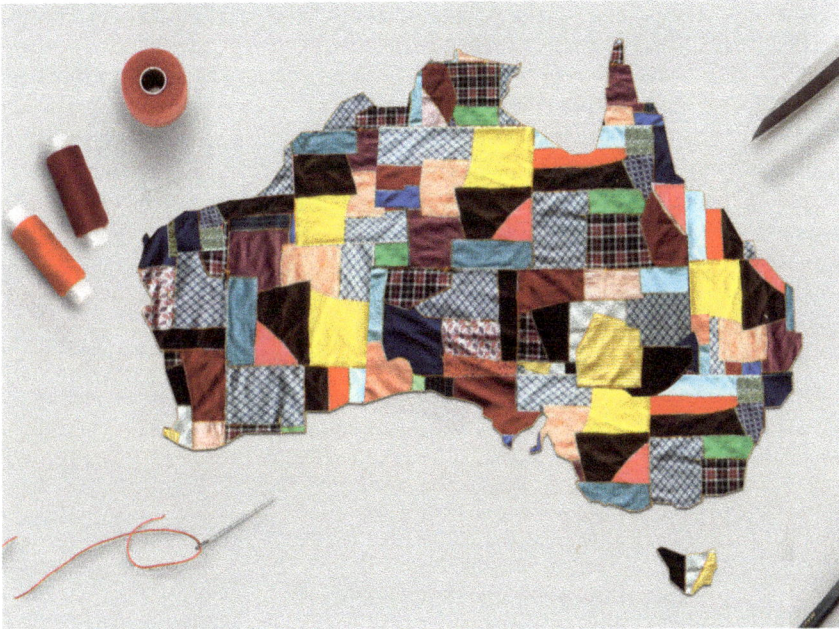

FIGURE 7.2: AUSTRALIA'S CURRENT PLANNING, AT THE NATIONAL SCALE, IS LIKE A PATCHWORK QUILT. IMAGE BY SHUBHAM GAUTAM.

is understandable because policymakers do not comprehensively review strategies at set intervals, but rather according to different political and economic cycles and circumstances within their jurisdictions. As a result, different policy documents address different geographic scales of jurisdiction and institutional rubrics and work to different timeframes (like a house full of old clocks) and projections.[31] We also note that it is part of Australia's grand political tradition that, when a difficult decision is made, the buck is passed from one level to another – generally federal to state and then back again.[32]

State government planning frameworks for managing population growth and related settlement patterns also have a comparatively low capacity to absorb population growth, sometimes not commensurate with higher-end Australian Bureau of Statistics forecasts. Moreover, much state-scale planning – where it exists – is not the product of extensive community engagement, so directives at that level, while capturing state-driven objectives, are not necessarily aligned with community preferences and sentiment.

31 Bolleter et al., "Preparing Australia:"
32 Aitken

State government planning for population growth in the capitals typically focuses on metropolitan infill and greenfield development. The latter, often pejoratively known as 'sprawl', is regarded as a necessary evil accommodating popular preference and housing shortages. What has often been missing in these essentially binary policy debates is the discussion of a third way: population decentralisation to satellite and regional centres. This situation is partly due to the failure of the growth centres within the guise of the new cities program idealistically launched by the Whitlam government, but with a muddled rationale disconnected from a complete understanding of economic drivers.[33] This policy failure casts a long shadow over similar attempts, which were also subsequently undermined by neoliberalism, the prevailing political orthodoxy since the 1980s. In this canon, government-sponsored population decentralisation is regarded as ineffective against centralising economic forces, and from this perspective, has been frequently viewed as a 'waste of expenditure'.[34] Nonetheless, the 'urban sprinkle' of regional centres, some growing quickly due to their environmental assets and proximity to major metropolitan centres, are crying out to be embedded in some sort of NSS.

HOW A NATIONAL STRATEGY COULD INFLUENCE SETTLEMENT PATTERNS

But how could an NSS seek to shape settlement patterns, given that market forces exert such a tremendous influence on the eventual shape of urban settlements? In partnership with the states, territories, city commissions and local governments, an NSS could be devised and deployed to influence settlement patterns in at least two main ways.[35] First, national guidance can delineate future urban growth areas and establish spatial limits for existing cities to effectively reduce the growth rate of city populations.[36] Second, it can coordinate federal, state and local government investments in enabling infrastructure, land development, urban services and employment generation to attract investors and incentivise the population to migrate and relocate to these areas.[37] This kind of NSS could be the basis for 'more logical, coordinated investment decisions at the national level'.[38] One example could be coordinating high-speed rail lines connecting state or territory capitals.

33 Seamer
34 Painter, 344
35 Gleeson, Lifeboat Cities; Lacquian
36 Haratsis
37 Laquian
38 Beatley, 'The Vision of Green Urbanism'

REQUIREMENTS OF AN AUSTRALIAN
SETTLEMENT STRATEGY

In contrast to the relatively short planning horizons at a state level, national policy focused on settlement should have a planning horizon equal to credible population projections, which for Australian capital cities is the 2060s.[39] This timeline is recognised in the Commonwealth's Intergenerational Report, published in mid-2023.[40] Such a planning horizon will address the situation where government decision-making is typically reacting to yesterday's problems rather than pre-empting tomorrow's challenges.[41] Settlement pattern planning is a very long-term process that is poorly understood, particularly by governments.[42] An Australian NSS needs to be long-range in outlook to ensure it looks beyond today's issues towards those that might, in time, be critical but are only just emerging. Likewise, successive federal governments must commit to a vision that will not bear fruit until long after their period in office ends.[43] It is no small ask of politicians wedded to short-term electoral cycles. Brian Haratsis's vision of a series of regional-economic plans spanning the continent to effect a transition toward a new national grid of cities underscores the importance of a partnership between the Commonwealth, the states, the private sector and the community.[44]

Policymakers should ensure that a prospective NSS that envisages value-adding interventions into the national settlement pattern is based on a comprehensive suitability analysis of prevailing climatic, environmental, economic and infrastructural factors. This book offers a first cut of this sort of analysis at a continental scale. Detailed studies are currently missing. This lacuna is critical because urbanisation without appropriate research-driven analysis can lead to urban development outcomes that incur ongoing environmental, societal or economic costs. Poorly conceived planning can fail to manifest in positive urban outcomes yet still incur high economic costs.[45]

Given Australia's risks, the International Panel on Climate Change (IPCC) identifies that developing specific and practical adaptation strategies to climate change at a national scale is urgent.[46] Nonetheless, adaptation progress in Australia mostly occurs at the local government level; is patchy and half-hearted; and adaptation planning, implementation, and evaluation are lagging. Indeed, Australia needs a governance shift from incremental and reactive to anticipatory decision-making, with more community-based and transformative adaptation within an overarching national framework.[47]

39 Australian Bureau of Statistics, Population Projections, Australia, 2017 (Base) - 2066'
40 Australian Government, Intergenerational Report 2023
41 Seamer
42 Seamer
43 Pacione
44 Haratsis
45 Bolleter et al., 'Informing Future Australian Settlement Planning'
46 IPCC
47 IPCC

Stalling implementing adaptation and emission reductions will stymie climate-resilient development, resulting in more costly climate impacts and brutal future adjustments.[48] Indeed, with more extreme levels of warming, adaptation costs increase, loss and damages grow, and governance and institutional responses have reduced capacity to adapt. The built environment is a heavy, fixed thing that is slow and expensive to change,[49] and the adaptation task is 'vast, almost unquantifiable, but the quicker we confront it, the better we will be able to manage'.[50] This proactive, yet long-term view is critical as 'adaptation will be an ongoing process of responding to change with no "end" point'.[51] Indeed, the worst projected climate change scenarios leave many of Australia's human and natural systems at 'very high risk and beyond adaptation limits'.[52]

However, an NSS could proactively respond by diverting population growth away from vulnerable regions. How would it do this? Firstly, such a policy can influence population growth rates by making selected centres more desirable to investors by offering infrastructure, energy, housing and other inputs.[53] Secondly, it could also carefully direct investment to vulnerable centres to retrofit the urban structure to be more resilient to projected future climatic conditions without necessarily fuelling population growth.

HURDLES AHEAD

We acknowledge there are headwinds to be confronted. An NSS may prove problematic for political reasons (e.g., because of state governments' power vis-a-vis the Commonwealth under the Australian Constitution). Indeed, even the process of achieving Federation is instructive considering the challenges of 'inducing six jealous, sovereign colonies to come together and forge one nation'.[54] We also note contentious debate on the issue of whether federal governments should have a direct role in urban management, which, as we have noted, is considered the exclusive domain of state and local governments.[55]

Furthermore, we acknowledge the classic administrative dilemma explained by Painter: 'The more you attempt to centralize formal control, the more you lose effective touch with the operations on the periphery that you seek to control.'[56] As Aitken explained: 'It is a task better suited to the dictator, the Generalissimo and the tyrant. However, it is a task which

48 IPCC
49 Gleeson, 'Waking from the Dream'
50 O'Neil and Watts
51 Hurlimann et al., 84
52 IPCC
53 Laquian
54 Day, 40
55 Oakley
56 Painter, 344

in Australia will have to be done democratically.'[57] We do not regard such dilemmas and challenges as fatal flaws within the DNA of a prospective NSS, but as issues that the policy will need to address in a calculated and careful manner.

In the messy democratic process required to build a groundswell of support behind an NSS, it will be critical that not only collaborative inter-governmental frameworks are put in place, but genuine engagement is conducted with Australians to solicit their opinions (our Plan *My* Australia surveys are just one of many forms this could take). This engagement should remind policymakers that, when discussing disembodied concepts like population and migration, we are talking about 'real lives: people and their needs, wants, capabilities and fears'.[58] Too often, in Australia, governments 'consult' residents to provide a veneer of respectability to a pre-determined outcome rather than genuinely responding to the thrust and nuances of community priorities.[59]

Such processes are critical concerning planning, potentially imposed on regional areas from the introspective isolation of Canberra.[60] It is vital to avoid the perception – and reality – that external interests with limited local knowledge drive a region's strategic planning and, despite best intentions, risk no personal loss if community outcomes go awry.[61] Beyond the urban-regional divide is a divide between current and future Australians. With all the different stakeholders drawn into planning our cities, we can forget the most critical group.[62] As Seamer explains:

> We don't know who they are or what they want as individuals, and we can only make judgements or suppositions about them. These are the people who will be living in our new suburbs or developments in the future, possibly for hundreds of years into the future.[63]

Finally, a prospective NSS needs to be a shared vision for Australia upheld by Indigenous and non-Indigenous Australians. Indigenous Australians have been virtually scripted out of planning history through the Eurocentrism of the field.[64] Despite advances in native title, the result is a situation where two coexisting systems of place-making and place

57 Aitken
58 Mares, 41
59 Kelly and Donegan
60 Day
61 Regional Australia Institute
62 Seamer
63 Seamer, 169
64 Freestone, 'Progress in Australian Planning History'

governance exist. Yet, one operates in a domineering manner to the almost total exclusion of the other, with deeply unfair consequences.[65] Libby Porter reminds us:

> *In Australia, the planning profession has never acknowledged that it coexists with another system of place-making and place-governance, nor has much effort been given to rethinking planning from the departure point of shared coexistence.*[66]

Genuine engagement with Indigenous communities about a prospective NSS is not only the right thing to do, but also the necessary thing. As Brendan Gleeson explains:

> *Our urban vessels have carried us very well through our short history, but we have also used them to run right over the original owners of this land. This was unjust and foolish …. we will have to turn to our indigenous brothers and sisters with humility in a quest for knowledge about country, and to learn to see the productive, nurturing Earth in new ways. This would be real enlightenment. We will need to gaze back with doubt upon all we hastily created, recognising bad and good within it all, and then seek new knowledge, which might include ancient wisdom in its energetic surviving forms.*[67]

65 Porter
66 Porter
67 Gleeson, Lifeboat Cities, 130

CONCLUSION

This book has presented findings from twin national-scale Plan *My* Australia surveys of laypeople and experts and a multi-factorial suitability analysis that examined receptive geographies for urbanisation in the twenty-first-century and beyond. The surveys were the first of their kind in collating community and expert opinions to assess settlement planning at the national scale. As a result, this book offers a preliminary examination of opinions from a broad spectrum of Australians that policymakers should consider in a national settlement strategy that would complement the national urban policy.

Suppose projections for Australia's population growth are borne out. In that case, Australia needs to consider planning, designing and inhabiting networks of regional cities into the next century in the most sustainable, liveable and productive ways possible. The challenge is immense. Gough Whitlam seemed up to it half a century ago and fell short. Still, he was fond of quoting the Canadian urbanist Humphrey Carver in rallying the troops:

> *Building cities is far the most difficult, complex and majestic thing that [people] do. In this we come nearest in scale to what God does in creating the stars and the hills and the forests.*[68]

68 Whitlam

BIBLIOGRAPHY

AECOM, *High Speed Rail Study, Phase 2 Report: Key Findings and Executive summary*, Report for the Department of Infrastrcture and Transport, AECOM, Sydney, 2013.

Aitken, D, 'The political likelihood of new towns in Australia', *Toward Cities of the Twenty-first Century: Proceedings of Canberra Forum 1970*, 23-30 May 1970, Goldsmith, John and James Conner, Eds, The Royal Australian Institute of Architects and The Royal Planning Institute, Canberra, 54-60.

Alonso, W, 'The mirage of new towns.' *The Public Interest* 19 (1970): 3-17.

Amati, M, *The City and the Super-Organism: A History of Naturalism in Urban Planning*, Palgrave Macmillan, Singapore, 2021.

American Association for the Advancement of Science, 'Old cities, new cities, no cities.' *Science* vol. 75, no. 4023, 1972, pp. 790.

Angel, S, *Planet of Cities*, Lincoln Institute of Land Policy, Cambridge, 2012.

Archer, J, Houghton, K and Vonthethoff, B, *Regional Population Growth – Are We Ready? The Economics of Alternative Australian Settlement Patterns*, Regional Australia Institute, Canberra, 2019.

Arman, OM, Clark, JL, Cocks, KD, Davis, JR, Hinde, CV, Parvey, CA, et al., *Finding Sites for New Cities: A Demonstration of the Search Capabilities of the Australian Resources Information System*, CSIRO Division of Land Use Research, Canberra, 1981.

Arnot, RH, 'Population and resources: a national spatial ordering concept plan', *Archetype* vol. 2, no. 1, 1974, pp. 16-30.

Aurigi, A, 'No need to fix: strategic inclusivity in developing and managing the smart city', *Digital Futures and the City of Today: New Technologies and Physical Spaces*, Caldwell, GA, Smith, C and Clift, E, Eds, Intellect, Bristol, 2016, pp. 9-28.

Australian Academy of Science, *The Risks to Australia of a 3°C Warmer World*, Australian Academy of Science, Canberra, 2021.

Australian Associated Press, 'Population to hit 55m by 2050: Triguboff', *Sydney Morning Herald*, 25 January 2010, <https://www.smh.com.au/national/population-to-hit-55m-by-2050-triguboff-20100125-mt45.html>.

Australian Bureau of Statistics. 'Western Australia: 2016 census all persons quickstats', ABS, 2017, <https://www.abs.gov.au/census/find-census-data/quickstats/2016/5>.

—— 'Population projections, Australia, 2017 (Base) - 2066', ABS, 2018. <https://www.abs.gov.au/statistics/people/population/population-projections-australia/latest-release>.

—— 'Population projections, Australia, 2012 (base) to 2101', ABS, 2013. <https://www.abs.gov.au/ausstats/abs@.nsf/lookup/3222.0main+features52012%20(base)%20to%202101#:~:text=Population%20size,and%2070.1%20million%20in%202101.>

—— 'Regional internal migration estimates, provisional', ABS, 2021, <https://www.abs.gov.au/statistics/people/population/regional-internal-migration-estimates-provisional/mar-2021>.

Australian Government, *National Urban Policy: Consultation Draft*. Commonwealth of Australia, Canberra, 2024a.

—— *National Urban Policy: A vision for the sustainable growth of our cities and suburbs*. Commonwealth of Australia, Canberra, 2024b.

—— *Intergenerational Report 2023: Australia's Future to 2063*. Commonwealth of Australia, Canberra, 2023.

—— *National Climate Resilience and Adaptation Strategy 2021-2025: Positioning Australia to Better Anticipate, Manage and Adapt to Our Changing Climate*, Commonwealth of Australia, Canberra, 2021.

—— 'Our Plan for Population, Migration and Better Cities', Liberal Party, 2019, <https://cdn.liberal.org.au/pdf/PlanningForAustFuturePopulation.pdf>.

—— *Planning for Australia's Future Population*, Commonwealth of Australia, Canberra, 2019.

—— *Building Up & Moving Out: Inquiry into the Australian Government's role in the development of cities*, House of Representatives Standing Committee on Infrastructure, Transport and Cities, Canberra, 2018.

—— *Our North, Our Future: White Paper on Developing Northern Australia*, Commonwealth of Australia, Canberra, 2015.

Australian Urban Design Research Centre, 'What might Australian cities look like by 2100?' The University of Western Australia, Perth, 2022, <https://www.audrc.org/bau-competition-results>.

Babb, J, 'Remembering 'populate or perish': Arthur Calwell', *News Weekly*, 21 May 2016, <https://newsweekly.com.au/nw-issue/2016-may-21/>.

Barrie, C, et al., 'Infrastructure and population', *Northern Development: Creating the Future Australia*, Roux, A, Daybell, M and McGauchie, D, Eds., ADC Forum, Melbourne, 2014, pp. 37-94.

Bean, CEW, *War Aims of a Plain Australian*, Angus and Robertson, Sydney, 1943.

Beatley, T, 'The Vision of Green Urbanism', *The City Reader*, LeGates, R and Stout, F, Eds., Routledge, London, 2015, pp. 399-408.

Beer, A and Clower, T, 'Specialisation and Growth: Evidence from Australia's Regional Cities', *Urban Studies*, vol. 46, no. 2, 2009, pp. 369-89.

Benson, S and Brown, G, 'Cities Fix: PM's Plan to Send Migrants to Regions for Five Years', *The Australian*, 29 August 2018, < https://www.theaustralian.com.au/subscribe/news/1/?sourceCode=TAWEB_WRE170_a_GGL&dest=https%3A%2F%2Fwww.theaustralian.com.au%2Fnation%2Fpolitics%2Fcities-fix-pms-plan-to-send-migrants-to-regions-for-five-years%2Fnews-story%2Fc8573e68a1438295818d5aab9de5471b&memtype=registered&mode=premium&v21=HIGH-Segment-1-SCORE&V21spcbehaviour=append>.

Berkley, GE, 'Britain's New Town Blues', *National Civic Review*, vol. 62, no. 9, 1973, pp. 479-85.

Bettini, G, 'Climate Barbarians at the gate? A critique of apocalyptic narratives on "climate refugees"', *Geoforum*, vol. 45, 2013, pp. 63-72.

Betts, K, 'Population growth: what do Australian voters want?' *People and Place*, vol. 18, no. 1, 2010, pp. 49-64.

Betts, K and Birrell, B, *Australian Voters' Views on Immigration Policy*, The Australian Population Research Institute, Research Report, 2017.

Biddle, N. *Big Australia, Small Australia, Diverse Australia: Australia's Views on Population*. Australian National University, ANUPoll, Report No 28, 2019.

Binks, B, Stenekes, N, Kruger, H, and Kancans, R, 'Snapshot of Australia's Agricultural Workforce', Australian Government, 2018.

Birrell, B, and Healy, E, *Immigration and the Housing Affordability Crisis in Sydney and Melbourne*, The Australian Population Research Institute, Research Report, 2018.

Black, R, Kniveton, D, Skeldon, R, Coppard, D, Murata, A and Schmidt-Verkerk, K, *Demographics and Climate Change: Future Trends and Their Policy Implications for Migration*, University of Sussex, Development Research Centre on Migration, Globalisation and Poverty, Working Paper No. T-27, 2008.

Blainey, G, *The Tyranny of Distance: How Distance Shaped Australia's History*, Sun Books, Melbourne, 1966.

Bohnet, IC and Pert, PL. 'Patterns, Drivers and Impacts of Urban Growth—a Study from Cairns, Queensland, Australia from 1952 to 2031', *Landscape and Urban Planning*, vol. 97, no. 4, 2010, pp. 239-48.

Bolleter, J, 'The Consequences of Three Urbanisation Scenarios for Northern Australia', *Australian Planner*, vol. 55, no. 2, 2018, pp. 103-125.

—— *The Ghost Cities of Australia: A Survey of New City Proposals and Their Lessons for Australia's 21st Century Development*, Cham: Springer, 2018.

Bolleter, J, Edwards, N, Cameron, R, Duckworth, A, Freestone, R, Foster, S, et al., 'Implications of the Covid-19 Pandemic: Canvassing Opinion from Planning

Professionals', *Planning Practice and Research,* vol. 37, no. 1, 2021, pp. 13-34.

Bolleter, J, Edwards, N, Freestone, R, Nichols, D, Oliver, G and Hooper, P, 'Long-Term Settlement Scenarios for Australia: a Survey and Evaluation of Community Opinions', *Urban Policy and Research,* vol. 40, no. 1, 2022, pp. 15-35.

Bolleter, J, Edwards, N, Freestone R, Nichols, D and Hooper, P, 'Evaluating Scenarios for Twenty-first-century Australian Settlement Planning: a Delphi Study With Planning Experts', *International Planning Studies,* vol. 27, no. 3, 2022, pp. 231-252.

Bolleter, J, Grace, B, Foster, S, Duckworth, A and Hooper, P, 'Projected Extreme Heat Stress in Northern Australia and the Implications for Development Policy', *Planning Practice and Research,* vol. 37, no. 5, 2021, pp. 601-23.

Bolleter, J, Grace, B, and Freestone, R, 'Preparing Australia for a Potential Surge in Environmental Migration', *Australian Planner,* vol. 58, no. 1-2, 2022, pp. 11-24.

Bolleter, J, Grace, B, and Freestone, R and Hooper, P, 'Informing Future Australian Settlement Planning Through a National-scale Suitability Analysis', *International Planning Studies,* vol. 27, no. 1, 2022, pp. 18-43.

Bolleter, J, Myers, Z and Hooper, P, 'Delivering Medium-density Infill Development Through Promoting the Benefits and Limiting Background Infill', *Journal of Urban Design,* vol. 26, no. 4, 2021, pp. 441-66.

Bolleter, J and Weller, R. *Made in Australia: The Future of Australian Cities.* University of Western Australia Publishing, Perth, 2013.

Bourne, LS and Simmons, JW, Eds., *Systems of Cities: Readings on Structure, Growth and Policy,* Oxford University Press, Perth, 1978.

Boyd, R, *The Australian Ugliness,* Cheshire, Melbourne, 1961

Brady, E, *Australia Unlimited,* George Robertson, Melbourne, 1918.

Brodie-Hall, L, *Mining,* Paper presented at the A Seminar on Decentralisation, The Town of Geraldton, 1972.

Bureau of Meteorology, 'Maps and Gridded Spatial Data', Australian Government, 2020, <http://www.bom.gov.au/climate/austmaps/about-agcd-maps.shtml>.

Burnley, I, *The Australian Urban System: Growth, Change and Differentiation*, Longman Cheshire, Melbourne, 1980.

Burnley, I and Murphy, P, *Sea Change: Movement from Metropolitan to Arcadian Australia*, UNSW Press, Sydney, 2004.

Butler, CD, 'Human Carrying Capacity and Human Health', *PLoS Medicine,* vol. 1, no. 3, 2004, pp. e55. https://doi.org/10.1371/journal.pmed.0010055.

Button, J, and Rizvi, A, 'The Great Transformation: Hooked on Migration', *Griffith Review,* vol. 61, 2018, pp. 11-29.

Cathcart, M, *The Water Dreamers: The Remarkable History of Our Dry Continent*, Text Publishing, Melbourne, 2010.

Chakrabortty, A, 'Paul Romer Is a Brilliant Economist– but His Idea for Charter Cities Is Bad', *The Guardian,* 27 July 2010, <https://www.theguardian.com/science/2010/jul/27/paul-romers-charter-cities-idea>.

Chan, G, *Rusted Off: Why Country Australia Is Fed Up*, Vintage Australia, Sydney, 2018.

Chapman, R, Tonts, M and Plummer, P, 'Resource Development, Local Adjustment, and Regional Policy: Resolving the Problem of Rapid Growth in the Pilbara, Western Australia', *Journal of Rural and Community Development,* vol. 9, no. 1, 2014, pp. 72-86.

Charles, MB, Ryan, N and Kivits, RA, 'Moving Towards Sustainable Intercity Transport: A Case Study of High-Speed Rail in Australia', *International Journal of Sustainable Development,* vol. 15, no. 1-2, 2012, pp. 125-47.

Chen, S, 'Land-Use Suitability Analysis for Urban Development in Regional Victoria: A Case Study of

Bendigo', *Journal of Geography and Regional Planning*, vol. 9, no. 4, 2016, pp. 47-58.

Cheung, R, *Balanced Development: A Case for Community Concern*, Balanced Development: A Case For Community Concern Conference, Balanced Development, 1972.

Christian Aid. *Human Tide: The Real Migration Crisis.* Christian Aid, London, 2007.

Chrysanthos, N and Ding, A, 'Food Fault Lines: Mapping Class through Food Chains', *Honi Soit,* 22 September 2017, <https://honisoit.com/2017/09/food-fault-lines-mapping-class-division-through-food-chains/>.

Cities Commission, *Report to the Australian Government: A Recommended New Cities Programme for the Period 1973-1978*, Cities Commission, Canberra, 1973.

Climate Council of Australia, *The Great Deluge: Australia's New Era of Unnatural Disasters*, Climate Council, Sydney, 2022.

Cocks, D, *Use with Care: Managing Australia's natural resources in the twenty first century,* New South Wales University Press, Sydney, 1992.

Cohen, SB, 'The Polyurban Frontier in Post-Industrial Israel', *Developing Frontier Cities*, Lithwick, H and Yehuda, G, Eds., Springer, Dordrecht, 2000, pp. 255-71.

Colman, J, *Decentralisation - Could it Help Our Fast Growing Cities?* Henry Halloran Trust, University of Sydney, Sydney, 2019.

Consolidated Land and Rail Australia, 'The Clara Plan' n.d., <https://www.clara.com.au/the-clara-plan/>.

Cooper, JAG and Lemckert, C, 'Extreme Sea-Level Rise and Adaptation Options for Coastal Resort Cities: A Qualitative Assessment from the Gold Coast, Australia', *Ocean & Coastal Management,* vol. 64, 2012, pp. 1-14.

Costanza, R, Kubiszewski, I, Cork, S, Atkins, PWB, Bean, A, Diamond, A, et al., 'Scenarios for Australia in 2050: A Synthesis and Proposed Survey', *Journal of Futures Studies,* vol. 19, no. 3, 2015, pp. 49-76.

Coutts, A, Beringer, J and Tapper, N, 'Changing Urban Climate and CO2 Emissions: Implications for the Development of Policies for Sustainable Cities', *Urban Policy and Research,* vol. 28, no. 1, 2010, pp. 27-47.

CSIRO. Climate Change in Australia, CSIRO, 2022, <https://www.climatechangeinaustralia.gov.au/en/>.

—— *An Assessment of the Historic Bradfield Scheme to Divert Water Inland from North Queensland*, CSIRO, Canberra, 2020.

Dale, A, *Beyond the North-South Culture Wars: Reconciling Northern Australia's Recent Past with Its Future,* Springer, New York, 2014.

Dale, A, Campbell, A, Douglas, M, Robertson, A, Wallace, R and Davies, P, 'From Myth to Reality: New Pathways for Northern Development', *Northern Development: Creating the Future Australia*, Roux, A, Faubell, M and McGauchie, Eds., ADC Forum, Melbourne, 2014, pp. 7-17.

Daley, P, 'Transforming the Bush: At Home on the Farm, with Robots', *Griffith Review*, vol. 52, 2016, pp. 269-282.

Danaher, D and Williamson JD. "New Town Blues': Planning Versus Mutual', *International Journal of Social Psychiatry*, vol. 29, no. 2, 1983, pp. 147-52.

Davidson, W, *Geographic Information System (Gis) Dataset for the Australian Feedlot Sector*, Meat and Livestock Australia Limited, Sydney, 2007.

Davison, G, *City Dreamers: The Urban Imagination in Australia.* NewSouth Publishing, Sydney, 2016.

—— 'Fatal Attraction? The Lure of Technology and the Decline of Rural Australia 1890-2000', *Tasmanian Historical Studies*, vol. 9, no. 1, 2003, pp. 40-55.

Day, PD, 'The Regional Mirage - and Problems That Won't Go Away', *Royal Australian Planning Institute Journal*, vol. 15, no. 2, 1977, pp. 38-42.

Department of Home Affairs, 'Regional Migration', Australian Government, 2023, n.d., <https://immi.homeaffairs.gov.au/visas/working-in-australia/regional-migration>.

Department of Infrastructure, Local Government and Planning, *Shaping SEQ: South East Queensland Regional Plan 2017*, Queensland Government, Brisbane, 2017.

Department of Infrastructure, Transport, Regional Development, Communications and the Arts, 'Cities', Australian Government, n.d., <https://www.infrastructure.gov.au/territories-regions-cities/cities>.

Department of Planning, Lands and Heritage, *Perth and Peel @3.5 Million*, Western Australian Planning Commission, Perth, 2018.

Department of Planning, Transport and Infrastructure, *The 30-Year Plan for Greater Adelaide: 2017 Update*, Government of South Australia, Adelaide, 2017.

Department of Regional Development, *Royalties for Regions: Progress Report July 2015- June 2016*, Government of Western Australia, Perth, 2016.

—— *Western Australia's Supertowns*, Government of Western Australia, Perth, 2011.

Diamond, J, *Collapse: How Societies Choose to Fail or Survive*, Penguin Books, London, 2011.

Dovey, K, *Urban Design Thinking: A Conceptual Toolkit*, Bloomsbury Academic, London, 2016.

Dovey, K and Woodcock I, Eds., *Intensifying Melbourne: Transit-Orientated Urban Design for Resilient Urban Futures*, Melbourne School of Design, The University of Melbourne, Melbourne, 2014.

Duranton, G and Puga D, 'The Growth of Cities', *Handbook of Economic Growth*, Aghion, P, and Durlauf S Eds., Elsevier, Oxford, 2013, pp. 751-853.

Economist, The, 'The Global Liveability Index 2021', Economist Intelligence Unit, 2021, *The Economist*, <https://www.eiu.com/n/campaigns/global-liveability-index-2021/>.

Economist Intelligence Unit, *The Global Liveability Index 2022: Recovery and Hardship*, Economist Intelligence Unit, London, 2023.

Einstein, KL, Palmer, M and Glick, DM, 'Who Participates in Local Government? Evidence from Meeting Minutes', *Perspectives on Politics,* vol. 17, no. 1, 2019, pp. 28-46.

Farrelly, E, *Killing Sydney: The Fight for a City's Soul*, Picador, Sydney, 2021.

Fincher, R, 'Population Growth in Australia: Views and Policy Talk for Possible Futures', *Geographical Research,* vol. 49, no. 3, 2011, pp. 336-47.

Flannery, T, *The Climate Cure: Solving the Climate Emergency in the Era of Covid-19*, Text Publishing, Melbourne, 2020.

Florida, R, 'Megaregions: The Importance of Place', *Harvard Business Review,* vol. 86, no. 3, 2008, pp. 18-19.

—— *Rise of the Creative Class*, Basic Books, New York, 2002.

Freestone, R, 'Progress in Australian Planning History: Traditions, Themes and Transformations', *Progress in Planning,* vol. 91, 2014, pp. 1-29.

—— 'Back to the Future', *Made in Australia: The Future of Australian Cities,* Bolleter, J and Weller, R, Eds., University of Western Australia Press, Perth, 2013, pp. 236-43.

—— 'The Garden City Idea in Australia.', *Geographical Research,* vol. 20, no. 1, 1982, pp. 24-48.

Freestone, R, Nichols, D and Bolleter, J, 'Pragmatic Utopianism: Tracking the Australian New Town Ideal from the 19th to the 21st Centuries', Paper presented to the *Ngā Pūtahitanga/Crossings* Conference, SAHANZ and the Australasian UHPH Group, Auckland, December 2022.

Freestone, R and Pullan, N, 'Sydney Post-War Metropolitan Planning: The Rise and Fall of the Satellite Town as a Spatial Imaginary', *Urban Policy and Research,* vol. 39, no. 4, 2021, pp. 315-33.

Freestone, R, Randolph, R and Steele, W, Eds. *Australian Urban Policy: Prospects and Pathways*, ANU Press, Canberra, 2024.

Frost, W, 'Australia Unlimited? Environmental Debate in the 'Age of Catastrophe, 1910-1939', *Environment and History,* vol. 10, no. 3, 2004, pp. 285-303.

Fuller, RB, *Utopia or Oblivion: The Prospects for Humanity*, Bantam Books, New York, 1969.

Gazzard, D, Ed., *Australian Outrage: The Decay of a Visual Environment*, Ure Smith, Sydney, 1966.

Geoscience Australia, 'Geodata Topo 250k Series 3 - (Personal Geodatabase Format)', Australian Government, 2018.

Gilbert, AD, 'Cities and Suburbs', *Australians from 1939*, Curthoys, A, Martin, AW and Rowse, T, Eds., Fairfax, Syme and Weldon Associates, Sydney, 1987, pp. 77-97.

Gleeson, B, *The Urban Condition*, Routledge, London, 2015.

—— 'The Greatest Spoiler: Salvation in the Cities', *Griffith Review 29: Prosper or Perish*. Schultz, J, Ed., 2010, pp. 57-66.

—— *Lifeboat Cities*, UNSW Press, Sydney, 2010.

—— 'Waking from the Dream: An Australian Perspective on Urban Resilience', *Urban Studies*, vol. 45, no 13, 2008, pp. 2651-2892.

—— 'Rescuing Urban Regions: The Federal Agenda', *Federalism and Regionalism in Australia: New Approaches, New Institutions*, Brown, A and Bellamy, J, Eds., ANU e-Press, Canberra, 2007, pp. 71-82.

Gottman, J. *Megalopolis: The Urbanized Northeastern Seaboard of the United States*, MIT Press, Cambridge, 1964.

Graham, H, *Decentralisation: A Policy for Action. Seminar on Decentralisation*. The Town of Geraldton, Geraldton, Department of Development and Decentralisation, 1972.

Greater Cities Commission, *The Six Cities Region Discussion Paper: Delivering Global Competitiveness and Local Liveability*, Greater Cities Commisison, Sydney, 2022.

Greater Sydney Commission, *City-Shaping Impacts of Covid-19: Towards a Resilient Greater Sydney*, Greater Sydney Commission, Sydney, 2020.

—— *Greater Sydney Region Plan: A Metropolis of Three Cities*, Greater Sydney Commission, Sydney, 2018.

Guaralda, M, Hearn, G, Foth, M, Yigitcanlar, T, Mayere, S and Law, L, 'Towards Australian Regional Turnaround: Insights into Sustainably Accommodating Post-Pandemic Urban Growth in Regional Towns and Cities', *Sustainability*, vol. 12, no. 24, 2020, pp. 1-13.

Gubernot, DM, Anderson, GB and Hunting, KL, 'The Epidemiology of Occupational Heat Exposure in the United States: A Review of the Literature and Assessment of Research Needs in a Changing Climate', *International Journal of Biometeorology*, vol. 58, no. 8, 2014, pp. 1779-88.

Gussen, B, 'A Proposal for a Singaporean "Charter City" in Australia', *The Straits Times*, 24 January 2017, p. A21, <https://eresources.nlb.gov.sg/newspapers/digitised/issue/straitstimes20170124-1>.

Hall, P, 'Enterprise Zones: A Justification', *International Journal of Urban and Regional Research*, vol. 6, no. 3, 1982, pp. 416-21.

Hall, P and Pain, K, *The Polycentric Metropolis: Learning from Mega-City Regions in Europe*, Routledge, 2006.

Hallsworth, EG, 'Feasibility of the Australian Desert Coast for Future Urban Settlements', *Desert Planning: International Lessons*, Golany, G, Ed., Architectural Press, London, 1982, pp. 43-49.

Haratsis, B, *Australia 2050: Big Australia?* Digital Print Australia, Adelaide, 2010

Harding, R, 'The Debate on Population and the Environment: Australia in the Global Context', *Journal of the Australian Population Association*, vol. 12, no. 2, 1995, pp. 165-195.

Hellicar, M, 'Populate or Perish?' *The Sydney Papers*, vol. 13, no. 3, 2001, pp. 35-42.

Hill, S, Cumpston, Z and Vigiola, GQ, 'Urban', In *Australia State of the Environment*, Commonwealth of Australia, Canberra, 2021.

Hopkins, D, 'Planning Metropolitan Perth through "Dialogue": Participatory Democracy or Manufactured Consent?' *Planning Perspectives from Western Australia: A Reader in Theory and Practice*, Alexander, I, Greive, S and Hedgcock, D, Fremantle Press, Perth, 2010, pp. 190-204.

Hopper, S and Gioa, P, 'The Southwest Australian Floristic Region: Evolution and Conservation of a Global Hotspot of Biodiversity', *Annual Review of Ecology, Evolution, and Systematics*, vol. 35, 2004, pp. 623-50.

Hugo, G, 'Change and Continuity in Australian International Migration Policy', *International Migration Review*, vol. 48, no. 3, 2014, pp. 868-90.

—— *Population Distribution, Migration and Climate Change in Australia: An Exploration*, Australian Climate Change Adaptation Research Network for Settlements and Infrastructure (ACCARNSI), Discussion Paper-Node 2, revised, 2012.

Hurlimann, A, Barnett, J, Fincher, R, Osbaldiston, N, Mortreux, C and Graham, S, 'Urban Planning and Sustainable Adaptation to Sea-Level Rise', *Landscape and Urban Planning*, vol. 126, 2014, pp. 84-93.

Hyndman, B, 'The Heat in Northern Australian Classrooms Could Impede Learning', *The Conversation*, 7 August 2015, <https://theconversation.com/the-heat-in-northern-australian-classrooms-could-impede-learning-44592>.

Idriess, I, *Onward Australia: Developing a Continent*, Angus and Robertson, Sydney, 1944.

International Organization for Migration, *Migration and Climate Change*, International Organization for Migration, Geneva, 2008.

IPCC, *Climate Change 2022: Impacts, Adaptation and Vulnerability, Working Group II Contribution to the Sixth Assessment Report*, International Panel on Climate Change, 2022.

Ittimani, L, 'High-Speed Rail Agency to Appoint Board', *Australian Financial Review*, 24 February 2023, <https://www.afr.com/companies/transport/high-speed-rail-agency-to-appoint-board-20230223-p5cn53>.

Kelly, J-F and Donegan, P, *City Limits: Why Australian Cities Are Broken and How We Can Fix Them*, Melbourne University Press, Melbourne, 2015.

King, C, 'High Speed Rail Gathers Speed', Press Release, 8 September 2022, <https://minister.infrastructure.gov.au/c-king/media-release/high-speed-rail-gathers-speed>.

King, M, 'Speech to CEDA: The Future of Australia's Resources Sector and Northern Australia', 19 April 2023, <https://www.minister.industry.gov.au/ministers/king/speeches/speech-ceda-future-australias-resources-sector-and-northern-australia>.

Klocker, N, Hodge, P, Dun, O, Crosbie, E, Dufty-Jones, R, McMichael, C, et al., 'Spaces of Well-Being and Regional Settlement: International Migrants and the Rural Idyll', *Population, Space and Place*, vol. 27, no. 8, 2021, pp. e2443.

Kullmann, K, 'Design for Decline Landscape Architecture Strategies for the Western Australian Wheatbelt', *Landscape Journal*, vol. 32, no. 2, 2013, pp. 243-60.

Lane, M, 'Exploring Short-Term and Long-Term Time Frames in Australian Population Carrying Capacity Assessment', *Population and Environment*, vol. 38, no. 3, 2017, pp. 309-24.

Laquian, AA, *Beyond Metropolis: The Planning and Governance of Asia's Mega-Urban Regions*, Woodrow Wilson Center Press, Washington, DC, 2005.

Lewis, G, '"Million Farms" Campaign, NSW 1919-25', *Labour History*, vol. 47, 1984, pp. 55-72.

Llewellyn-Smith, M, 'Canberra Forum 1970—Towards the Cities of the 21st Century', *Royal Australian Planning Institute Journal*, vol. 8, no. 3, 1970, pp. 86-87.

Lloyd, C and Anderton, N, 'From Growth Centres to Growth Centres?' *Australian Planner*, vol. 28, no. 3, 1990, pp. 6-15.

Lonsdale, RE, 'Manufacturing Decentralization: The Discouraging Record in Australia', *Land Economics*, vol. 48, no. 4, 1972, pp. 321-28.

—— 'Decentralization: The American Experience and Its Relevance for Australia', *The Australian Journal of Social Issues*, vol. 6, no. 2, 1971, pp. 116-27.

Lowy Institute, 'Lowy Institute Poll 2022', Lowy Institute, 2022, <https://poll.lowyinstitute.org/report/2022/>.

MacFarlane, R, 'Generation Anthropocene: How Humans Have Altered the Planet Forever', *The Guardian*, 1 April 2016, < https://www.theguardian.com/books/2016/apr/01/generation-anthropocene-altered-planet-for-ever>.

Mares, P, 'Monday Morning in Mernda: A Land of Plenty, or Plenty in the Land?' *Griffith Review 29: Prosper or Perish*, Schultz, J, Ed., 2010, pp. 13-45.

McAdam, J, and Blocher, J 'Factcheck Q&A: As the Climate Changes, Are 750 Million Refugees Predicted to Move Away from Flooding?' *The Conversation,* 4 August 2020, <https://theconversation.com/factcheck-qanda-as-the-climate-changes-are-750-million-refugees-predicted-to-move-away-from-flooding-63400>.

McCrea, R and Walters, P, 'Impacts of Urban Consolidation on Urban Liveability: Comparing an Inner and Outer Suburb in Brisbane, Australia', *Housing, Theory and Society,* vol. 29, no. 2, 2012, pp. 190-206.

McGregor, R, 'Developing the North, Defending the Nation? The Northern Australia Development Committee, 1945-1949', *Australian Journal of Politics and History,* vol. 59, no. 1, 2013, pp. 33-46.

—— *Environment, Race, and Nationhood in Australia: Revisiting the Empty North,* Palgrave Macmillan, New York, 2016.

McGuirk, J, 'Can Cities Make Us Better Citizens?' *The New Yorker,* 26 April 2018, <https://www.newyorker.com/books/page-turner/can-cities-make-us-better-citizens>.

McNee, G and Pojani, D, 'Nimbyism as a Barrier to Housing and Social Mix in San Francisco', *Journal of Housing and the Built Environment,* vol. 37, 2022, pp. 553-573.

Megarrity, L, *Northern Dreams: The Politics of Northern Development in Australia,* Australian Scholarly Publishing, Melbourne, 2018.

—— '"Necessary and Urgent?": The Politics of Northern Australia 1945-75', *Journal of the Royal Australian Historical Society,* vol. 97, no. 2, 2011, pp. 136-160.

Merlin, T, 'The Traditional Housing Model Isn't Working – Is "Subscription Living" the Future?' *Architect's Journal,* 6 June 2019, <https://www.architectsjournal.co.uk/news/opinion/the-traditional-housing-model-isnt-working-is-subscription-living-the-future>.

Mirams, S, '"The Attractions of Australia": E.J. Brady and the Making of *Australia Unlimited*', *Australian Historical Studies,* vol. 43, no. 2, 2012, pp. 270-86.

Mittermeier, RA, Turner, WR, Larsen, FW, Brooks, TM and Gascon, C, 'Global Biodiversity Conservation: The Critical Role of Hotspots.' *Biodiversity Hotspots: Distribution and Protection of Conservation Priority Areas.* Zachos, E and Habel, JC, Eds., Springer-Verlag, Berlin, 2011, pp. 3-22.

Morgan, R, 'Western Water Dreamers Rise Again with Colin Barnett's Canal Vision', *The Conversation,* 3 August 2012, <https://theconversation.com/western-water-dreamers-rise-again-with-colin-barnetts-canal-vision-8625>.

Mullins, P, 'Cities for Pleasure: The Emergence of Tourism Urbanization in Australia', *Built Environment,* vol. 18, no. 3, 1992, pp. 187-98.

—— 'Tourist Cities as New Cities: Australia's Gold Coast and Sunshine Coast', *Australian Planner,* vol. 28, no. 3, 1990, pp. 37-41.

Murphy, K, '"The Modern Idea Is to Bring the Country into the City": Australian Urban Reformers and the Ideal of Rurality, 1900-1918', *Rural History,* vol. 20, no. 1, 2009, pp. 119-36.

Murphy, P, 'The Metropolis', *Planning Australia: An Overview of Urban and Regional Planning,* Maginn, P and Thompson, S, Eds., Cambridge University Press, Melbourne, 2012, pp. 155-79.

Murray, D, *The Strange Death of Europe: Immigration, Identity, Islam,* Bloomsbury Publishing, London, 2017.

Myers, N, 'Environmental Refugees in a Globally Warmed World', *Bioscience,* vol. 43, no. 11, 1993, pp. 752-61.

—— 'Environmental Refugees: An Emergent Security Issue', *13th Economic Forum,* 2005.

Nathan, M and Overman, H, 'Agglomeration, Clusters, and Industrial Policy', *Oxford Review of Economic Policy,* vol. 29, no. 2, 2013, pp. 383-404.

—— 'Will Coronavirus Cause a Big City Exodus?' *Environment and Planning B: Urban Analytics and City Science,* vol. 47, no. 9, 2020, pp. 1537-42.

National Native Title Tribunal, 'Data Downloads', Australian Government, 2019 <http://www.nntt.gov.au/assistance/Geospatial/Pages/DataDownload.aspx>.

Neutze, GM, 'The Case for New Cities in Australia', *Urban Studies,* vol. 11, no. 3, 1974, pp. 259-75.

Newman, P, 'The City and the Bush—Partnerships to Reverse the Population Decline in Australia's Wheatbelt', *Crop and Pasture Science,* vol. 56, no. 6, 2005, pp. 527-35.

Newton, P and Brealey, T, 'Remote Communities in Tropical and Arid Australia', *Design for Arid Regions,* Golany, G, Ed., Van Nostrand Reinhold, New York, 1983, pp. 223-54.

Newton, PW, 'Beyond Greenfield and Brownfield: The Challenge of Regenerating Australia's Greyfield Suburbs', *Built Environment,* vol. 36, no. 1, 2010, pp. 81-104.

Nichols, D, Freestone, R and Walker, P, 'Towards the Cities of the 21st Century.' Paper presented to the Australian History Association Conference, Ballarat, July 2016.

Norman, B, *Urban Planning for Climate Change*, Routledge, London, 2023.

Norman, B, *Sustainable Pathways for Our Cities and Regions: Planning within Planetary Boundaries*, Routledge, London, 2018.

Northern Australia Infrastructure Facility, 'Investing for Impact Across the North', 8 August 2016, < https://www.naif.gov.au/media-centre/naif-project-updates-investing-for-impact-across-northern-australia/>.

—— 'New Government Commits to Northern Australia Development', 16 June 2022, <https://www.naif.gov.au/media-centre/new-government-commits-to-northern-australia-development/>

O'Neil, C and Watts, T, *Two Futures: Australia at a Critical Moment*, Text Publishing, Melbourne, 2015.

Oakley, S, 'Politics of Recollection: Examining the Rise and Fall of DURD and Better Cities through Narrative', *Urban Policy and Research,* vol. 22, no. 3, 2004, pp. 299-314.

OECD, UN Habitat, and Cities Alliance, *Global State of National Urban Policy 2021: Achieving Sustainable Development Goals and Delivering Climate Action. Synthesis Brochure*, OECD, Paris, 2021.

Office of Northern Australia, and Department of Industry, Innovation and Science, *Our North, Our Future: Developing Northern Australia 2017 Implementation Report*, Commonwealth of Australia, Canberra, 2017.

Pacione, M, 'Where Will the People Go?—Assessing the New Settlement Option for the United Kingdom', *Progress in Planning,* vol. 62, no. 2, 2004, pp. 73-129.

Painter, M, 'Urban Government, Urban Politics and the Fabrication of Urban Issues: The Impossibility of Urban Policy' ,*Australian Journal of Public Administration,* vol. 38, no. 4, 1979, pp. 335-46.

Paris, C, 'New Patterns of Urban and Regional Development in Australia: Demographic Restructuring and Economic Change', *International Journal of Urban and Regional Research,* vol. 18, no. 4, 1994, pp. 555-72.

Parish, K, 'A Charter City for Refugees?' *Club Troppo,* 20 October 2014, <https://clubtroppo.com.au/2014/10/20/a-charter-city-for-refugees/>.

Pearson, DM and Gorman, JT, 'Managing the Landscapes of the Australian Northern Territory for Sustainability: Visions, Issues and Strategies for Successful Planning', *Futures,* vol. 42, no. 7, 2010, pp. 711-22.

Pegler, C, Li, H and Pojani, D, 'Gentrification in Australia's Largest Cities: A Bird's-Eye View', *Australian Planner,* vol. 56, no. 3, 2020, pp. 191-205.

Pennay, B, *Making a City in the Country: The Albury-Wodonga National Growth Centre Project 1973-2003*, UNSW Press, Kensington, 2005.

Pettit, CJ, Klosterman, RE, Delaney, P, Whitehead, AL, Kujala, H, Bromage, A, et al., 'The Online What If? Planning Support System: A Land Suitability Application in Western Australia', *Applied Spatial Analysis and Policy,* vol. 8, no. 2, 2015, pp. 93-112.

Pilbara Development Commission, 'Pilbara Cities Initiative', Government of Western Australia 2016, <https://www.pdc.wa.gov.au/>.

Planning Institute of Australia, *Through the Lens: The Tipping Point*, Planning Institute of Australia, Canberra, 2018.

Plummer, P, Tonts, M and Argent, N, 'Sustainable Rural Economies, Evolutionary Dynamics and Regional Policy', *Applied Geography,* vol. 90, 2018, pp. 308-20.

Porter, L, 'Indigenous People and the Miserable Failure of Australian Planning', *Planning Practice & Research,* vol. 32, no. 5, 2017, pp. 556-570.

Potts, A, 'The Power of the City in Defining the National and Regional in Education. Reactions against the Urban: Universities in Regional Australia', *Paedagogica Historica*, vol. 39, no. 1, 2003, pp. 135-52.

Powell, JM, 'Home Truths and Larrikin Prophets, "Australia Unlimited": The Inter-War Years', *Populate and Perish? The Stresses of Population Growth in Australia*, Birrell, B, Hill, D and Nevill, J, Eds., Australian Conservation Foundation, Melbourne, 1984, pp. 80-99.

Pred, AR, 'Growth Transmission within the Australian System of Cities: General Observations and Study Recommendations', *Cities Commission Occasional Paper No 3*, 1975, pp. 30-55.

Productivity Commission, *Performance Benchmarking of Australian Business Regulation: Planning, Zoning and Development Assessments*, Productivity Commission, Canberra, 2011.

Ramalho, CE, Laliberté, E, Poot, P and Hobbs, RJ, 'Complex Effects of Fragmentation on Remnant Woodland Plant Communities of a Rapidly Urbanizing Biodiversity Hotspot', *Ecology*, vol. 95, no. 9, 2014, pp. 2466-2478.

Randolph, B, 'Delivering the Compact City in Australia: Current Trends and Future Implications', *Urban Policy and Research*, vol. 24, no. 4, 2006, pp. 473-90.

Raupach, MR, McMichael, AJ, Alford, K, Cork, S, Finnigan, JJ, Fulton, EA, et al., 'Living Scenarios for Australia as an Adaptive System', *Negotiating Our Future: Living Scenarios for Australia to 2050*, Raupach, M, McMichael, AJ, Finnigan, JJ, Manderson, L and Walker, BH, Eds., Australian Academy of Science, Canberra, 2012, pp. 1-53.

Rees, W and Wackernagel, M, 'Urban Ecological Footprints: Why Cities Cannot be Sustainable—and Why They are a Key to Sustainability', *Environmentl Impact Assessment Review*, vol. 16, no. 4-6, 1996, pp. 223-48.

Regional Australia Institute, *Rethinking the Future of Northern Australia's Regions: More Than Mines, Dams and Development Dreams*, Regional Australia Institute, Canberra, 2013.

Remplan, 'Economy, Jobs and Business Insights', Remplan, 2023, <https://www.remplan.com.au/>.

Rinehart, G, *Northern Australia and Then Some: Changes We Need to Make Our Country Rich*, Executive Media, Melbourne, 2012.

Robb, A, 'The Australian Government's Long-Term Vision for Developing Australia's North', *Northern Development: Creating the Future Australia*, Roux, A, Faubell, M and McGauchie, D, Eds., ADC Forum, Melbourne, 2014, pp. 173-179.

Romer, P, 'Opportunities for Population Growth to Drive Development of Australia's North', *Northern Development: Creating the Future Australia*, Roux, A, Faubell, M and McGauchie, D Eds., ADC Forum, Melbourne, 2014.

Roux, A, Faubell, M and McGauchie, D, *Northern Development: Creating the Future Australia*, ADC Forum, Melbourne, 2014.

Rushman, G, 'Towards New Cities in Australia', *Town Planning Review*, vol. 47, no. 1, 1976, pp. 4-25.

Rutherfurd, I and Finlayson, B, 'Whither Australia: Will Availability of Water Constrain the Growth of Australia's Population?' *Geographical Research*, vol. 49, no. 3, 2011, pp. 301-16.

Salt, B, *The Big Tilt*, Hardie Grant Books, Melbourne, 2011.

Sarkissian, W, 'Wendy Sarkissian on Nimbyism, Community Resistance and Housing Density', *The Fifth Estate*, 7 March 2013, <https://thefifthestate.com.au/articles/nimbyism-community-resistance-and-housing-density/>.

Scanlon Foundation Research Institute, 'The 2017 Mapping Social Cohesion Report', Scanlon Foundation Research Institute, 2017, <https://scanloninstitute.org.au/publications/mapping-social-cohesion-report/2017-mapping-social-cohesion-report>.

Schech, S, 'Silent Bargain or Rural Cosmopolitanism? Refugee Settlement in Regional Australia', *Journal of Ethnic and Migration Studies*, vol. 40, no. 4, 2014, pp. 601-18.

Seamer, P, *Breaking Point: The Future of Australian Cities*, Nero, Melbourne, 2019.

Sennett, R, *The Fall of Public Man*, Alfred A. Knopf, New York, 1977.

Seto, KC, Güneralp, B and Hutyra, LR, 'Global Forecasts of Urban Expansion to 2030 and Direct Impacts on Biodiversity and Carbon Pools,' *PNAS*, vol. 109, no. 40, 2012, pp. 16083-88.

SGS Economics and Planning, *Reimagining Australia's South-East*, Prepared for the Committee for Melbourne, SGS Economics and Planning, 2020, <https://sgsep.com.au/assets/main/SGS-Economics-and-Planning_Reimagining-Australias-South-East.pdf>.

Sharifi, E, Sivam, A and Boland, J, 'Resilience to Heat in Public Space: A Case Study of Adelaide, South Australia', *Journal of Environmental Planning and Management*, vol. 59, no. 10, 2016, pp. 1833-54.

Sherwood, SC and Huber, M, 'An Adaptability Limit to Climate Change Due to Heat Stress', *Proceedings of the National Academy of Sciences*, vol. 107, no. 21, 2010, pp. 9552-55.

Siedentop, S, Fina, S and Krehl, A, 'Greenbelts in Germany's Regional Plans—an Effective Growth Management Policy?' *Landscape and Urban Planning*, vol. 145, 2016, pp. 71-82.

Southphommasane, T, *Don't Go Back to Where You Came From: Why Multiculturalism Works*, NewSouth, Sydney, 2012.

Southwest Australia Ecoregion Initiative, *The Southwest Australia Ecoregion: Jewel of the Australian Continent*, Southwest Australia Ecoregion Initiative, Perth, 2006.

Spearritt, P, 'The 200 KM City: Brisbane, the Gold Coast, and Sunshine Coast', *Australian Economic History Review*, vol. 49, no. 1, 2009, 87-106.

Spilhaus, A, 'The Experimental City', *Science*, vol. 159, no. 3816, 1968, pp. 710-15.

Steadman, RG, 'The Assessment of Sultriness. Part I: A Temperature-Humidity Index Based on Human Physiology and Clothing Science', *Journal of Applied Meteorology*, vol. 18, no. 7, 1979, pp. 861-73.

Steele, W, 'Indonesia Isn't the Only Country Planning New Cities. Why Not Australia?' *The Conversation*, 2 May 2019, <https://theconversation.com/indonesia-isnt-the-only-country-planning-new-cities-why-not-australia-116266>.

Stone, J, 'Empty or Full? The Debate over the Population of Australia', Paper Presented at the Symposium of the 1994 Annual General Meeting of the Australian Academy of Science. *Issues*, vol. 37, 1996.

Storey, K, 'Fly-in/Fly-out and Fly-Over: Mining and Regional Development in Western Australia', *Australian Geographer*, vol. 32, no. 2, 2001, pp. 133-48.

Strange, C and Bashford, A, *Griffith Taylor: Visionary Environmentalist Explorer*, National Library Australia, Canberra, 2008.

Stretton, H, *Ideas for Australian Cities*, Georgian House, Melbourne, 1970.

Taylor, G, 'Possibilities of Settlement in Australia', *Limits of Land Settlement*, Bowman, I, Ed., *Limits of Land Settlement: A Report on Present-day Possibilities*, Council on Foreign Relations, New York, 1937, 195-227.

Technic 10, and Crooks Michael Peacock Stewart, *Pilbara Town Planning Study*, Government of Western Australia, Perth, 1972.

Tuli, S, 'Migrants Want to Live in the Big Cities, Just Like the Rest of Us', *The Conversation*, 1 April 2019, <https://theconversation.com/migrants-want-to-live-in-the-big-cities-just-like-the-rest-of-us-113911>.

Tuli, SC and Hu, R, 'Knowledge Economy and Migrant Knowledge Workers in the Global City: A Case Study of Melbourne, Australia', *Australian Planner*, vol. 55, no. 2, 2018, pp. 126-44.

Twitchett, WA, 'Habitat Principles: Australian Practice?' *Royal Australian Planning Institute Journal*, vol. 15, no. 4, 1977, pp. 134-137.

United Nations, 'World Population Prospects', United Nations, 2022, <https://population.un.org/wpp/>.

—— 'National Urban Policy', United Nations, 2022, <https://unhabitat.org/programme/national-urban-policy>.

—— 'Sustainable Cities: Why They Matter', United Nations, 2016, <www.un.org/sustainabledevelopment/wp-content/uploads/2018/09/Goal-11.pdf>.

—— *Draft Outcome Document of the United Nations Conference on Housing and Sustainable Urban Development (Habitat III)*: Document A/CONF, United Nations, 2016, <https://digitallibrary.un.org/record/1290312?ln=en>.

Urban Taskforce Australia, 'Planning for Sydney's Future Apartments', Urban Taskforce Australia, 2017, <https://www.urbantaskforce.com.au/urban-ideas-2>. [no longer available online]

Victorian State Government, *Plan Melbourne 2017-2050*, Victorian State Government, Melbourne, 2017.

Vij, A, Ardeshiri, A, Li, T, Beer, A and Crommelin, L, *Understanding What Attracts New Residents to Smaller Cities*, Australian Housing and Urban Research Institute Final Report, No. 375, 2022.

Walker, M, 'Population Growth in Australia: How Environmental Groups Are Responding', *People and Place*, vol. 18, no. 1 2010, pp. 39-48.

Watson, D, *The Bush: Travels in the Heart of Australia*, Penguin, Melbourne, 2014.

Weller, R, *Boomtown 2050*, UWA Publishing, Perth, 2009.

Weller, R and Bolleter, J, *Made in Australia: The Future of Australian Cities.*, UWA Publshing, Perth, 2013.

Wennersten, JR and Robbins, D, *Rising Tides: Climate Refugees in the Twenty-First Century*, Indiana University Press, Bloomington, 2017.

Whitaker, SD, 'Did the Covid-19 Pandemic Cause an Urban Exodus?' Federal Reserve Bank of Cleveland, 2021, <https://www.clevelandfed.org/publications/cleveland-fed-district-data-brief/cfddb-20210205-did-the-covid-19-pandemic-cause-an-urban-exodus>.

Whitlam, G, 'An Urban Nation', First Annual Leslie Wilkinson Lecture, University of Sydney, 2 July 1969, Parliament of Australia, <https://parlinfo.aph.gov.au/parlInfo/search/display/display.w3p;query=Id:%22media/pressrel/760054%22;src1=sm1>.

Wilkinson, G, McKenzie, FH, Bolleter, J and Hooper, P, 'Political Centralization, Federalism and Urbanization: Evidence from Australia', *Social Science History*, vol. 47, no. 1, 2023, pp. 11-39.

Wilmoth, D, Purdon, R, Strickland, A and Logan, MI, '"Towards a National Strategy for Urban and Regional Development", *Australian Urban Economics: A Reader*, McMaster, JC and Webb, GR, Eds., Australia and New Zealand Book Company, Sydney, 1976, pp. 9-45.

Woinarski, J, Mackey, B, Nix, H and Traill, B, *The Nature of Northern Australia: Natural Values, Ecological Processes and Future Prospects*, ANU Press, Canberra, 2007.

World Counts, The, 'World Population', The World Counts, 2023, <https://www.theworldcounts.com/populations/world/people>.

World Population Review, 'World City Populations 2023', World Population Review, 2023, <https://worldpopulationreview.com/>.

Ye, R and Ma, L, 'Australian City Workers' Average Commute Has Blown out to 66 Minutes a Day. How Does Yours Compare?' *The Conversation*, 30 July 2019, <https://theconversation.com/australian-city-workers-average-commute-has-blown-out-to-66-minutes-a-day-how-does-yours-compare-120598>.

ACKNOWLEDGEMENTS

This book grew out of an Australian Research Council Discovery Project (DP190101093). Chief investigators on the project were Professor David Nichols (lead), Professor Robert Freestone, Professor Paul Walker, Dr Elizabeth Taylor and Dr Julian Bolleter. Our particular thanks to David Nichols for supporting this book venture.

The authors are grateful to Dr Paula Hooper and Dr Nicole Edwards from the Australian Urban Design Research Centre (AUDRC) for their help in designing the pivotal Plan *My* Australia surveys and crunching the resulting data. Thanks to Bill Grace from AUDRC for his guidance in conducting the suitability analysis. Thanks to Nicole Edwards for also venturing the Inland Cities scenario (what an omission this would have otherwise been). The authors acknowledge Shubham Gautam and Nur Mohd Rozlan, also from AUDRC, for assisting with the book's graphics and breathing life into the various visions of future Australian cities. We also thank Shlomo Angel, Brendan Gleeson, Peter Newton and Barbara Norman for underscoring in their words the value in investigating future urban settlement on the Australian continent.

The discussion of the Plan *My* Australia survey results in this book (in chapters 3 to 5) builds upon the foundations laid down in a previous paper by the authors and their colleagues: Bolleter J, Edwards N, Freestone R, Nichols D, Oliver G, Hooper P. 'Long-term settlement scenarios for Australia: a survey and evaluation of community opinions'. *Urban Policy and Research,* vol. 40, no. 1, 2021, pp. 15-35. Thank you to the authors and Taylor and Francis for permitting us to draw from and integrate this material in this book.

Various parts of this book build upon the foundations laid down in previous books and papers by the authors and their colleagues. The background and discussion sections of chapters 3, 4 and 5 build upon: Bolleter J. *The Ghost Cities of Australia: A Survey of New City Proposals and Their Lessons for Australia's 21st Century Development. Cham:* Springer, 2018.

The 'scenario suitability' described in chapters 3, 4 and 5 are documented in more detail in: Bolleter J, Grace B, Freestone R, Hooper P. 'Informing future Australian settlement planning through a national-scale suitability analysis'. *International Planning Studies,* vol. 27, no. 1, 2021, pp. 18-43.

To a lesser degree, the book also draws on other previous publications by the author/s:

- Bolleter J, Grace B, Freestone R. 'Preparing Australia for a potential surge in environmental migration'. *Australian Planner,* vol. 58, no. 1-2, 2022, pp. 11-24.
- Bolleter J, Edwards N, Cameron R, Duckworth A, Freestone R, Foster S, Hooper P. 'Implications of the Covid-19 Pandemic: Canvassing Opinion from Planning Professionals'. *Planning Practice and Research,* vol. 37, no. 1, 2022, pp. 13-34.
- Bolleter J, Edwards N, Freestone R, Nichols D, Hooper P. 'Evaluating Scenarios for Twenty-First-Century Australian Settlement Planning: a Delphi Study With Planning Experts'. *International Planning Studies,* vol. 27, no. 3, 2022, pp. 231-52.
- Bolleter J. 'The Consequences of Three Urbanisation Scenarios for Northern Australia'. *Australian Planner*, vol. 55, no. 2, 2019, pp. 1-23.
- Bolleter J. 'The Limits of Spatial Design in Delivering Inland Decentralisation in Western Australia's SuperTowns'. *Australian Planner,* vol. 56, no. 1, 2019, pp. 1-21.
- Bolleter J, Weller R. *Made in Australia: The Future of Australian Cities*. Perth: University of Western Australia Publishing; 2013.

The authors would like to acknowledge co-authors and collaborators who contributed to this related research, notably Robert Cameron, Nicole Edwards, Sarah Foster, Bill Grace, Paula Hooper, David Nichols, Grace Oliver and Richard Weller.

The book incorporates material from winning submissions in a national ideas competition, 'Business as Unusual: Imagining a Future Australian City', conducted by AUDRC and supported by the Planning Institute of Australia. The authors would like to acknowledge Dr Robert Cameron from AUDRC for providing invaluable assistance with the conceptualisation, administration and promotion of the competition, and the winners and general participants for entrusting us with their urban dreams. Thanks to the competition jurors: Abel Feleke, Beth George, Robin Goodman, Perry Lethlean, Rebecca Moore and Richard Weller.

The authors would also like to thank David Ponton for his generous drone tuition and fantastic photography. Thanks also to James and Kent Lyon for providing drone photos for Bunbury and Antoinette Carrier for her evocative image of Big Bell.

Thanks to Ivan Rijavec for generously allowing us to use building imagery in the montages of future cities from his 2011 exhibition 'Boyd's Error: Planning's Curse, Reflections on the Australian Ugliness' described below:

Presented by Rijavec Architects, Boyd's Error: Planning's Curse was an ambitious exhibition that aspires to change the way in which we perceive Australian urbanism. The exhibition comprised of a photographic collage of each building circumscribing the Gertrude, Brunswick, Johnston and Smith Street Fitzroy blocks in inner Melbourne. This extraordinary three-kilometre 'unravelling' re-evaluates the way we interpret our streetscapes, re-examining Boyd's treatise and neighbourhood character and heritage planning policies. The existing streetscapes were photographed by John Gollings Photography, and the montages were produced by students in one of Ivan Rijavec's design studios at RMIT.

Julian would like to thank AUDRC advisory board Chairs David Maclennan and Fred Chaney for their support and guidance over the years. Finally, thanks to Rose Bolleter and Dr Sally Appleton for supporting yet another book project. Rose, when it is 2101 (and you are 89!), you can dust off this book and see how wide of the mark your dad was. Sending love to your future self.